M000285539

THREE SPANISH *QUERELLE* TEXTS

The Other Voice in Early Modern Europe:
The Toronto Series, 21

The Other Voice in Early Modern Europe: The Toronto Series

SERIES EDITORS Margaret L. King *and* Albert Rabil, Jr.
SERIES EDITOR, ENGLISH TEXTS Elizabeth H. Hageman

Previous Publications in the Series

MADRE MARÍA ROSA
Journey of Five Capuchin Nuns
Edited and translated by Sarah E.
Owens
2009

GIOVAN BATTISTA ANDREINI
Love in the Mirror: A Bilingual Edition
Edited and translated by Jon R. Snyder
2009

RAYMOND DE SABANAC AND
SIMONE ZANACCHI
Two Women of the Great Schism: The
Revelations *of Constance de Rabastens
by Raymond de Sabanac and* Life of
the Blessed Ursulina of Parma *by
Simone Zanacchi*
Edited and translated by Renate
Blumenfeld-Kosinski and Bruce L.
Venarde
2010

OLIVA SABUCO DE NANTES
BARRERA
The True Medicine
Edited and translated by Gianna
Pomata
2010

LOUISE-GENEVIÈVE GILLOT DE
SAINCTONGE
Dramatizing Dido, Circe, and Griselda
Edited and translated by Janet Levarie
Smarr
2010

PERNETTE DU GUILLET
Complete Poems: A Bilingual Edition
Edited by Karen Simroth James
Translated by Marta Rijn Finch
2010

ANTONIA PULCI
*Saints' Lives and Bible Stories for the
Stage: A Bilingual Edition*
Edited by Elissa B. Weaver
Translated by James Wyatt Cook
2010

VALERIA MIANI
Celinda, A Tragedy: A Bilingual Edition
Edited by Valeria Finucci
Translated by Julia Kisacky
Annotated by Valeria Finucci and
Julia Kisacky
2010

*Enchanted Eloquence: Fairy Tales by
Seventeenth-Century French Women
Writers*
Edited and translated by Lewis C.
Seifert and Domna C. Stanton
2010

GOTTFRIED WILHELM LEIBNIZ,
SOPHIE, ELECTRESS OF HANOVER
AND QUEEN SOPHIE CHARLOTTE
OF PRUSSIA
*Leibniz and the Two Sophies: The
Philosophical Correspondence*
Edited and translated by Lloyd
Strickland
2011

The Other Voice in
Early Modern Europe:
The Toronto Series

SERIES EDITORS Margaret L. King *and* Albert Rabil, Jr.
SERIES EDITOR, ENGLISH TEXTS Elizabeth H. Hageman

Previous Publications in the Series

Three Spanish *Querelle* Texts: *Grisel and Mirabella, The Slander against Women,* and *The Defense of Ladies against Slanderers*

A Bilingual Edition and Study

PERE TORRELLAS
and JUAN DE FLORES

~

Edited and translated by

EMILY C. FRANCOMANO

ITER

Iter Inc.
Centre for Reformation and Renaissance Studies
Toronto
2013

Iter: Gateway to the Middle Ages and Renaissance
Tel: 416/978–7074   Email: iter@utoronto.ca
Fax: 416/978–1668   Web: www.itergateway.org

Centre for Reformation and Renaissance Studies
Victoria University in the University of Toronto
Tel: 416/585–4465   Email: crrs.publications@utoronto.ca
Fax: 416/585–4430   Web: www.crrs.ca

© 2013 Iter Inc. & Centre for Reformation and Renaissance Studies
All rights reserved.
Printed in Canada.

Iter and the Centre for Reformation and Renaissance Studies gratefully acknowledge the generous support of James E. Rabil, in memory of Scottie W. Rabil, toward the publication of this book.

Iter and the Centre for Reformation and Renaissance Studies gratefully acknowledge the generous support of the National Endowment for the Humanities toward the publication of this book.

Library and Archives Canada Cataloguing in Publication
Three Spanish querelle texts : Grisel and Mirabella, The slander against women, and The defense of ladies against slanderers : a bilingual edition and study / Pere Torrellas and Juan de Flores ; edited and translated by Emily C. Francomano.

(The other voice in early modern Europe. Toronto series ; 21)
Includes bibliographical references and index.
Contents: Maldezir de mugeres ; The slander against women / Pere Torrellas — Razonamiento de Pere Torrella en defensión de las donas contra los maldezientes ; The defense of ladies against slanderers — Grisel y Mirabella ; Grisel and Mirabella / Juan de Flores.
Issued also in electronic format.
Text in English and Spanish; translated from the Spanish.
Co-published by: Iter Inc.
ISBN 978-0-7727-2134-1

1. Torroella, Pere, ca. 1420–ca. 1492—Translations into English. 2. Flores, Juan de, 15th/16th cent—Translations into English. 3. Spanish literature—To 1500—Translations into English. 4. Women—Spain—Literary collections. 5. Misogyny—Spain—Literary collections. 6. Middle Ages—Literary collections. I. Francomano, Emily C. II. Victoria University (Toronto, Ont.). Centre for Reformation and Renaissance Studies III. Iter Inc. IV. Title: Grisel and Mirabella, The slander against women, and The defense of ladies against slanderers. V. Title: Spanish querelle texts. VI. Title: Querelle texts. VII. Series: Other voice in early modern Europe. Toronto series ; 21

PQ6174.A3T57 2013
860.8'002   C2013-900313-4

Cover illustration: Juana or Joanna of Castile, called 'The Mad' (1479–1555) daughter of Ferdinand II of Aragon (1452–1516) and Isabella of Castile (1451–1504), 1500 (panel), Juan de Flandes (c. 1465–1519) / Kunsthistorisches Museum, Vienna, Austria / The Bridgeman Art Library XAM 68656.

Cover design:
Maureen Morin, Information Technology Services, University of Toronto Libraries.

Typesetting and production:
Iter Inc.

Contents

Acknowledgments

I was first drawn into the dark, fascinating world of the Spanish sentimental romances in a graduate seminar taught by Patricia E. Grieve at Columbia University. I am extremely grateful to her for the introduction, even if at times I am not sure whether to praise or *maldecir* her for the resulting life-long obsession. Discussions with Mark Johnston, Sol Miguel Prendes, Isidro Rivera, Ron Surtz and Barbara Weissberger over the years have also been invaluable to me. I wish to thank Joe Gwara, who most generously shared material in press and his 1988 University of London dissertation with me. I wish also to thank Yvette Neisser Moreno and Pat Fisher, teacher and fellow classmate in several translation workshops at Bethesda Writers Center. I am especially indebted to my most constant and long suffering readers, who happen also to be family members, Nina Rulon-Miller and Eugenio Ibarz.

The National Endowment for the Humanities Scholarly Editions and Translations Grant Program and a Georgetown University Summer Research Grant provided key support for the completion of this project. The Department of Spanish and Portuguese at Georgetown University permitted me to draw upon the talents of graduate assistants during the preparation of the manuscript of this book. I am grateful to Laura Manrique Gómez for her help researching Pere Torrellas' *Slander* and the many responses his contemporaries wrote to it, to Silvia Marijuan for her devotion to the transcription of *Grisel y Mirabella*, and also to Clara Pascual Argente, Maureen Russo, María José Navia, Yoel Castillo Botello, and Estefanía Tocado Orviz for their assistance with references, the preparation of the volume manuscript, and responses to drafts of the translations. Thanks go as well to an undergraduate assistant, Joseph Pearson. The Rubbetino Press kindly permitted the use of Robert Archer's editions of two of Pere Torrellas' works in this volume. Sincere thanks go to Albert Rabil for his forbearance and continuing support of the project.

Introduction

The Other Voice

This volume of the Other Voice brings together the two most influential voices in the Spanish *querelle des femmes*, Pere Torrellas (ca. 1420– ca. 1492) and Juan de Flores (d. ca. 1503). Although their names and works are not well known today outside of Hispanic Studies, Torrellas's *Slander against Women* (*Maldezir de mugeres*) (ca. 1445) and Flores's short romance *Grisel and Mirabella* (*La historia de Grisel y Mirabella*) (ca. 1475) circulated widely among Spanish readers from the time of their composition through the sixteenth century.[1] *Grisel and Mirabella* also achieved considerable success in translation and was read across Europe. Pere Torrellas and Juan de Flores in all likelihood never met, but their works have more in common than their participation in the *querelle*, for Torrellas appears as a misogynist, libertine character in *Grisel and Mirabella*. Indeed, *The Slander against Women*, Flores's *Grisel and Mirabella*, and Torrellas's lesser-known *Defense of Ladies against Slanderers* together circumscribe the Spanish *querelle*, a debate that blurs the lines between literature and history.

In the debate about women in Spanish poetry and prose that flared in the second half of the fifteenth century, the name "Torrellas" was synonymous with misogyny.[2] Pere Torrellas, a Catalonian courtier and poet in the service of the Crown of Aragon, may or may not have wanted to throw down a gauntlet when he composed the poem

---

1. Although both writers may be considered "Spanish" in the present day by virtue of their use of the Castilian language and homes within what is now Spain, the political map of the mid- and late-fifteenth century was quite different from today. While "Spain" as a political unit did not exist in the Middle Ages, *España* (Spain) did exist as a geographic and cultural concept, embracing the many kingdoms of the Iberian Peninsula, including those of Castile, Aragon, Navarre, Portugal, and the last remnant of al-Andalus, the Kingdom of Granada. The Crown of Aragon, moreover, had expanded into a Mediterranean empire that included much of the Italian peninsula. Consequently, I use the terms "Spain" and "Spanish" in a broad sense.

2. In the texts of the period—and in modern scholarship as well—Torrellas's name appears in several different forms: Torrellas, Torrella, Torroella, Torroellas. The first spelling is used throughout this study.

1

that would come to be known as the *Maldezir de mugeres,* or *Slander against Women,* which begins with the cautionary verses, "the man in love who courts / a woman, destroys himself."[3] Whatever the poet's true intentions, his twelve stanzas on the dangerous and devious nature of "Woman," followed by one concluding stanza in praise of a "Lady" who is an exception to the rule, incited many of his contemporaries, as well as future generations of writers, to take up their pens in the defense or defamation of women. The exact date and circumstances of the poem's composition are unknown, but it was raising hackles in the courts of Aragon, Navarre, Naples, and Castile by the 1450s. The *Slander* incited a *querelle* in its day: at least twelve contemporary poets wrote responses to it, defaming Torrellas and ostensibly defending women, or praising and agreeing with his depiction of women and their wiles. Torrellas, provoked by his fellow courtiers and poets—and perhaps by the unwritten and now lost reactions of the women present in his original audiences as well—penned a self-consciously ironic retraction in prose, *The Defense of Ladies against Slanderers.*[4] Among the many late-medieval Spanish works that define and question gender roles and relations, the *Slander* and the texts that respond directly to it and to its author stand out as an exchange of directly related texts. Importantly, not only are beliefs about the nature of women central to the polemic; these literary exchanges also discuss the character of men who debate about women.

Torrellas's historical and literary legacy as an enemy of women was sealed for future generations by Juan de Flores, author of several short romances and royal chronicler to Isabel I and Fernando V of Castile, known as the Catholic Monarchs. Flores's extremely popular *Grisel and Mirabella,* written in the 1480s and first printed in 1495, is a fictional response to Torrellas's *Slander* and *Defense.* The plot of *Grisel and Mirabella,* in which Torrellas is resurrected as a character, turns upon the polemic about gender relations: Torrellas, as an "expert on

---

3. "Quien bien amando persigue / dona, a sí mesmo destruye."

4. In addition, Torrellas wrote two poetic sequels to the *Slander: A quien basta el conocer* (To the man whose knowledge is sufficient), a poem justifying the *Slander* as a call to reform women, and *Entre las otras sois vos* (You are among the others), a gloss upon the *Slander's* final stanza, in honor of the Queen of Naples. Pere Torroella, *Obras completas,* ed. Robert Archer (Soveria Mannelli, Italy: Rubbettino, 2004), 242–48.

women," is called upon to prove women's universal guilt in sexual seduction in a trial by jury. *Grisel and Mirabella* turns Torrellas's poetic diatribe, which Flores clearly knew, into a farce of forensic rhetoric. His opponent in the trial is the beautiful and worldly-wise Braçayda, a character from the Homeric tradition, who argues in defense of women. Braçayda echoes both Christine de Pizan and Chaucer's Wife of Bath when she insists that the jury's decision to condemn women is a foregone conclusion because men write the laws by which women must live and judge them according to those laws. Grisel and Mirabella concludes with the sadistic revenge unleashed upon Torrellas by aggrieved women, thus creating a legend of his "martyrdom" when he dies at their hands.

Grisel and Mirabella, dedicated to an unnamed female reader who may have been none other than Queen Isabel I, not only imagines a woman taking part in the debate, but also uses the medium of narrative fiction to show that the *querelle* could have real effects upon the lives of women and men. Nevertheless, *Grisel and Mirabella* leaves the debate open, at once suggesting that it can never be resolved and encouraging the romance's historical readers—male and female—to continue the debate and lend their voices to the *querelle*.

Torrellas and Flores's first audiences were limited to the rarefied cultural settings of late-medieval courts. Nevertheless, both *The Slander against Women* and *Grisel and Mirabella* appeared in multiple print editions, thus reaching a wider readership. Torrellas's *Defense of Ladies against Slanderers* reached far fewer readers in the fifteenth and sixteenth centuries and has received little scholarly attention in the present day. Nevertheless, it serves as an important bridge between the two more famous works.

Grisel and Mirabella was not only popular in the Spanish context. In the sixteenth century, *Grisel* was translated into Italian, French, English, and Polish. Presses across Europe produced multiple editions well into the seventeenth century, when it was also translated into German. Translations were also published in bilingual, trilingual and quadrilingual formats for use as tools for language learning. In addition to its influence on other seventeenth-century works, *Grisel* eventually became the basis for the anonymous Jacobean play *Swetnam the Woman Hater* (ca. 1620), which was part of the historical de-

bate on women in England.[5] Thus, in one form or another, *Grisel and Mirabella* was perhaps the most widely disseminated work of fiction in the sixteenth-century pan-European *querelle des femmes*.

The broad and lasting influence of both Torrellas's *Slander* and Flores's *Grisel and Mirabella* merit their inclusion among the titles included in *The Other Voice*. To date, neither work has been available to students and scholars in modern English translation, nor is *Grisel and Mirabella* easily accessible in Spanish.[6] The inclusion of Torrellas's *Defense of Ladies against Slanderers* also makes a lesser-known intertext of *Grisel and Mirabella* available to readers. Torrellas went down in history as the ultimate misogynist and Flores was long considered by critics a staunch defender of women. Recent scholarship has added nuance to our understanding of these two polar positions, particularly in the case of Flores.[7] Torrellas's literary engagement in the *querelle* as

5. Joseph Swetnam's pamphlet *The Arraignment of Lewde, idle, forward, and unconstant women* (1615), like Pere Torrellas's *Slander*, provoked contemporary rejoinders. Three direct replies all published under female names (Rachel Speght, Ester Sowerman, and Constantia Munda, this last clearly a pseudonym) appeared in print in 1617. The play *Swetnam the Woman-hater, Arraigned by Women* followed soon after the pamphlets. See *Swetnam the Woman-Hater: The Controversy and the Play*, ed. Coryl Crandall (West Lafayette, IN: Purdue University Press, 1969) and *Female Replies to Swetnam the Woman-Hater*, ed. Charles Butler (Bristol, UK: Thoemmes Press, 1995).

6. Two published critical editions exist: *Grisel y Mirabella: edizione critica, introduzione e note de Maria Grazia Ciccarello Di Blasi* (Rome: Bagatto, 2003) and *La historia de Grisel y Mirabella*, ed. Pablo Alcázar López and José A. González Núñez. (Granada: Editorial Don Quijote, 1983). Joseph J. Gwara also edited *Grisel and Mirabella* in "A Study of the Works of Juan de Flores, with a critical edition of *La Historia de Grisel y Mirabella*" (Ph.D. diss., Westfield College, University of London, 1989), 2:513–708. Barbara Matulka included a transcription in *The Novels of Juan de Flores and their European Diffusion: A Study in Comparative Literature* (New York: Institute of French Studies, 1931), 331–71.

7. The classic studies are Matulka's *The Novels of Juan de Flores and Their European Diffusion* and Jacob Ornstein's "La misoginia y el profeminismo en la literatura castellana," *Revista de filología española* 3 (1941): 219–32. Both Matulka and Ornstein see Flores as a committed defender of women. Antony Van Beysterveldt was one of the first readers of the debate to question the validity and usefulness of assigning authors to either the pro- or anti-feminist sides of the polemic in his "Revisión de los debates feministas," *Hispania* 64 (1981): 1–13. More recent scholarship, to which I will refer below, includes Patricia E. Grieve, *Desire and Death in the Spanish Sentimental Romance (1440–1550)* (Newark, DE: Juan de la Cuesta, 1987), Antonio Pérez-Romero, *The Subversive Tradition in Spanish Renaissance Writing* (Lewisberg, PA: Bucknell University Press, 2005), Mercedes Roffé, *La cuestión del género en*

a defender as well as a detractor of women points to the ambiguity of authorial intentions in these central texts of the Spanish debate on women, which, with the exception of the *Slander*, cannot be easily classified as either misogynist or profeminine.[8] The *Slander, Defense,* and *Grisel and Mirabella* exude a sense of literary delight in re-staging the old arguments concerning women's chastity, mercy, goodness, and power over men. At the same time, they reveal the urgency with which writers continued to engage in what seemed to be an endless and intractable debate. The lasting popularity of the *Slander* and *Grisel and Mirabella*, moreover, shows how readers remained eager for debate texts and works about the *querelle*.

The Historical Context for The Slander against Women, The Defense of Ladies against Slanderers, *and* Grisel and Mirabella: *Iberian Politics and the Debate on Women 1440–1500*

The heyday of the Spanish debate on women lasted from the time Torrellas composed his *Slander* until the turn of the sixteenth century. In those decades, which were marked by great changes in the political fortunes of the Iberian Kingdoms of Castile, Aragon, Portugal, and Granada, male courtly and clerical writers produced an extraordinary number of works on women. Despite the intensity and persistence of the production of *querelle* texts, there are no known Spanish debate texts written by women. Julian Weiss's recent inventory of clerical treatises, poetry, conduct books, catalogs of women, narrative fiction, drama, and translations contributing to the debate during the period includes over fifty works.[9] They range from the scathing misogynist

---

Grisel y Mirabella *de Juan de Flores* (Newark, DE: Juan de la Cuesta, 1996), and Barbara F. Weissberger, *Isabel Rules: Constructing Queenship, Wielding Power* (Minneapolis: University of Minnesota Press, 2004), Chapter Six.

8. The terms "profeminine" and "profeminist" describe medieval defenses of women that praise women according to the traditional definitions of gendered roles in society, thus avoiding the anachronistic connotations of the word "feminist" when applied to medieval texts about women. Alcuin Blamires, *The Case for Women in Medieval Culture* (New York: Oxford University Press, 1997), 12.

9. "Bibliography of Primary Texts in Spanish," in *Gender and Debate from the Early Middle Ages to the Renaissance*, ed. Thelma Fenster and Clare Lees (New York: Palgrave, 2002),

treatise of Alfonso Martínez de Toledo, called the *Corbacho* (1438), in honor of its ideological debt to Boccaccio's *Corbaccio*, and to Álvaro de Luna's catalog, the *Book of Famous and Virtuous Women* (ca. 1444), to Fray Martín de Córdoba's conduct book dedicated to the future Queen Isabel I, *The Garden of Noble Damsels* (ca. 1468). Many authors, like Juan de Flores, also embedded the debate within longer fictional works, such as *The Prison of Love*, a short romance by Diego de San Pedro that, like *Grisel and Mirabella*, became an international success. Flores is, however, the only known Spanish author who turned the debate itself into the central plot of a work of fiction. He is also one of the few to imagine a female character participating in the debate, speaking on behalf of women.

Torrellas's *Slander* and *Defense* and Flores's *Grisel and Mirabella* epitomize the critical challenge of late-medieval texts that rehearse and refute misogynist discourse. Profeminine and misogynist texts from the later Middle Ages and Early Modern period often sound alike; the parroting effect of diatribes against and defenses of women is easily mistaken for a lack of historical specificity. Moreover, humor abounds in the texts of the Spanish *querelle*, leading many readers to consider medieval debate texts as part of a courtly game, entertainment without serious cultural importance or consequences. Defining, vituperating, and praising women may well have been a ludic and even lubricious activity, but behind the sly laughter serious issues are at stake. Notwithstanding the repetitive—and seemingly timeless—nature of the terms of the debate on women and its often jocular register, each text is in reality grounded in particular ideologies, in the historical, political, and economic circumstances, as well as in the literary trends of its time and place. The texts, Robert Archer concludes, "are all characterized by a real concern with the viability of the authoritative view of women [which is] essentially contradictory and self undermining," resulting in the "strong sense of indeterminacy" that runs through late-medieval Hispanic texts that address issues of sexuality and gender identity.[10]

275–81.

10. Archer concludes, "the localized context in which each of the texts is written ensures that the combination of common ideas about women they contain ... is nearly always unique."

The outpouring of texts on the subject of gender identity in Spanish literature of the fifteenth century was at once part of the ancient and on-going misogynist and profeminine traditions—defining women as inferior beings, dangerous to men; defining women as the sum of virtues, necessary for men's comfort and survival—and also a phenomenon relating to the political upheaval and civil strife among many of the kingdoms and powerful families of Iberia during the period.

In Castile, the reigns of three successive monarchs of the Trastamaran dynasty—Juan II (1406–1454), Enrique IV (1454–1474), and Isabel I (1474–1504)—brought questions of sexuality and gender into the forefront of political life. Juan II's long reign began under the shared regency of his uncle Fernando of Antequera (d. 1416) and his mother Catherine of Lancaster (1373–1418), known for her "manly" qualities.[11] Even after reaching the age of majority, Juan II was essentially a puppet king, who left most decision-making and power in the hands of his favorite, Álvaro de Luna (ca. 1390–1453), rumored to be both a sorcerer and the king's lover. Luna's *Book of Famous and Virtuous Women*, mentioned above, which was perhaps an attempt to demonstrate his own appreciation for and courtly protection of women, was dedicated to Juan's first wife María of Aragon. Luna's power came to an abrupt end in 1453 when Juan II's second wife, Isabel of Portugal, convinced her husband to order his execution. Ironically, Álvaro de Luna had forced Juan II to marry Isabel. Juan II died soon after the execution of his favorite.[12] His son Enrique IV, who came to be known as "the impotent," succeeded him and, like his father, was also under the sway of a favorite, Juan Pacheco.[13] Both Juan II and Enrique IV were portrayed as weak, effeminate, heterodox, and sexually deviant by chroniclers wishing to elevate Isabel I as the savior of her kingdom.

The Problem of Woman in Late-Medieval Hispanic Literature (Woodbridge, Suffolk, UK: Tamesis, 2005), 204.

11. Fernán Pérez de Guzmán, *Generaciones y semblanzas*, ed. José Antonio Barrio Sánchez (Madrid: Cátedra, 1998), 77–78.

12. For the career of Álvaro de Luna, see Nicholas G. Round, *The Greatest Man Uncrowned: A Study of the Fall of Álvaro de Luna* (London: Tamesis, 1986).

13. For the reign of Enrique IV, see William D. Phillips, *Enrique IV and the Crisis of Fifteenth-Century Castile 1425–1480* (Cambridge, MA: Medieval Academy of America, 1978).

Isabel I, daughter of Juan II, convinced her brother Enrique IV to name her as his successor to the throne after the death of their other brother Alfonso, because Enrique was apparently unable to father an heir of his own. Enrique, after repudiating his first wife Blanca of Navarre, married Juana of Portugal, who did eventually have a daughter. However, that daughter, Juana (1462–1530), was soon known as "la Beltraneja" due to the relationship between her mother Queen Juana and the nobleman Beltrán de la Cueva. Isabel rose to power following a civil war pitting her supporters against those of her niece Juana.

Other royal and noble women played important roles in the Iberian kingdoms of Castile, Navarre, and Aragon during this period, empirically demonstrating political and also martial abilities that gave the lie to definitions of women shared by misogynist and profeminine arguments alike. In addition to Isabel I and Catherine of Lancaster, who ruled during her son Juan II of Castile's minority, María of Castile served as queen-lieutenant of Aragon during her husband Alfonso V of Aragon's (1416–1458) conquest of and residence in Naples.[14]

Spanish debate literature thus burgeoned against a background of dynastic upheaval that challenged traditional gender roles. In Castile, where women could inherit the throne and reign as queens in their own right, gender issues in discussions of monarchy were particularly charged. Isabel I's ascension to the throne followed the reigns of two kings accused of effeminacy as well as a civil war pitting Isabel against her niece as rival for the crown. The presence of a strong female monarch in Spain in the last decades of the fifteenth century clearly generated anxiety that found its expression in the literature of the day.[15] In addition to the overt gender issues involved in succession and regency, the period was also one of transition for the definition of nobility itself. Arguing the "Woman Question" was

---

14. See Theresa Earenfight, "Absent Kings: Queens as Political Partners in the Medieval Crown of Aragon," in *Queenship and Political Power in Medieval and Early Modern Spain*, ed. Theresa Earenfight (Burlington, VT: Ashgate, 2005), 33–51.

15. See Weissberger, 'Deceitful Sects': The Debate about Women in the Age of Isabel the Catholic," in *Gender and Debate from the Early Middle Ages to the Renaissance*, ed. Thelma S. Fenster and Clare A. Lees (New York: Palgrave, 2002), 207–36; and chapter one of *Isabel Rules: Constructing Queenship, Wielding Power* (Minneapolis: University of Minnesota Press, 2004).

an important way in which courtiers and clerics could jockey for position in the court in a continual game of symbolic one-upmanship, which at once assuaged and revealed "men's anxiety that their identity rests on the shaky foundations of a female Other, who by their own definition, is mutable and beyond absolute control."[16] Thus, as Julian Weiss asserts, debating about women served as a way for men to gain cultural and symbolic capital at court during a period in which many cultural boundaries were being redrawn, in particular the respective positions of clerical and secular learned men at court.[17] Torrellas and Flores, who both held important posts in their respective courts, were writers for whom composing entertaining poetry and prose about sex and gender identities was perfectly compatible with political careers. Indeed, at the time, writing for the entertainment of the court was a significant factor in social and political advancement.[18]

At the turn of the sixteenth century, however, Spain entered an era of unprecedented power and stability, following the unification made possible by the marriage of Isabel I of Castile to Fernando II of Aragon in 1479 (when he also became Fernando V of Castile), the conquest of Granada in 1492, and the expansion of the Spanish Empire into the New World. This expansion continued in 1516, when, Charles I, the grandson of Isabel and Fernando, ascended the Spanish throne, and the Empire also extended to the Low Countries. In addition to Spain's increased visibility and power, the sixteenth century saw a concentrated number of reigning queens and queens regent throughout Europe, including, but not limited to, Catherine de Medici and the two Tudors, Mary and Elizabeth. The printed editions of *Grisel and Mirabella* and the *Slander* circulated in this dual context of Spanish international hegemony and the "Age of Queens."[19]

---

16. Weiss, "'¿Qué demandamos de las mugeres?': Forming the Debate about Women in Late Medieval Spain (With a Baroque Response)," in *Gender and Debate from the Early Middle Ages to the Renaissance*, ed. Thelma S. Fenster and Clare A. Lees (New York: Palgrave, 2002), 237–75; 240.

17. Weiss, "'Qué demandamos de las mugeres?'" 238–40.

18. Archer, *The Problem of Woman*, 132.

19. The epithet is Sharon L. Jansen's. *Debating Women, Politics and Power in Early Modern Europe* (New York: Palgrave Macmillan, 2008), 1–9.

The Literary Contexts of the Torrellas Querelle *and*
Grisel and Mirabella

Pere Torrellas's *Slander* and the responses it provoked were composed and first circulated in a very particular mid- to late-fifteenth-century literary and courtly context. Juan II of Castile, Alfonso V "The Magnanimous" of Aragon, and his nephew, Carlos de Viana, were all avid patrons of the arts and letters. In Naples, Alfonso V established a brilliant court that attracted many of the leading lights of Italian humanism, as well as Castilian writers who had fallen out of favor with King Juan II of Castile.[20] Writers in the courts of Castile, Navarre, Aragon and Naples cultivated a vast corpus of lyrics compiled in anthologies of court entertainment known today as the *cancioneros* or "song books."[21] Much more than collections of verse, the *cancioneros* contain religious poetry, debates in verse on both weighty philosophical topics and lighter fare, collections of *motes* (cryptic mottoes), *letras* (brief poems) and *devisas* (emblematic verses), love poetry, moral allegories, poetry celebrating or vituperating individuals of note, advice, social and sexual satire, letters, and short treatises. Some *cancioneros* represent the output of a particular court, like the *Cancionero de Herberay*, which is closely linked to the court of Navarre, and others were compiled around a group of texts that had first circulated among an original readership and then was reconfigured for new readers. Some *cancioneros* are thematically unified, others miscellanea. Of the over 190 known manuscript *cancioneros*, some were clearly produced as luxury items made for luminaries, such as Juan II of Castile, and others as little more than rough copies. What is perhaps most homogenous about this group of texts and manuscripts is its courtliness and social nature—two elements that form recognizable *cancionero* poetics.

---

20. For politics and literary patronage at the court of Alfonso The Magnanimous, see Roger Boase, *The Troubadour Revival: A Study of Social Change and Traditionalism in Late Medieval Spain* (Boston: Routledge & Kegan Paul, 1978), 95–102.

21. The term *cancionero* means "songbook," but, as Dorothy Severin has rightly observed, the term is too limiting and specific to describe the heterogeneous nature of the texts copied in anthologies for a range of purposes, both public and private. "Cancionero: un género malnombrado," *Cultura Neolatina* 54 (1994): 95–105.

Cancionero poetry, particularly amatory poetry, was long held in low esteem by scholars, branded as impersonal, artificial, and insignificant.[22] Nevertheless, it was clearly highly valued by contemporary audiences. In the early sixteenth centuries *cancionero* poetry was re-edited and repackaged for new readers, in the 1511 printing of the bestselling *Cancionero general*, which was followed by eight successive editions printed in Spain and the Netherlands.[23] The resulting broader circulation transformed the *cancionero* from a distinctly courtly corpus to one that reached an urban, non-noble public. *Cancionero* lyric was praised in the seventeenth century by Baltasar Gracián for its *agudeza* (sharp wit), a combination of cleverness, conciseness, punning, and allusion.[24] *Cancionero* poets employed a markedly limited vocabulary, exploiting polysemy and syntactical obscurity; most of their verses contain multiple—sometimes contrary—meanings. Whatever one's evaluation of the aesthetic quality of *cancionero* poetry, it is clearly of cultural and historical interest, a record of one of the most salient non-martial methods available for self-promotion and self-fashioning in court.

The poems and other texts in the *cancionero* corpus show the imaginary world of courtly love created by the old elite as well as its recreation and re-evaluation by new generations of courtiers, both noble and non-noble. The idealization and deflation of courtly ideals reside side by side in the *cancioneros*. *Cancionero* poetry, as Roger Boase argues, consisted of a "revival" of troubadour poetic and chivalric ideas in a time when social changes were continually shedding light on their irrelevance.[25] As E. Michael Gerli similarly observes, the *cancioneros* are "evidence of a baronial culture in decline," the "last

22. Keith Whinnom provides a good overview of criticism on *cancionero* poetry in *La poesía amatoria cancioneril* (Durham, UK: University of Durham, 1981), 1–20.

23. Hernando del Castillo, comp. *Cancionero General*, ed. Joaquín González Cuenca (Madrid: Castalia, 2004), 5 vols.

24. Baltasar Gracián, *Arte de ingenio: tratado de la agudeza*, ed. Emilio Blanco (Madrid: Cátedra, 1998), 356–360.

25. *The Troubadour Revival*, 151–2.

vestiges of the decentralized landowning elite" that "signal its substitu-
tion by a centralized, bourgeois and lettered society."[26]

Cancionero poetry was popular in Flores's milieu and provided a sort of glossary for the emerging novelistic tradition in which
he wrote. Flores's *Grisel and Mirabella* belongs to the loosely defined
genre known as the Spanish sentimental romance. The sentimental
romances are a group of twenty or so short fictions produced in the
second half of the fifteenth and first decades of the sixteenth centuries.
Debate about the existence and limits of the genre itself is ongoing
in Spanish literary studies, but the general critical consensus defines
a sentimental romance as a short, formally hybrid, and fictional text
about love that is unrequited or that ends badly. In this sense, many of
the romances are stories worthy of inclusion in Day Four of Boccaccio's *Decameron*, in which Filostrato, whose very name means "pros-
trated by love," orders his companions to tell tales of "those whose
love ended unhappily," and indeed, many of the Spanish sentimental romances are clearly indebted to the work of Boccaccio.[27] All of
the sentimental romances, because of their thematic focus on het-
erosexual love, are profoundly concerned with gender and sexuality
and often portray the tensions that inevitably arise between personal
passion and political interests, thus putting both courtly and political ideals into question. In addition to incorporating varied literary
forms, from letters, debates, and allegory to lyric poetry, many of the
sentimental romances introduce a first-person narrator who is called
"The Author." The sentimental romances are also self-consciously literary, featuring metafictional scenes of writing, reading, translation,

---

26. "Introducción" in *Poesía cancioneril castellana* (Madrid: Akal, 1994), 12 (translation
mine). For further reading on the cultural politics and milieu of the *cancioneros*, see Weiss,
The Poet's Art: Literary Theory in Castile c. 1400–60 (Oxford: The Society for Mediaeval
Languages and Literature, 1990) and *Poetry at Court in Trastámaran Spain: From the* Can-
cionero de Baena *to the* Cancionero general, eds. E. Michael Gerli and Julian Weiss, (Tempe,
AZ: MRTS, 1998).

27. Giovanni Boccaccio, *The Decameron*, trans. G. H. McWilliam (1972; repr., New York;
Penguin, 1995), 280. As Marina Scordilis Brownlee notes, the lovers' situation in *Grisel and
Mirabella* is quite similar to that of Ghismonda and her lover Guiscardo in the first story of
Day Four in the *Decameron*. *The Severed Word: Ovid's* Heroides *and the Novela Sentimental*
(Princeton, NJ: Princeton University Press, 1990), 192.

and interpretation.[28] Like the *cancioneros*, most of the Spanish sentimental romances were first intended for select and courtly audiences,
but thanks to the introduction and spread of printing, they became
available to an ever-widening readership.

Lives and Works of Pere Torrellas and Juan de Flores

PERE TORRELLAS

The historical Pere Torrellas and the character that emerges from the
Slander and *Grisel and Mirabella* are two very distinct figures. Born
circa 1420 in La Bisbal, in the north of what is today Catalonia, Torrellas was the youngest son of a landowning family of the lower nobility.[29] As such, he was sent to be educated and serve as a squire in the
retinue of Carlos of Viana, nephew of Alfonso V of Aragon and son
of King Juan II of Navarre, future king of Aragon.[30] The young squire's
service in the prince's household initiated a successful political career
and, from that time forward, he was linked to the courts of Navarre
and Aragon in the Iberian Peninsula and in Naples. Torrellas's association with these courts brought him into contact with many important
literati of the day and also drew him into the political conflicts that
were continually arising between and within the Iberian Peninsula's
most powerful families.

Torrellas traveled frequently in the service of the royal houses
of Navarre and Aragon. In 1441 he fought at the side of Juan II of
Aragon in the battle of Medina del Campo, against the forces of his

28. See Emily C. Francomano, "The Spanish Sentimental Romance," in *Women and Gender in Medieval Europe: An Encyclopedia*, ed. Margaret C. Schaus (New York: Routledge, 2006), 734–36; Joseph J. Gwara, "Preface," in *Studies on the Spanish Sentimental Romance (1440–1550): Redefining a Genre*, ed. Gwara and E. Michael Gerli, (Rochester, NY: Tamesis, 1997), vii–xii; Gerli, "Introduction," in *Studies on the Spanish Sentimental Romance (1440–1550)*, xiii–xvii; and Gerli, "Toward a Poetics of the Spanish Sentimental Romance," *Hispania* 72.3 (1989): 474–82.

29. For the outline of Torrellas's biography I have drawn upon Martí de Ríquer, *Història de la literatura catalana* 2 (Barcelona: Ariel, 1980), 161–86; Archer, "Introducció," in Pere Tor- roella, *Obra Completa*, vii–xv; and Francisco Rodríguez Risquete, "Pere Torroella i les corts dels Infants d'Aragó al segle XV," *Llengua & literatura* 13 (2002): 209–220.

30. Historical documents place Torrellas at Carlos' court in 1438. Ríquer, *Història*, 175.

cousin Juan II of Castile. Torrellas was wounded and taken prisoner while protecting the king's person and later paid his own ransom. Torrellas was sent with Juan II of Aragon's secretary to the court of Alfonso V in Naples in 1445. In 1450 we find him listed as the *oficial del cuchillo* (master of the knife; seneschal) in Juan's household, and he is referred to in various documents as seneschal and counselor to both Juan II and Carlos de Viana. In 1456 Torrellas was once more at the court in Naples, serving as the seneschal to Juan of Aragon, son of Juan II from an extra-marital relationship and future bishop of Saragossa. In 1458 Juan II recognized Torrellas's service, calling him "magnificum et dilectum consiliarium et maiordomum nostrum Pere Torroella militem" (Our noble and beloved counselor and majordomo Pere Torroella, knight) and granted him the income from the windmills attached to the Castle of Bellcaire near Torrellas's family home in northern Catalonia. The documents praising Torrellas and granting the income also refer to his recent marriage to Yolant de Levià. In the 1460s Torrellas was active in the civil wars pitting Dom Pedro of Portugal (1429–1466) against Juan II for rule of Catalonia, which took place when the Castilian nobility, backed by Juan II, challenged the throne of Enrique IV of Castile. In 1475 Juan II named his former seneschal Lord of Empordà.

All of Torrellas's known work is preserved in the *cancioneros*, where forty-six poems in Spanish and Catalan are attributed to him directly and eleven more poems may be the products of his pen.[31] In addition to the poems, his *Defense of Ladies against Slanderers* and thirteen other short prose works are also preserved in *cancionero* manuscripts. Many of the poems in Catalan are addressed to a female figure Torrellas calls by the code name, or *senhal*, "*Bé de mos mals*," which can be loosely translated as "Good of my ills." The name is a play upon the language of courtly love, in which love is a pleasurable malady and the beloved, who causes the illness, is the source of both favor and suffering. The majority of Torrellas's poems in Spanish are also love poems. Like the *Slander*, Torrellas's prose works are also intimately related to his life at court, including short pieces mourning the

---

31. Archer, "Introducció," x. For Torrellas's complete works in Spanish and Catalan see Pere Torroella, *Obra completa*, ed. Robert Archer (Soveria Mannelli, Italy: Rubbettino, 2004) and *Obra completa*, ed. Francisco Rodríguez Risquete, 2 vols. (Barcelona: Barcino, 2011).

deaths of prominent figures, an imaginary letter from Demosthenes to Alexander the Great, and exchanges of letters with other writers, notably a series of letters on the nature of love with Pedro de Urrea.

JUAN DE FLORES

Other than the conjecture that "Juan de Flores was a Castilian noble," little was known about Flores's life until the archival investigations of Joseph J. Gwara and Carmen Parrilla demonstrated that he was nothing less than an official chronicler to the Catholic Monarchs, a *corregidor*, or royal administrator, and may have also served as a rector at the University of Salamanca.[32] The identification of Juan de Flores as the author of the previously anonymous *Crónica incompleta de los Reyes Católicos* (Unfinished Chronicle of the Catholic Monarchs) and the discovery of new works also attributable to his pen reveal him to have been a major figure in Castilian letters, indeed one of, if not *the* most "prolific, versatile, and influential writer of late-fifteenth-century Spain."[33]

Flores is the author of two short romances, *Grisel and Mirabella*, presented here, and *Grimalte and Gradissa*, a continuation of Boccaccio's *The Elegy of Lady Fiammeta*. In *Grimalte*, the title character attempts to unite Fiametta and her beloved Panfilo as a test of his love for Gradissa and proof of his worthiness. Grimalte's project is unfruitful; Fiametta's love for Panfilo remains unrequited, as does Grimalte's for Gradissa. Although it was not as widely disseminated as *Grisel and Mirabella*, *Grimalte and Gradissa* also enjoyed an international readership in the sixteenth century, when it was translated into French.

Flores's unfinished *Chronicle of the Catholic Monarchs* covers the tumultuous time leading to Isabel I's marriage to Fernando II of

32. See Gwara, "The Identity of Juan de Flores: The evidence of the *Crónica incompleta de los Reyes Católicos*," *Journal of Hispanic Philology* 11.2 (1987): 103–29; and "The Identity of Juan de Flores: The evidence of the *Crónica incompleta de los Reyes Católicos* (concluded)," *Journal of Hispanic Philology* 11.3 (1987): 205–22; as well as Carmen Parrilla, "Un cronista olvidado: Juan de Flores, autor de la *Crónica incompleta de los Reyes Católicos*," in *The Age of the Catholic Monarchs, 1475–1516: Literary Studies in Memory of Keith Whinnom*, ed. Alan Deyermond and Ian Macpherson (Liverpool: Liverpool University Press, 1989), 123–33.

33. Gwara, "The Identity of Juan de Flores (concluded)," 222.

Aragon and the early years of their reign. In addition to the discovery of Flores's official role in the court of the Catholic Monarchs, in recent decades, more works attributed to him have come to light. In 1976 *Triunfo de amor* (The Triumph of Love) previously thought to be a lost or even non-existent work, was recovered.[34] *The Triumph of Love* is an allegory in which a civil war breaks out between all the subjects, both living and dead, of the God of Love. When the war ends, Love mandates a new courtly code, ordering that men no longer court women. Rather, women must forever more court men. Composed at roughly the same time as Flores's chronicle, *The Triumph of Love* allegorizes the civil war preceding Isabel I's consolidation of power and the challenge to traditional gender roles inherent in her presence on the throne. A fourth work, *La coronación de la Señora Gracisla* (The Coronation of the Lady Gracisla), which was recovered at the same time as the *Triumph of Love*, can also be reliably attributed to Flores.[35] *The Coronation* relates the story of a beauty contest and, like the *Triumph of Love*, contains elements suggesting its intention as a *roman à clé*.

Flores's fictional works, with the exception of *The Coronation*, are all dedicated to female readers. As an official historian, he was writing for a very particular female reader, Isabel I, who was in many ways his "most privileged reader."[36] Appointed chronicler in 1476, Flores would undoubtedly have had personal contact with his royal patrons and personal knowledge of the affairs of their court.[37]

---

34. Grieve, "Juan de Flores Other Work: Technique and Genre of *Triumpho de Amor*," *Journal of Hispanic Philology* 5 (1980): 25–40. On history and the politics of gender in *Triunfo*, see Francomano, "Juan de Flores Delivers a Bull," in *"De ninguna cosa es alegre posesión sin compañía": Estudios celestinescos y medievales en honor del profesor Joseph Thomas Snow*, ed. Devid Paolini (New York: Hispanic Seminary of Medieval Studies, 2010), 2:151–161; Gerli, "Gender Trouble: Juan de Flores's *Triunfo de Amor*, Isabel la Católica, and the Economies of Power at Court," *Journal of Spanish Cultural Studies* 4.2 (2003): 169–84; and Weissberger, Isabel's 'Nuevas leyes': Monarchic Law and Justice in *Triunfo de Amor*," in *Juan de Flores: Four Studies*, ed. Gwara (London: Department of Hispanic Studies, Queen Mary and Westfield College, 2005), 91–113.

35. Gwara "Another Work by Juan de Flores: *La coronación de la señora Gracisla*," in *Studies on the Spanish Sentimental Romance*, 75–110.

36. Weissberger, "Isabel's 'Nuevas leyes'," 92.

37. Gwara, "The Identity of Juan de Flores," 108; and "The Identity of Juan de Flores (concluded)," 206.

Content and Analysis of Pere Torrellas's Slander *and* Defense

THE SLANDER AGAINST WOMEN

"The man in love who courts / a woman, destroys himself." So begins the poem that would come to be called the *Slander*. Although it is impossible to know with certainty, at our centuries-long remove from the genesis and first audiences of the poem, it is likely that it was intended to entertain a courtly gathering of men and women in Naples in the 1440s.[38] It was probably meant to be provocative in the same mischievous way that much *cancionero* lyric is. Twelve stanzas declaim the vices and defects of women: they are ungracious, capricious, lascivious, obsessive, greedy, fickle, cunning, often physically repugnant, liars and schemers who deceive and disappoint men at every turn. In the words of Robert Archer, the *Slander* is a "a rosary of neatly phrased misogynistic ideas."[39] Torrellas cleverly couched the all-too familiar accusations in the octosyllabic rhyming verses that are commonplace in *cancionero* poetry. Yet, as readings of debate literature continually reveal, misogynist humor, no matter how "innocently" and playfully presented, gave audiences serious food for thought.[40] The *Slander* certainly fanned the flames of discord.

The *Slander* is a product of cultural and geographic confluence. Such poetic invectives were familiar in Catalan-Occitan literary circles, but were unprecedented in Castilian *cancioneros*, where individual women were sometimes made the targets of vituperation, but never in the context of courtly love itself, and where the "Woman Question" was a theme the courtly poets did not address.[41] The

---

38. Although most scholars date the poem's composition between 1440 and 1460, Weiss, following Brian Dutton, argues for an earlier date, circa 1435. "'¿Qué demandamos de las mugeres?'" 268n. Rodríguez Risquete posits that it could not have been composed any earlier than 1436. *Obra completa*, 2: 96.

39. *The Problem of Woman*, 170.

40. As Blamires cautions, in speaking about literary defenses of women "a distinction should be made between the seriousness with which the views are held by the writers … and the seriousness which a reader is able to find in the views constructed." *The Case for Women*, 31. The same, I would argue, is true for invective texts.

41. Rosanna Cantavella, *Els cards i el llir: una lectura de l'Espill de Jaume Roig* (Barcelona: Quaderns Crema, 1992), 36. This idea is fully explored by Archer in "Las coplas 'De las

querelle Torrellas provoked, which is as much a debate about masculine courtliness as it is about women, shows the tension between older and newer court identities.

The poem begins as a courtly lover's complaint, but quickly veers off the well-known course of describing or remonstrating a *belle dame sans merci*. This familiar conceit places the poet and unnamed ladies in the standard positions of lover and object of courtly love. And, as Robert Archer notes, the first five stanzas maintain this relationship between poetic subject and female love object.[42] Unlike clerical diatribes such as the Martínez de Toledo's *Corbacho*, Torrellas does not deplore the apotheosis of women in the courtly "religion of love;" nor does the *Slander* concern itself with the state of man's soul before God.[43] Rather, the poem is almost entirely concerned with the behavior of women toward men in amorous matters. On the other hand, accusations of heresy were not only wielded by moralists critical of courtly love; poets who criticized Torrellas and others who speak ill of women as *maldizientes* (slanderers) called them heretics against the religion of love. Such accusations were akin to accusations of homosexuality, thus recalling the frequent association of so-called deviant sexuality with religious heterodoxy.[44]

In the third stanza, Torrellas turns from the commonplace complaints of a slighted lover to proverbial wisdom. Women, he says, "are just like she-wolves / when they choose a mate."[45] He does not mean that they are bloodthirsty predators, as the English suggests, but rather, refers to the Spanish adage that women, like she-wolves in heat, always choose the least attractive male to be found. This proverb

---

calidades de las donas' de Pere Torroella y la tradición lírica catalana," *Boletín de la Real Academia de Buenas Letras de Barcelona* 47 (1999–2000): 405–23.

42. *The Problem of Woman*, 175.

43. Gerli discusses the connections between courtly love and clerical misogyny in "La 'religión del amor' y el antifeminismo en las letras castellanas del siglo XV," *Hispanic Review* 49.1 (1981): 65–81.

44. Weissberger, "'A Tierra Puto!' Alfonso de Palencia's Discourse of Effeminacy," in *Queer Iberia: Sexualities, Cultures, and Crossings from the Middle Ages to the Renaissance*, ed. Josiah Blackmore and Gregory S. Hutcheson (Durham, NC: Duke University Press, 1999), 291–24.

45. "De natura de lobas son / ciertamente, en escoger."

equating women with wolves when they choose a mate is glossed by Juan Luis Vives in *The Education of A Christian Woman*:

> I have seen women who do not recoil from men whose nature is worse than that of brute beasts—dirty drunk, wrathful, stupid, imprudent, idiotic, cruel, and blood-thirsty, who have less in common with men than wild beasts, [and women] who flee and avoid the company of wise and temperate men. This conduct inspired one of our own writers, using the vernacular tongue to attack them, saying that they have the instinct of she-wolves in choosing a mate, since they are said to choose the vilest and most foul-smelling of the males that follow after them. From this characteristic the name of she-wolf has been assigned to women.[46]

Vives' reference to Torrellas, written in 1523, attests to the long-lived reputation of the poet. Torrellas turns the proverb into an extended simile, elaborating upon the proverb with animal lore that is not normally connected to sexual activity:

> Truly, women are just like she-wolves
> when they choose a mate,
> like eels, when hooked into the bait,
> when they resist, like porcupines;
> they think nothing of virtue or ability,
> intelligence, kindness, or wisdom
> rather, they look for advantage,
> comely ways, and generosity,
> where riches may be had.[47]

---

46. *The Education of a Christian Woman: A Sixteenth-Century Manual*, trans. Charles Fantazzi, (Chicago: University of Chicago Press, 2000), 161.

47. "De natura de lobas son / ciertamente, en escoger, / de anguillas en retener, / e en contrastar, de erisón; / no estiman virtud ni abteça, / seso, bondat, nin saber, / mas catan abinenteza, / talle de obrar e franqueza, / do puedan bienes aver."

The second verse of the stanza is emblematic of the concise yet obscure syntax characteristic of *cancionero* lyric. Women are "de anguillas en retener;" literally, they are "in holding, like eels." The line yields two, opposite interpretations. On the one hand women may be like eels because they are slippery and hard to hold on to.[48] However, the line may also refer to the hooked teeth common to some types of eels, which allow them to snag the flesh of their prey.[49] Both interpretations further the poem's invective. Torrellas next equates women with porcupines, who, according to medieval bestiaries, when attacked roll into a ball and shoot out their quills.

The invective escalates, as it moves from the register of courtly love to definitions of women's nature in stanzas six through twelve. Torrellas includes a scabrous double entendre when he claims that women lead men on only to disappoint them because they need to keep hidden physical defects a secret. However, *secreto* means both "secret," and was also used in medieval Castilian as a noun referring to a small bag or purse kept hidden within the skirts of a garment. The implication is that the hidden defect is genital. Rodríguez Risquete further remarks that the defect alluded to may be the loss of virginity.[50]

Throughout the poem, Torrellas aligns himself and men with cultural authority, opposing male humanity to female subhumanity. In the eleventh stanza, Torrellas returns to the concept of women's animal nature, announcing in the first line that "Woman" is an animal. The second line, however, reveals that the poet is paraphrasing the Aristotelian theory on the generation of women:

> Woman is that animal
> we call an imperfect man,
> procreated by defect
> of nature's good heat.[51]

48. Archer and Rodríguez Risquete both interpret the line in this manner. Archer, ed., *Obra completa*, 204n and Rodríguez Risquete, ed., *Obra completa*, 2:107.

49. This is Nicasio Salvador Miguel's reading. "La tradición animalística en las *Coplas de las calidades de las donas*, de Pere Torrellas," *El crotalón* 2 (1985): 215–24.

50. *Obra completa*, 2:108.

51. "Mujer es un animal / que se diz' hombre inperfecto / procreado en el defecto / del buen calor natural."

Thus, in the same way that prior verses yielded dual meanings, this one too doubly advances Torrellas's invective. The idea that women were malformed men, the results of gestational damage to the normative male fetus, is a medieval commonplace, traceable to Aristotle and Galen.

The greater part of Torrellas's cleverly couched litany of female vices contains few surprises for readers and listeners attuned to the misogynist tradition. However, stanza nine suggests a glimmer of true insight into gender relations in fifteenth-century court society, a glimmer that will intensify into a warm, if heavily ironic, glow in Torrellas's prose retraction of the *Slander*, to which we will return below. Stanza nine makes a move away from the sphere of male-female romantic relations, revealing an awareness of the political and social status of women. Women recognize their own powerlessness, Torrellas says, and this is why they use tricks, hypocrisy and cosmetics in order to gain the upper hand in their relationships with men:

> Feeling that they are subjugated
> and lacking any power
> in order to take control
> women form shady sects.[52]

Here, as Weissberger observes, the poem "tacitly acknowledge[s] the inequities inherent in the traditional gender hierarchy and express[es] fear that the subjected gender may seek to correct them."[53] Women, Torrellas implies, know perfectly well that the apotheosis of the courtly beloved lady is a sham, and he knows it too. This is not to say that Torrellas here makes any objection concerning real women's lack of power. Rather, the stanza is offered as a caution to men, as a safeguard for the "normal" hierarchy. I would not go so far as Nicasio Salvador Miguel's assertion that the poem demonstrates Torrellas's profound knowledge of women, but this stanza and the later *Defense* do indeed contain social commentary suggesting that the

---

52. "Sintiendo que son subjectas / e sin negund poderío, / a fin de aver señorío / tienen engañosas sectas."

53. "'Deceitful Sects': The Debate about Women in the Age of Isabel the Catholic," in *Gender in Debate*, 213.

status of women is problematic.[54] The texts in the *querelle* provoked by the *Slander*, like the Italian defenses of women studied by Pamela Benson, are "less comfortably patriarchal" than it would seem.[55] Indeed, no defamation of women is comfortably patriarchal; rather their reiteration of misogynist diatribe belies what Mark Breitenberg terms "anxious masculinity," expressed as the need to continually protect and reaffirm male superiority and authority. Masculine pre-eminence is supposedly unquestionable, as is the right of men to rule, but the hyper-orthodoxy of defamations and negative definitions of women, indeed their very existence, shows that such rights were continually in question.[56]

The final stanza offers a palinode: the litany of vices only serves, Torrellas claims, to exalt his beloved, who is "unlike all the others." Whereas Torrellas's fellow men were the audience imagined in the preceding stanzas, here, he addresses a single woman, who he claims gives the lie to the universal definition of Woman just asserted.

> You, Lady of this my life,
> are unlike all the others;
> far from the common lot,
> you, alone in a world of two,[57]

54. *La poesía cancioneril: El Cancionero de Estúñiga* (Madrid: Alhambra, 1977), 228.

55. *The Invention of the Renaissance Woman* (University Park, PA: Pennsylvania State University Press, 1992), 4.

56. Masculinity, Mark Breitenberg suggests, is "inherently anxious," and the cultural productions that construct masculinity within patriarchal contexts inevitably express anxiety because they construct male subjects as superior, yet also in need of the "constant defense" of their privileged position: "masculine subjectivity constructed and sustained by a patriarchal culture—infused with patriarchal assumptions about power, privilege, sexual desire, the body—inevitably engenders varying degrees of anxiety in its male members." *Anxious Masculinity in Early Modern England* (Cambridge, UK: Cambridge University Press, 1996), 1–3. As Weissberger asserts, the concept of "anxious masculinity" is certainly not limited to English literature. Rather, it can be seen in "any discursive strategy that expresses, articulates, and/or contains a perceived loss of masculine power and privilege" and is a particularly useful concept for understanding the literary productions associated with the reign of Isabel I of Castile. *Isabel Rules*, xv.

57. Casas Rigall suggests that Torrellas' description of his lady as "alone in a world of two" is meant as a comparison between the lady praised in the poem and the Virgin Mary. *Agudeza y retórica en la poesía amorosa de cancionero* (Santiago de Compostela, Spain: Universidade

are she who undoes
all that my verses contain.[58]

Thus, the diatribe moves from a description of dangerous *donas* (ladies), to accusations against all women, to a definition of Woman, only to conclude with praise for one *dona*, who stands out from the reprehensible common lot of women.

This technique of rhetorical about-face, or *suspensio*, is common to *cancionero* poetry.[59] In Keith Whinnom's words, it constitutes a "defraudación del lector," a purposeful disappointment of readerly expectations cultivated from the outset of the poem.[60] Nevertheless, the palinode is not necessarily a retraction. Readers and listeners are left to decide if the existence of this one woman does indeed "undo" Torrellas's verses or if she is the exception that proves the rule so piquantly and exhaustively expounded in the rest of the poem.

THE DEFENSE OF LADIES AGAINST SLANDERERS

Following the circulation of the *Slander*, Torrellas apparently saw himself obliged to apologize in writing. Nevertheless, his recantations continue the general ambivalence of the debate as a whole. The full title of Torrellas's retraction is *A Treatise by Pere Torrellas in Defense of Ladies against Slanderers in Recompense for Some Verses He Composed in Which He Defames The Aforementioned Ladies*.[61] In the three surviving manuscript versions the *Defense* is always introduced with a statement that the piece was written as reparation for the *Slander*. In one manuscript, the *Cancionero Coimbra Universitaria*, the *Defense* follows directly upon the heels of the *Slander*.

---

de Santiago de Compostela, 1995), 209. Archer, on the other hand, argues that Torrellas means that his *dama* is so rare, there are only two like her in the world (*Obra completa*, 216). Both meanings could in fact be present in the final stanza.

58. "Entre las otras sois vós, / dama de aquesta mi vida, / del traste común salida, / ... vós sois la que desfaséis / lo que contienen mis versos."

59. Casas Rigall, *Agudeza y retórica*, 209

60. *La poesía amatoria cancioneril*, 71.

61. *Razonamiento de Pere Torrella en defensión de las donas contra los maldezientes, por satisfación de unas coplas qu'en dezir mal de aquellas compuso.*

The prose *Defense* begins with a disquisition on the difference between the terms "woman" (*muger*) and "lady" (*dona*) and then revisits each of the arguments inveighed against both women and ladies in the *Slander*, cunningly turning them into causes for praise. This is precisely the rhetorical strategy used in many profeminine texts described by Alcuin Blamires as redoctrination.[62] Torrellas glosses *dona* as "she who must be obeyed" in the demand for an apology for the *Slander*. *Muger*, on the other hand, signifies *mansedumbre* (gentleness, pliability), which Torrellas claims means the promise of pardon. Torrellas draws upon Isidore of Seville's highly influential but false etymology of the Latin *mulier* (woman), from which the Spanish muger derives. Isidore's etymology and explanation of the differences between men and women is relevant to the *querelle des femmes* on the whole and also to the terms of the debate in Juan de Flores's *Grisel and Mirabella*. Consequently, it is worth quoting at length here:

> A man (*vir*) is so called, because in him resides greater power (*vis*) than in a woman—hence also 'strength' (*virtus*) received its name—or else because he deals with a woman by force (*vis*). But the word woman (*mulier*) comes from softness (*mollities*), as if *mollier* (cf. *mollior*, "softer"), after a letter has been cut and a letter changed, is now called mulier. These two are differentiated by the respective strength and weakness of their bodies. But strength is greater in a man, lesser in a woman, so that she will submit to the power of the man; evidently this is so lest, if women were to resist, lust should drive men to seek out something else or throw themselves upon the male sex. As I was saying, woman (*mulier*) is named for her feminine sex, not for a corruption of her innocence, and this is according to the word of Sacred Scripture, for Eve was called woman as soon as she was made from the side of her

---

62. Blamires's discussion of "redoctrination" appears in "Refiguring the 'Scandalous Excess' of Women: The Wife of Bath and Liberality," in *Gender in Debate from the Middle Ages to the Renaissance*, ed. by Thelma S. Fenster and Clare A. Lees (New York: Palgrave, 2002), 57–78.

man, when she had not yet had any contact with a
man as is said in the Bible.[63]

Torrellas's comparison of *dona* and *muger* is not without irony,
as the two words were often used interchangeably in his day, *dona* de-
riving from Torrellas's native Catalan. *Dona* was also used in Spanish
as a synonym for *dueña* (a woman of high status). However, Torrellas
wants to make a critical distinction that echoes the defenses of courtliness with which he was attacked for the *Slander*. Authorities such as
Solomon, Ovid, and Boccaccio who defame women, Torrellas argues,
were not speaking of *donas*, but of *fembras* (females). More importantly, he also echoes the *Slander*, which begins by alerting readers
to the perils of courting a *dona* and proceeds to define *muger* as an
"imperfect animal." The rhetorical force of the *Slander* in part derives
from the elision of the distinction between courtly *donas* and the universal category of Woman. What had been joined for rhetorical effect
in the *Slander* is sundered in the *Defense*. To these two terms, Torrellas
adds a third: *señoras*, used to address part of his collective inscribed
audience.

In the *Slander*, Torrellas addressed male courtly lovers and
then the unnamed "Lady of this my life," identifying himself with men
who find themselves rejected, in the thrall of, and threatened by wom-
en throughout the poem. In the *Defense*, Torrellas addresses *maldizientes* (slanderers) as well as women, and explicitly places himself in
the ambiguous position of being both a *maldiziente* and a defender of
women. He refers to the *maldizientes* as both "you" and "we" and also
ardently claims his desire to serve women in a courtly fashion.

Following the definitions of ladies and women, the *Defense*
paraphrases classic arguments on the superiority of woman extrapo-
lated from the Creation story: Eve was created from superior material and in a superior place than was Adam. Torrellas next turns to
the subject of Woman and women, saying that any *maldiziente* who
claims to be speaking of all women is clearly in the wrong, and then
producing a list of over one hundred "good" women. This catalog includes individual women from legends and biblical narratives, as well

---

63. *The Etymologies of Isidore of Seville*, ed. and trans. by Stephen A. Barney, W. J. Lewis, J. A.
Beach, and Oliver Berghof (Cambridge, UK: Cambridge University Press, 2006), IX.ii., 242.

as from ancient and recent history, such as Sappho, Minerva, Lucretia, the Virgin Mary and the Spanish María Coronel, famous either for staving off the sexual advances of Pedro The Cruel (1334–1369) by disfiguring her face with boiling oil, or for combating her sexual appetites during her husband's absence by mutilating her genitals with a burning brand. Torrellas also cites the behavior of entire nations of women, such as Indians, the Sabine women, and the Israelites. As in other late-medieval profeminine works, self-mutilation and the practice of *sati*, or the immolation of widows upon their husband's funeral pyres, are praised as heroic feats of chastity and proof of women's superior love.

In addition to commonplaces of heroic chastity, Torrellas includes some ambiguous figures in his catalog, such as Sempronia, who appears both in his short list of bad women and in his list of women to be praised for their singular wisdom. Among the women who gave up their lives for love, Torrellas mentions a "Spanish Zamorana," which may be a reference to Queen Urraca of Zamora (1033 or 1034–1101), who was rumored to be her brother Alfonso's lover.[64] Moreover, Torrellas adds characters from popular late-medieval fiction, such as the faithful but star-crossed Ghismonda from the fourth day of Boccaccio's *Decameron*, to his list. Unlike the catalogs of good women that Torrellas draws upon for his examples, such as Boccaccio's *Famous Women*, Álvaro de Luna's *Book of Famous and Virtuous Women*, and Diego de Valera's *Defense of Virtuous Women*, Torrellas does not give the details of each famous woman's or group of women's lives and deeds. His examples would have been well known to readers of his day. Nevertheless, by merely enumerating rather than describing and praising his examples, Torrellas allowed his readers to recall that many of the names he includes were often also listed in catalogs of "bad" women.[65]

64. Rodríguez Risquete posits the identity of the "Zamorana" as Queen Urraca. *Obra completa*, 2.197.

65. For late-medieval catalogs of women, see Glenda McLeod, *Virtue and Venom: Catalogs of Women from Antiquity to the Renaissance* (Ann Arbor: University of Michigan Press, 1991).

Torrellas then proceeds to take up and "spin" many of the accusations leveled at women in the *Slander* into motives for defense.[66] The direct parallels that can be drawn between the two texts suggest that the apology was composed with tongue in cheek, as the *Slander* may have been as well. In addition to close relationship between the *Slander* and the *Defense*, many of the arguments that Pere Torrellas uses ostensibly to defend women are echoed in *Grisel and Mirabella* when Braçayda attacks men in general and the character Torrellas. Flores may well have been familiar with Torrellas's *Defense* as well as his *Slander*.

The *Defense*, however, enters into more serious and critical waters when Torrellas, speaking now as a fellow *maldiziente* to a male audience, considers the very real issues of marriage, family relations, and domestic abuse:

> But tell me, you unmanly man, if accusing women
> pleases you, if all the crimes that you impute to wom-
> en were true, could any one equal that crime for which
> God said, "It repenteth me that I have made man"? Of
> course not. But we men, taking counsel from malice,
> as if forgetting our own defects, make women's little
> flaws out to be huge, their doubtful defects certain,
> and their hidden ones public. We are not satisfied by
> having turned women from companions into slaves.
> It is not enough for us that we marry them off without
> their consent, that we give many women to lords and
> masters who would hardly be worthy of being their
> vassals. It is not enough for us that, as lawmakers,
> favoring ourselves and putting women at a disadvan-
> tage, we define our own criminal offenses as civil ones,
> and women's civil offenses as criminal. No, it is not
> enough for us that—some by jealous husbands, others
> by malicious mothers-in-law, others by spiteful moth-
> ers, others by whomever, for they are never lacking
> in superiors—women be continually abused. We are

---

66. Archer, "'Tus falsas opiniones e mis verdaderas razones': Pere Torroella and the Woman-Haters," *Bulletin of Hispanic Studies* 78 (2001): 551–66.

not satisfied by the thousands of other injuries, injustices, accusations, and even more attacks on women, so now we seek their dishonor with an onslaught of new insults.

Lest we attribute too much sincerity to this barrage of accusations against men, it is important to note that Torrellas also refers to women's "hidden defects" here, recalling stanza six of the *Slander*, where he accuses women of leading men on but stopping short of granting their favors in order to hide their physical defects. When speaking of women and gender relations, Torrellas is never "comfortably patriarchal," nor entirely serious; the irony of the two works allows the contradictions of slander and defense to coexist.

Jill Mann asks whether apologies to women are "as conventional as the antifeminism for which they purportedly attempt reparation," or if we might see in them any "evidence of a genuine sensitivity to what real-life women might be thinking and feeling[.]"[67] In Torrellas's contributions to the *querelle*, the answers to both questions are qualified affirmatives. Torrellas was skilled at using the "protective shield of rhetoric" that an apology offered, but he also seems to have had a keen eye for the pathologies of gender relations in fifteenth-century aristocratic society.[68] The final impression left from the two works is a blend of strident, traditional misogyny, anxious masculinity, sardonic profeminism and, in the end, a critical diagnosis of gender relations that unmasks courtly love as an attractive yet ultimately impotent construct, a courtly game that in its elevation of "women" to "ladies" does not change the domestic and political order of society.

Afterlife of the Slander

As Robert Archer concludes in his study of Spanish texts that address issues of gender identity and relations, "It can be stated confidently that there were few readers or writers of Hispanic vernacular texts between the mid-fifteenth century and the mid-sixteenth who did not know

67. *Apologies to Women: Inaugural Lecture Delivered 20th November, 1990* (Cambridge, UK: Cambridge University Press, 1991), 3.

68. Mann, *Apologies to Women*, 30.

Torrellas's poem."[69] Although the *Slander* first appeared and circulated in courtly, aristocratic settings, the growth of the printing industry, particularly in the first decades of the sixteenth century, facilitated the spread of both his poem and his fame as the Spanish-speaking world's ultimate misogynist. Torrellas's *Defense* was quickly forgotten, but the *Slander* was copied into many manuscript anthologies of court poetry, seventeen of which are now extant, dating from the 1460s to the middle of the sixteenth century, and was also reproduced in the nine editions of the *Cancionero general*, published in both Spain and in the Netherlands, although some editions attributed the diatribe against women to another poet.[70] Indeed, Torrellas became a commonplace for those wishing to attack women or criticize misogynist discourse, for they "could do so with reference to a specifically Hispanic *maldiziente* rather than the more distant figures of Solomon or Boccaccio, and could refer to a Hispanic text."[71]

The Responses

At least twelve poets wrote responses to the *Slander*, and to other misogynist texts, in the years between Torrellas's incendiary poem's first appearance and the publication of the *Cancionero general*. Some of the responses are addressed—slung may be a better term—at Torrellas directly, while others are more generalized and attack any and all *maldizientes*. The responses are representative of the ways that cancionero poets formulated the debate about women as a debate about male courtliness. These replies to Torrellas, like so much of the *cancionero* tradition, portray the poets in a continual competition of courtly one-upmanship in which old ideals and new social realities come into conflict.

---

69. *The Problem of Woman*, 170.

70. Dutton and Jineen Krogstad provide the texts of all known versions of the *Slander* as well as of the poetic responses to Torrellas in *El cancionero del siglo XV, ca. 1360–1520*, 7 vols. (Salamanca: University of Salamanca, 1990–1991). The poems are also available on the University of Liverpool, UK, website, "An Electronic Corpus of 15th Century Castilian *Cancionero* Manuscripts," http://cancionerovirtual.liv.ac.uk.

71. Archer, *The Problem of Woman*, 170.

Suero de Ribera (ca. 1410–1475) and another poet active in the 1450s and 1460s known only as Carvajal, who both may have known Torrellas personally through their mutual connections to the Neapolitan court, attacked the *Slander* by writing defenses of the courtly code and courtly love rather than of women. Ribera, a prolific author and Neapolitan courtier from a powerful Castilian family, charges that *maldizientes* have no right to call themselves gentlemen because "noble men must be the protectors of women" (los fidalgos han de ser / defensa de las mujeres). Ribera asserts that it is a blight upon the good name of a man's lineage if he maligns women publicly; courtesy and nobility demand that men keep silent even about "base women" (las baxas).[72] Ribera's response concludes by equating all men who do not protect women from slander with the slanderers, who deserve to be ill treated by women. Carvajal, who was possibly a *converso* or New Christian, calls an unnamed *maldiziente* a heretic who has blasphemed against the religion of courtly love and deserves to be stoned for his apostasy. In response to the complaint that women do not requite the love that is offered to them or favor their suitors, Carvajal declares, "It is the man who loves and not the one who is beloved who is called virtuous" (al amante et non al amado / se atribuye la virtud).[73]

Whereas Suero de Ribera took aim at Torrellas's lack of gentility, Antón de Montoro (1404–ca. 1477), a convert to Christianity known as "The Tailor of Cordoba," launches an even more pointed attack upon Torrellas's lineage in his cutting "I know not who you are, Torrellas" (Yo non sé quién soys, Torroellas).[74] Other poets praised Montoro in their verses, but also made fun of his origins as a Jew and a merchant, two social identities that would have seemed incompatible with courtly poetry to many of his contemporaries. It is important, however, to note that Montoro was not alone in his susceptibility to accusations of "unclean blood" by other poets. Many of the literati of

72. *Respuesta de Suero de Ribera en defensión de las donas* (Suero de Ribera's Response in Defense of Ladies), in *El cancionero del siglo XV*, 2:7–8 and 364–65; 4:58 and 370.

73. *Respuesta en defensión de amor* (Response in Defense of Love), in *El cancionero del siglo XV*, 2:362 and 4:56; 367–68.

74. Julio Rodríguez-Puértolas, "Introducción," in Antón de Montoro, *Cancionero*, ed. Marcella Ciceri (Salamanca: Universidad de Salamanca, 1990), 14–15.

the time came from families who had converted to Christianity and *cancionero* poetry was one of the forums in which lettered men aired their suspicions and cast aspersions upon one another. Montoro does not accuse Torrellas of Jewish roots. Rather, he lambasts Torrellas as barely human, a monster pulled from the ground like a mandrake, engendered when a lowly shepherd masturbated into the dirt. Montoro's aspersions on Torrellas's lineage are a potent reminder that, in the *cancioneros* and courts of the second half of the fifteenth century, the debate on women is also a forum for debates about social origins: racial, religious, and nobiliary. Montoro's attack is paired with an ironic retraction in which he admits that Torrellas is right about women. The insult, however, is not withdrawn. Montoro's ambivalence is emblematic of the tenor of the *querelle* texts found within the *cancionero* context.[75]

Gómez Manrique (ca. 1412–1490), another prolific poet and one of the first known playwrights in Spanish letters, was a highly placed noble and a trusted ally to Isabel I. Manrique responded to the *Slander* by using a classic strategy of poetic competition, matching each of Torrellas's stanzas with a refutation that follows the same rhyme and meter. The rebuttal, conserved in four *cancionero* manuscripts, begins with the lines "It is fitting that the man who argues against women be taught a lesson" (Conviene que castigue quien contra damas arguye).[76] What follows is a lengthy but anodyne encomium of women.

While there may never have been a formal debate on the question of women and the slander of women held at the courts Torrellas and his poetic respondents frequented, the *cancionero* tradition clearly constructs a debate between them.[77] Indeed, the internal organization

75. For Montoro's responses, see Antón de Montoro, *Cancionero*, 161–63 and *El cancionero del siglo XV*, 2:7 and 181; 3:18.

76. Gómez Manrique's *Respuesta al mal dicho de mossen Pedro Torrella catalano* (Response to Pedro Torrellas's Slander) is found in the two anthologies the poet probably compiled of his own work, *Obras de Gómez Manrique* and the *Cancionero de Gómez Manrique*, both of which date from circa 1475, and also in two Catalan *cancioneros*. For the full texts of each of the four copies, see *El cancionero del siglo XV*, 1:2–4 and 33–34; 2:208–09 and 469–70.

77. Although, as Archer argues, there "was no debate [on gender] in any real sense" in medieval and Early Modern Spanish literature, and that individual authors did not see themselves

of many *cancionero* manuscripts transmits the concept of an ongoing *querelle*. For example, Manrique's response is presented with the *Slander* in alternating stanzas in three anthologies and follows upon the heels of the *Slander* in one. The *mise en page* in the manuscripts thus heightens the debate effect.

When the *Slander* and Manrique's challenge are intertwined, moreover, the stridency of Torrellas's invective is attenuated, and it cannot build upon its own rhetorical force and escalation. The exchange ends with Manrique's praise for "Woman" as "Among the works of God, she is the very most favored" (Entre las obras de Dios / es la muy más escogida). If his *respuesta* (response) ended here, Manrique would already have had the last word, but he adds a concluding stanza for good measure, affirming that "Among ladies / there are many of good fame / and if others are not / it is because you provoke them / by plotting against them." (de las damas / hay muchas de buenas famas / y si algunas no lo son / será por vuestra ocasión / que urde las tales tramas). Once again, it is not so much the nature of women, but the behavior of men that concerns the poet in the end.

The material design of a debate is most evident in the manuscripts that present the *Slander* and Manrique's response under a single rubric. Nevertheless, other *cancioneros* create a similar image of an exchange of views on women and the men who slander them. The *Cancionero de Estúñiga* and the *Cancionero de Hixar* contain the *Slander*, followed directly by the *respuestas* of Suero de Ribera and of Antón de Montoro, respectively. Other manuscripts pair the *Slander* with Ribera's retort, with Montoro's responses, and with Hugo de Urriés' lengthy defense of women, *Señora discreta e mucho prudente* (Discreet and most prudent lady) written in *arte mayor* (lines of twelve syllables), a meter generally reserved for weighty issues in *cancionero* poetics.[78] In the *Cancionero Coimbra Universitaria*, the *Slander* is followed by Torrellas's own *Defense*.

The *querelle* ignited by the *Slander* continued throughout the fifteenth century and into the sixteenth. Hernan Mexía, another *cancionero* poet whose works were published in the *Cancionero general*,

---

as "participating in a form of disputational forum" (*The Problem of Woman*, 204), the format of the *Cancioneros* envisions the poets as if they were participating in a face to face debate.

78. *El cancionero del siglo XV*, 2:1–21.

wrote both against the *maldizientes* and in praise of Torrellas, whom he invokes as the "son of Boccaccio."[79] Juan del Encina, Pedro Manuel de Urrea, and Íñigo Beltrán de Valdelomar all wrote poems against *maldizientes* in the late fifteenth and early sixteenth centuries. In the anonymous sentimental romance *Triste deleytación*, written in the late 1450s or 1460s, two women discuss gender relations, naming Torrellas as the author of "abominable verses" and praising Juan Rodríguez del Padrón for the high opinion of women pronounced in his work.[80] The misogynist opinions voiced in the *Slander* were continued in prose as well, notably in *Celestina*.[81] Luis de Lucena used the *Slander* as the springboard for his parodic sermon against courtly love, *Repetición de amores* (Declamation on Love), published in the late fifteenth century, similarly elevating Torrellas to the status of authority on the subject of women and love.[82] Thus, by the end of the fifteenth century, the name of Torrellas had become commonplace in texts about the nature of women, men, and love. Given the great popularity of both the *Cancionero general* and *Grisel and Mirabella*, Flores's short romance would have been considered a contemporary allusion and extension of the debate for many readers.

Content and Analysis of Grisel and Mirabella

Juan de Flores's novella *Grisel and Mirabella* was composed in the 1480s and was probably first printed in Lérida in 1495.[83] From 1495 on, it was a "best seller" in the sixteenth-century sense. Unlike the

79. *Otras suyas en que descubre los defectos de las condiciones de las mugeres* (Other Verses by the Same Poet in which He Reveals the Defects of Women's Character), in *El cancionero del siglo XV*, 5:196–200.

80. F.A.d.C., *Triste deleytación: An Anonymous Fifteenth-Century Castilian Romance*, ed. E. Michael Gerli (Washington, D.C.: Georgetown University Press, 1982), 54.

81. Rojas, Fernando de, *Celestina*, ed. Dorothy Severin (Madrid: Cátedra, 1987).

82. *Repetición de Amores*, ed. Jacob Ornstein (Chapel Hill, NC: University of North Carolina Press, 1954).

83. This first known edition contains neither the date nor the publisher's location, but the type used indicates with near certainty that it was printed in Lérida by Henricus Botel in or circa 1495. See Gwara, "A Study of the Works of Juan de Flores, with a Critical Edition of *La historia de Grisel y Mirabella*" (Ph.D. diss., Westfield College, University of London, 1988), 452–56; and Maria Grazia Ciccarello Di Blasi, "Introduzione," in *Grisel y Mirabella*, 94–95.

cancionero poets and other writers who responded directly to the *Slander* by taking Torrellas to task or celebrating him, Flores used the *querelle* as the central plot in *Grisel*. Indeed, in the romance, oratory outweighs action. Building upon Torrellas's literary reputation and the abundance of connotations his very name elicited, Flores resuscitates the poet as a character who debates the nature of women. While the *cancionero* poems use the "Woman Question" as a topic that allows men to debate and fashion courtly manliness, Flores's sentimental romance of desire, suicide, and revenge brings women onto the stage as advocates in the debate concerning their natures. Women's voices are not heard in the *querelle* waged in *cancionero* poetry. Although the presence of vocal female characters in romance are at best "the fictional traces of voices in a dialogue whose words are lost,"[84] Flores's short prose romance, dedicated to an unnamed woman, but likely destined for Queen Isabel I and her court, opens the debate to women readers and characters.

Flores weaves the *querelle* into a complex and ironic story of the ill-fated Scottish lovers, Grisel and Mirabella. Mirabella is the only heir to the throne, but her father, who loves her too much to let her marry, has turned away all her suitors. He has also locked her away from sight because her unsurpassed beauty causes any and all men who see her to fall desperately in love and lose their lives competing for her. Despite the King's precautions, two knights persevere and manage to see Mirabella by scaling the walls of her prison at night. One evening, the two knights arrive at the same time, both intent on seeing Mirabella, and discover that they are intimate friends. Love triumphs over friendship, however, and after debating how to decide which of the two is more worthy of loving Mirabella, one knight kills the other. The victor is Grisel. Mirabella, overcome with sorrow for the deaths of so many knights and swayed by the force of Grisel's suit, falls in love with him and they find a way to engage in the "no less pleasing than perilous battle" of love in secret. The happy pair are discovered when Mirabella's maidservant tells her own lover, the *maestresala*—

84. Roberta Krueger, *Women Readers and the Ideology of Gender in Old French Verse Romance* (Cambridge, UK: Cambridge University Press, 1993), xiv.

the King's taster, a high-ranking household servant—about the affair, who in turn plots to catch Grisel and Mirabella *in flagrante.*[85]

Title Page of *Grisel y Mirabella*, Seville 1529

85. The chief duties of a *maestresala* concerned managing the king's table and tasting food to prevent poisoning. Real Academia Española, *Diccionario de la lengua española*, 22nd ed. s.v. "Maestresala." According to Ruperto de Nola, the *maestresala* occupied a position of slightly less importance than a majordomo and something like that of a butler; the *maestresala's* duties also included maintaining the smooth day-to-day operations of a noble household, the education of pages in arms and letters, and the maintenance of household furnishings. *Libro de guisados*, ed. Dionisio Pérez (Madrid: Nueva Biblioteca de Autores Españoles, 1929), 25–27.

At this point Flores alerts readers to the "Law of Scotland," which demands that when a couple is caught in an illicit affair, the partner most responsible for inflaming and acting upon sexual desire be executed and the other be banished for life. Both Grisel and Mirabella claim to be the one at fault, each saying that they forced the other. Despite torture, neither lover retracts their statement. Consequently, the King and his counselors decide that the only way to ascertain who is really at fault in this particular case of seduction is to find out once and for all if men seduce women, causing them to sin, or if, on the other hand, women seduce men, causing their perdition in the process. In the counselors' words, they wish to learn whether "men or women, females or males ... [are] more at fault for the sin of the other."[86] This question is central to the *querelle des femmes* and to the debate in the *cancioneros*, where the *Slander* claims that women trick and seduce men and the responses argue that if women commit offenses against morality, it is because men force them to. The King's counselors say that they are more knowledgeable about law than love; consequently the help of experts is needed. Torrellas and the Homeric character Braçayda are called in to argue the case.

The foul-tongued "Torrellas" in *cancionero* poetry and narrative prose was already a fiction, a poetic voice created by the historical poet and also a figure of the imagination of the authors who wrote against and in imitation of him. The narrator of *Grisel* describes Torrellas as "renowned for his knowledge of women," "quite daring in the business of love," and a "great wit," and thus an ideal participant in a formal debate against a woman that might serve as the final judgment upon all women. Torrellas's opponent is also a character resuscitated from popular literature: Braçayda, more commonly known as Briseide or Criseyde, who often appears in medieval retellings of the Trojan war both as a "symbol of woman's inconstancy" and a "wronged, long-suffering and constant woman."[87] Moreover, in medieval narratives of the Trojan war, Braçayda is often portrayed as eloquent and skilled in argumentation, traits which would have made her an apt choice for

---

86. "Si los hombres o las mujeres o ellas o ellos quál d'estos era más occasión del yerro al otro."

87. Matulka, *The Novels of Juan de Flores*, 88–89.

Flores's narrative.[88] Flores was not the first Castilian author to rewrite Braçayda's story. Juan Rodríguez de Padrón turned Braçayda into a sympathetic figure in his *Bursario*, an adaptation of Ovid's *Heroides* that also contains several original letters, including an exchange between Braçayda and Troilus. Flores's intended audience also may have recognized her as one of the few female voices in the *cancioneros*, the woman to whom the motto "O, if only I had never been born!" is attributed by the poet Gómez de Rojas.[89]

Flores's introduction of the known historical and literary figures Torrellas and Braçayda, in what had heretofore been the quasi-mythical time of romance and in the space of far-off Scotland, much like his resuscitation of Boccaccio's characters in *Grimalte and Gradissa*, and of both historical and literary characters in *The Triumph of Love*, blurs the boundaries between fiction and reality. This is important in the context of debate literature, because the *querelle des femmes* is not only textual and discursive—an academic debate taking place in books—but also part of the social fabric of the late medieval and Early Modern periods, a discourse in the broader sense that had real effects.

Indeed, Flores underlines the fact that the trial will determine the future of gender relations and set a precedent for future cases: Braçayda is motivated not only by Mirabella's plight, but by her "general love for all women;" the men of the court know that "men's honor" is at stake and that if Torrellas loses the case, "they would have lost everything to women forever more."[90] The ensuing debate, which involves four exchanges of accusations, is heavily drawn from the *Slander* and in part from the responses to the *Slander*. Significantly, the two advocates do not mention the case at hand, but speak in universal terms of "men" and "women." Braçayda also directs *ad hominem* attacks against Torrellas, thus mixing the general and the particular in

88. Ciccarello Di Blasi, "Introduzione" in *Grisel y Mirabella*, 46–47; see also Roberto Antonelli, "The Birth of Criseyde—An Exemplary Triangle: 'Classical' Troilus and the Question of Love at the Anglo-Norman Court," in *The European Tragedy of Troilus*, ed. Piero Boitani (Oxford: Clarendon Press, 1989), 21–48.

89. "¡O, si yo nunca nasçiera!" *Poesía feminina en los cancioneros*, ed. Miguel Ángel Pérez Priego (Madrid: Editorial Castalia, 1989), 67–69.

90. "Que si de allí quedassen condenados: para siempre con las mugeres quedavan perdidos."

her arguments. As in the Torrellas *querelle*, the content of the debate concerns courtly love, but the romance *Grisel and Mirabella* suggests that it is impossible to separate issues of gender in courtly love from questions of gender identity and relations writ large.

Braçayda bases her defense, like many a combatant in the *querelle* before her, on women's relative weakness, to which she adds women's lack of discursive power in a world where men control knowledge and the legal system. Her rhetorical strategy is related to profeminine redoctrination. Nevertheless, Braçayda is not so much making the case for women as making a case against men and Torrellas. Braçayda exploits commonplace accusations of feminine weakness and defects and echoes replies to the *Slander*, including Torrellas's own *Defense of Ladies against Slanderers*, saying that women, as the weaker, less educated, less discreet, less knowing half of humanity, cannot be at fault in cases of sexual seduction. Consequently, women cannot force men to engage in sexual relations, but men can easily force women, for which women should not be blamed. Again echoing the *Slander*, she acknowledges that women are subject to men. As the powerless subjects of male control, she argues, women cannot be to blame if they are easily led to sin by men. Virtue, Braçayda contends, is no benefit to women, because men will slander even the most virtuous of women, and women would rather sin in secret than be lambasted in public.

Whereas in the *Slander* Torrellas compared women to shewolves, eels, and porcupines, Braçayda turns to the animal world to support her claim that women do not seduce men. Rather, just as male animals are more attractive than females and they strut in pursuit of mates, so it is in the world of men and women, where nature makes it men's work to pursue and court women, and women's work to defend themselves against men's onslaughts. However, her claim that men are like peacocks gives Torrellas the perfect entry to attack women for their use of cosmetics. He counters that the peacock's fan is like women's "splendid clothes." He repeats the *Slander's* comparison of women to wolves and also likens women to bridled horses, who strain at the reins and bits that hold them back from their desires.

Braçayda also turns accusations generally hurled at women into complaints about men. Women, she argues, are unable to resist

the seductive wiles of men, their persuasive speech, their letters, and even their looks. Men are hypocrites, pretending to love when they do not. She takes aim at the rhetoric and posturing of courtly love, chiding men for their hyperbolic claims: "Oh, how many of you men come before us complaining that you are at death's door, so melancholy and lovesick, that we must take pity on you even if we do not love you! You, by begging us for your lives, condemn us to death."[91] Such begging for a lady's mercy as the remedy for lovesickness is a commonplace in the language of courtly love. However, in Braçayda's complaint against men and throughout *Grisel and Mirabella*, Flores's calls readers' attention to the conceits of courtly language. In the romance, the figurative terms of "dying of love" become literal.[92]

One of Braçayda's most forceful statements recalls the Wife of Bath's question, "who painted the lion?" from Chaucer's *Canterbury Tales*:[93] "For, in our ignorance, we have no one to write in our favor, while you men, who hold pen in hand, can say whatever you want."[94] Like the Wife of Bath, Braçayda points out to her listeners that invectives against women are not the work of impartial observers. Braçayda's closing statement reminds Torrellas and her audience that many women throughout history have died at the hands of men in defense of their chastity, while no men have done so. She also denounces the hypocrisy of the very debate in which she has been called to defend women. When Torrellas claims that men are powerless in seduction, Braçayda retorts, "Well, now it seems you do not want to be lords over us in everything, for that is why we have come here, so that at least in

---

91. "¡O quientos venís ante nos tan mortales y tristes: que sin amor era razón de os haver piedad! Y por daros la vida: buscáisnos agora la muerte."

92. It is possible that Flores alludes here to another popular sentimental romance, *Cárcel de Amor* (*The Prison of Love*), in which the lovesick Leriano begs Laureola to save his life by showing mercy even though she does not love him. In *Cárcel*, the consequences of Laureola's mercy, such as it is, are disastrous. Diego de San Pedro, *Cárcel de Amor*, ed. Parrilla (Barcelona: Crítica, 1995).

93. Geoffrey Chaucer, "The Wife of Bath's Prologue and Tale," v. 692, in *The Riverside Chaucer*, 3rd ed., ed. Larry Benson (New York: Oxford University Press, 2008), 105–22.

94. "Porque en nuestra simplicidad no hay quién scriva en favor nuestro. Y vosotros que tenéis la pluma en la mano: pintáis como queréis."

the eyes of justice we will be equals."[95] Her irony presages the outcome of the debate.

Torrellas counters that women love to be courted and that even if they do not declare their desires in words, they know how to use *gestos* (gestures) and *señales* (signals), making the same claim as his historical namesake does in stanza nine of the *Slander*. Introducing his second response, he jokes that just as women are easy to seduce, it will be easy to beat Braçayda in the debate. Boasting about the many women who have propositioned him, Torrellas paraphrases stanzas ten and twelve of the *Slander*, alleging that if women were freed from shame, they would court men just as expertly as men now court women.[96] Again paraphrasing the *Slander*, he accuses women of hypocrisy and hidden crimes. In response to Braçayda's claim that women are innocent and ignorant in the face of men's superior knowledge and thus vulnerable, Torrellas claims that in reality women are cunning and knowing, though it is true that ignorance favors chastity: "I have often seen from experience that simpleminded women are somehow more chaste; hence ignorance is good for you and knowledge harmful, as you can clearly see, since all the clever women follow the course of our desires: 'she who knows most, sins most.'"[97]

Both combatants claim that the other sex is the root of all evil. Torrellas returns to this accusation for his closing argument, which is his most conventional, and perhaps for that reason, most effective in the frame of the narrative. There are no Lucretias in today's world, he retorts. In fact, with each generation, women get worse. Eve, born innocent, but in the "evil form" of woman, sinned and caused Adam to sin, sealing the fate of gender relations for the ages. Ironically foretelling his own downfall, Torrellas repeats the old saw that not even the

95. "Pues ya no queráis en todo ser senyores. Que por esto venimos aquí: porque a lo menos en la justicia seamos iguales."

96. In *The Triumph of Love*, Flores puts Torrellas's hypothesis to the test: women do indeed become expert seducers once freed from the "strong rein of modesty." *Triunfo de amor*, ed. Antonio Gargano, 176. Flores's *The Triumph of Love*, like *Grisel and Mirabella*, cannot be easily classified as pro- or anti-feminine.

97. "Ya he yo visto por experiencia: que las mujeres más simples son en alguna manera más castas. Donde consiste que la simplesa os es salud. Y el saber danyoso. Como claro lo veis. Pues que todas las más agudas siguen la carrera de nuestros desseos: y la que más sabe yerra."

wisest of men can compete with the wiles of women. He concludes with a series of accusations taken directly from the *Slander*.

The King's twelve judges find Mirabella and all women guilty. Braçayda protests the fundamental futility of debating before men, whose laws "condemn the ravished victim to death—and long live the rapist!"[98] Men, who are the "judges, litigants, and lawyers in the same case," had come to a foregone conclusion despite all the trappings of a fair hearing.[99] The Queen attempts to intercede, but the King upholds his judges' decision, stating that justice must take precedence over affection and Mirabella is sentenced to death by fire. Grisel, however, throws himself on the pyre before she can be executed. Grisel's death is accepted by the King as evidence of God's will and ultimate judgment of the case. Mirabella subsequently commits suicide by throwing herself into a pit of lions.

Despite the fact that God seems to have reversed the judges' decision, the following episodes of the novella play out in ironic fashion many of the arguments made for and against women in the debate. Torrellas finds that he has been captivated by Braçayda's charms and now suffers from love for her. He has confidence in his own seductive powers and writes a letter to her, begging her to show him mercy and putting his life in her hands, using the rhetoric of courtly love that Braçayda had denounced. The fictional Torrellas's letter to Braçayda echoes the exordium of *The Defense of Ladies against Slanderers*, suggesting that Flores may have been familiar with the historical Torrellas's retraction. The Queen, her ladies, and Braçayda, intent on revenge, decide to play along and pretend that Braçayda cannot resist him. Torrellas, true to Braçayda's accusation that men slander women, boasts to the other men of the court that he has seduced her handily. However, Torrellas, like the wise men shamed by women to whom he alluded in the debate, is no match for the ladies' schemes: "But the wretched man had no way of knowing the fatal trick that hid within Braçayda's ready mercy, and he, thinking her easily seduced, was all the more easily, simple-mindedly, and stupidly overpowered."[100] The

---

98. "Que quieren que muera la que es forçada: y viva el forçador."

99. "Pues ellos son juezes y partes y avocados del mismo pleito."

100. "Pero el malaventurado non pudo conoçer aquell enganyo de la muerte: que en la presta piedad de Braçayda se scondía. Y éll juzgándola por ligera de vençer: fue éll más ligero sim-

ladies ambush Torrellas and turn all his talk of "dying of love" from metaphor into concrete reality. They bind, torture, and hurl insults at him, finally tearing him apart with instruments of torture, their nails, and even their teeth. As Maria Grazia Ciccarello Di Blasi points out, the angry ladies, who break for dinner and a detailed discussion of the punishment they plan for the misogynist, turn Torrellas's own instrument of attack—wounding words—against him, while he is gagged and unable to speak.[101] By including *maestresala* (taster or master of the chamber) among the names of the dishes served up for the dinner and remarking that the ladies leave no flesh on Torrellas's bones, Flores gives the execution a cannibalistic quality. Moreover, since the historical Torrellas had served in a similar position as master of the knife, and later as majordomo in the Neapolitan court, and the lovers Grisel and Mirabella were exposed by the King's *maestresala*, the presence of "taster" as part of the "bitter meal" the ladies give the misogynist seems fitting. The Queen, Braçayda, and the other women of the court conclude their vengeance by burning the poet's remains, keeping his ashes in amulets in order to better and more pleasurably recall the demise of the woman-hater.

Grisel and Mirabella thus presents three attempts to conclude the *querelle*: the trial, a divine proof, and the violent silencing of misogyny's champion. Nevertheless, the *querelle* remains inconclusive and indeterminate. The plot of the romance turns upon the unsatisfactory debate staged between Torrellas and Braçayda, which has almost nothing to do with the particular case of Grisel and Mirabella and which is rigged from the outset to find women universally guilty of men's sexual sins. As mentioned above, some readers have considered Flores a champion of women and the romance as a vision of feminine triumph. Antonio Pérez-Romero, for example, reads *Grisel and Mirabella* as part of a subversive tradition in Spanish letters and as a vision of women's resistance to patriarchy.[102] Patricia Grieve, on the other hand, suggests that in this work, "fraught with ambiguities," women are "merely living up to their unsavory reputa-

---

ple y neciamente vencido."

101. "Introduzione," in *Grisel y Mirabella*, 73–74.

102. *The Subversive Tradition in Spanish Renaissance Writing* (Lewisburg: Bucknell University Press, 2005), 70–83.

tion" propagated by misogynist writers.[103] As Helen Cathleen Tarp points out, Flores "makes each protagonist an advocate, witness and evidence in the great pro and anti-feminist debate contained in this text," yet because "each character embodies the best and the worst of the arguments presented ... the text offers no definitive answer to the question."[104] Still others, such as Mercedes Roffé, see the work as promoting a thoroughly conservative view of women.[105] The bloody and bestial revenge evokes scenes from Ovid's *Metamorphoses*, such as the death of the poet Orpheus at the hands of an angry horde of Bacchae as well as descriptions of cannibal witches in the *Hammer of Witches*.[106] The palinode appended to Martínez de Toledo's *Corbacho* imagines a similar physical attack upon a *maldiziente* by angry women.[107] What were Early Modern readers meant to conclude? And what are we today to conclude about this dark and strangely funny short romance? The indeterminacy of *Grisel and Mirabella*, which invites readers to continue to debate and question when the book is closed, is an important contributor to the lasting popularity of Flores's romance.

The Afterlives of Grisel and Mirabella

In addition to the eight known Spanish editions of *Grisel and Mirabella*, dating from 1495 to 1562, three manuscript versions have also

---

103. *Desire and Death in the Sentimental Romance*, 56 and 65.

104. "*Aurelio et Isabelle*: An Edition and Study of the 1556 Antwerp Spanish and English translations of Juan de Flores's *Grisel y Mirabella*" (Ph.D. diss., University of New Mexico, 1999), 79.

105. *La cuestión del género*, 12. See also Patricia Crespo Martín, "Violencia mitológica en *Grisel y Mirabella*," *La corónica* 29.1 (2000): 75–87; María Cruz Muriel Tapia, *Antifeminismo y subestimación de la mujer en la literatura medieval castellana* (Caceres, Spain: Editorial Guadiloba, 1991); and John T. Cull, "Irony, Romance Conventions, and Misogyny in *Grisel y Mirabella* by Juan de Flores," *Revista canadiense de Estudios Hispánicos* 22, no. 3 (1998): 415–30.

106. Lilian von der Walde Moheno, *Amor e ilegalidad*: Grisel y Mirabella *de Juan de Flores* (Mexico City: Universidad Nacional Autónoma de México, 1996), 238–39.

107. Alfonso Martínez de Toledo, *Arcipreste de Talavera o Corbacho*, ed. E. Michael Gerli (Madrid: Cátedra, 1992), 304–6.

survived.[108] These multiple editions and manuscript copies attest to the romance's considerable popularity among Spanish audiences, but this popularity pales in comparison with the romance's international diffusion. While Torrellas's *Slander* reached ever widening audiences in Spanish through the multiple reprintings of the *Cancionero general* in Spain and the Netherlands, *Grisel and Mirabella* enjoyed widespread international popularity in Spanish and in translation. In fact, the diffusion of *Grisel and Mirabella* is comparable to that of other translations of late medieval vernacular works of fiction such as *The Decameron*, *The Prison of Love*, and *Amadis of Gaul*, which, among a handful of other texts, all moved with relative ease across national and linguistic borders.[109] An Italian translation by Lelio Aletiphilo—probably a pseudonym for Lelio Manfredi, a translator and poet working in the sphere of the Gonzaga family—called *Aurelio and Isabella* appeared in at least thirteen editions between 1521 and 1554 and served as the basis for subsequent translations of the romance. An anonymous French translation, *The Judgment of Love*, appeared soon after the first printing of the Italian and was also followed by multiple editions. The Polish translation, known as *The Story of King Equanusie of Scotland*, appeared in 1578.

In the second half of the sixteenth century, bilingual Spanish-French and Italian-French, as well as trilingual French-Italian-English printings of the romance also appeared in multiple editions, indicating that the romance was being put to use as an aid for learning languages by its international readership. In these multilingual versions, the romance was known as *Aurelio and Isabelle*, and the Spanish version, when present, is a retranslation from the Italian. In 1556, a four-

---

108. Of the three manuscripts, only one, found in MS 940 of the Biblioteca Trivulziana in Milan, Italy, a miscellany dating from the first half of the sixteenth century, is complete. The other two, MS 5–3–20 of the Biblioteca Colombina in Seville, Spain and MS lat. 6966 of the Biblioteca Apostolica Vaticana in Rome, Italy, contain partial texts of the romance. For detailed descriptions of the manuscripts and editions, see Ciccarello Di Blasi, "Introduzione," in *Grisel y Mirabella*, 83–113; and Gwara, "A Study of the Works of Juan de Flores," 435–93; and also Gwara and Diane Wright, "A New Manuscript of Juan de Flores' *Grisel y Mirabella*: Biblioteca Apostolica Vaticana, Vat. Lat. MS 6966, ff. 68r–76v," *Bulletin of Hispanic Studies* 77.4 (2000): 503–26.

109. Andrew Pettegree, "Translation and the Migration of Texts," in *Borders and Travellers in Early Modern Europe*, ed. Thomas Betteridge (Aldershot, UK: Ashgate, 2007), 113–28.

language edition (Italian, French, Spanish and English) was published in Antwerp. This version is dedicated to Margarita Wolschaten, the daughter of a Dutch family active in the printing industry in Antwerp in the sixteenth century. The anonymous editor prefaces his offering with a short catalog of famous women who exerted evil power over men and nations, including Helen of Troy, Cleopatra, and Hecuba, whose lack of virtue he contrasts with that of both Hortensia and his dedicatee. The editor's catalog casts the story of Grisel and Mirabella as yet another cautionary tale of the danger women with power pose to men.[110]

Page from the Polyglot *Aurelio et Isabelle*, Antwerp, 1608

In addition to the English translation included in the polyglot edition, two freestanding English adaptations, both anonymous, appeared in the seventeenth century, *A Paire of Turtle Doves* (1602) and *Swetnam the Woman-Hater* (1620). The German *Historia von Aurelio und Isabella* appeared somewhat later in 1630. All in all, at least 60 edi-

110. *Histoire de Aurelio et Isabelle, fille du Roy d'Escoce, nouvellement traduict en quatre langues, italien, español, françois & anglois* (Antwerp: Steelsio, 1556), no pag.

tions, translations, and adaptations of *Grisel and Mirabella* circulated for the century and a half following its initial composition.

As the change in title from *Grisel and Mirabella* to *Aurelio and Isabelle* suggests, Aletiphilo's early Italian translation exercised considerable influence over most of the subsequent translations. Citing the poor quality of the printed Spanish edition he used, Aletiphilo explained that although his wish was to remain faithful to the sense of the Spanish author, he saw himself forced to makes some changes, additions, and guesses. Moreover, he considered it necessary to change the names of the protagonists in order to avoid barbarisms.[111] Aletiphilo may have wished to honor Isabella d'Este by renaming the heroine, and chose the more classical sounding Aurelio over Grisel, despite Flores's choice of a name with a clear allusion to the feminine heroine, patient Griselda. Aletiphilo also changed the names of Torrellas and Braçayda to Afranio and Hortensia. The change of the culturally specific name of Torrellas, on the one hand, removes the strong intertextual relationship between the romance and *cancionero* tradition as a whole and Torrellas's works in particular. The change thus would have made Aletiphilo's woman-hating advocate for men a more universal figure for readers unfamiliar with the Spanish *cancioneros*, even though many Italian readers would indeed have been familiar with the tradition due to the close ties between the two literary cultures. However, there is also a possible element of anti-misogynist irony in Aletiphilo's choice of Afranio. Afranio degli Albonesi was a canon in the service of the d'Este court in Ferrara who around 1521 invented the phagotus, a complicated double-reed musical instrument that used two pairs of bellows to produce a wide variety of sounds. If Aletiphilo decided to name his protagonist after the canon, he may have been making a sort of inside joke while also equating the woman-hater with a "wind-bag" or "blow-hard."[112] Aletiphilo's rechristening of Braçayda as Hortensia is most likely a reference to the daughter of the Roman orator Hortensius. Hortensia figures in

---

111. *Historia de Isabella e Aurelio composta da Giouanni de Fiori alla sua signora in castigliano tradutta in lingua volgare Italica per Meser Lelio Aletiphilo: e da lui dedicata al molto uertuoso L. Scipione Atellano* (Milan: Giannotto da Castiglione, 1521), no pag.

112. Cecil Forsyth, "The Phagotus of Afranio," in *Orchestration* (New York: Macmillan, 1944), 500–02.

medieval catalogs of famous women, including the *Book of Illustrious and Virtuous Women*, where she appears as a model of eloquence and modesty. Consequently, Hortensia is a less morally ambiguous figure than Braçayda, "a less problematic representation of female virtue."[113]

A Note on the Translations and Transcriptions

Lelio Aletiphilo, one of Flores's early translators, assures his Italian readers that he has followed the precepts of Horace and has translated "sense for sense" rather than "word for word," never straying from the intentions of the Spanish author except where the poor quality of the printed edition of *Grisel and Mirabella* that he used forced him to make assumptions about those intentions.[114] Aletiphilo also felt free to add descriptive adjectives, follow false cognates, and to change the names of his protagonists in order to enhance the elegance of his Italian *Aurelio and Isabelle*. In short, Aletiphilo made the text his own, a luxury to which I, as a twenty-first century academic translator of Torrellas's and Flores's fifteenth-century poetry and prose, cannot and will not aspire. Although a Renaissance translator seeking to advance his or her own vernacular through the process of translation would not approve of straying so far from the Horatian decree, I have not sought to render the *Slander* in snappy, rhyming verse; nor have I attempted to smooth out the rough edges of Flores's often long, serpentine sentences, in which the logic of clausal relationships is often somewhat oblique. Rather, and following the guiding principles of Greer and Rhodes in their translation of the works of María de Zayas for this series, I have translated Torrellas and Flores at "just one remove from a literal rendition, attempting to mimic the formal register of the prose without sacrificing ... readers' comfort."[115] The purpose here is

113. Tarp, "*Aurelio et Isabelle*: An Edition and Study," 100.

114. "Prologue," in *Historia de Isabella e Aurelio*, no pag.

115. Margaret R. Greer and Elizabeth Rhodes, "Volume Editors' Introduction," in María de Zayas y Sotomayor, *Exemplary Tales of Love and Tales of Disillusion*, ed. and trans. Margaret R. Greer and Elizabeth Rhodes, (Chicago: University of Chicago Press, 2008), 40–41. In addition to Green and Rhodes' discussion of translating Zayas, I have found Alan Turner's reflections on anachronism and vocabulary in translation extremely helpful. "Translation and Criticism: The Stylistic Mirror," *The Yearbook of English Studies* 36.1 (2006): 168–76.

not to imitate and improve upon Torrellas and Flores, but rather to give readers a sense of their late-medieval voices and style. I see staying close to the authors' late-medieval syntax, which is often a marker of orality, as a way of capturing the sense of pre-modernity in the text and conveying it to contemporary readers. Flores mixes short, pithy statements with long, winding sentences full of dependent clauses. I have tried to respect his rhetoric and belabored sentence construction, but have divided some of these sentences up to make for more legible and comprehensible English. Moreover, and again following Greer and Rhodes, I have used "mildly archaic" vocabulary and diction. I have also often turned for inspiration to the anonymous—and often impenetrable—sixteenth-century English translation of *Grisel and Mirabella*, John Minsheu's *Dictionarie in Spanish and English* (1599), the anonymous *A very profitable boke to learn the maner of redyng, writyng & speakyng English & Spanish* (1554), and the *Nuevo tesoro lexicográfico del español (S. XIV–1726)* compiled by Lidio Nieto Jiménez and Manuel Alvar Esquerra.

The double entendres that make up so much of the sharp wit of *cancionero* poetry and which are also used to great effect in the two prose pieces included here are particular challenges to both interpretation and translation. Moreover, late medieval and Renaissance vocabulary in both Spanish and English was less individuated than that of the modern day, and, consequently, single words are used in a variety of meanings in the original Spanish texts. In these three works of poetry and prose about the relations between the sexes, some of the most important terms are the most difficult to convey succinctly in English. For example, the late-medieval Castilian term *honestad* had a very wide range of interrelated meanings, including "honesty," "modesty," "moderation," "composedness," "decency," "chastity," "honorableness," "goodness," and "virtue." In general, I have translated *honestad* as *virtue* in order to reflect both Torrellas's and Flores's concentration on matters of sexual relations and because, although not as polysemic as the Castilian *honestad*, *virtue* does connote many of the same virtues as *honestad*. *Enganyar*, whose meanings range from "to trick" or "to beguile" to "to seduce," is another such term, which I have translated variously according to the context in which it appears. Flores plays upon the alliterative terms *fuerte* (strong), *fuerça*

(strength), and *flaqueça* (weakness, frailty), and the etymologically related terms *sforçar*, meaning "to strengthen," "to fortify," "to embolden," but also "to rape," *sforçado*, meaning "valiant," when used in the masculine form, and *sforçada*, "ravished" or "raped," when used in the feminine form. For example, when Mirabella insists that she "ravished" Grisel, Flores highlights the gendered use of the term. The equation of men with forcefulness and women with being the frail objects of force harkens back to Isidore of Seville's etymologies aligning men with strength and power and women with softness. Flores also created quite a few tongue twisters with his wordplays on force and frailty, which posed a particular challenge for translation into English. For example, when Grisel challenges another knight to a duel, he taunts that God will not favor the faint-hearted: "no en suertes como vuestro flaco coraçón y menos verdad pedía: por scusarse de la afruenta que hará enganyoso vuestro amor y flacas las fuerças que nunqua fueron fuertes" (He will not be on the side of chance, as you wrongly and faint-heartedly have claimed in order to avoid our duel; now your love shall be discovered to be false, and your strengths— which never were forceful—frail). Mirabella likewise pairs force and frailty when she attempts to convince Grisel to let her take the blame for their affair: "que lo flaco sfuerça sin fuerça lo fuerte" (frailty forcelessly gives force to the forceful). In the translation, whenever possible I have followed Flores's diction and used alliterative terms. Flores also uses many figures of repetition, such as "desseados desseos" (desired desires), which I have also rendered as repetitions in the English version offered here.

Because of their rarity in modern editions and so that readers familiar with Spanish can refer to the medieval texts in the original language, each of the three works is presented here in bilingual format. The Spanish versions of Pere Torrellas's *Maldezir* (Slander) and *Razonamiento* (Defense of Ladies against Slanderers) are reproduced from Robert Archer's edition of the complete works of the poet, with the generous permission of Rubbettino Editore.[116]

---

116. *Obra completa*, 199–200. The *Maldezir*, as reproduced in the *Cancionero general* 1511, contains 15 stanzas. Although it is possible that Torrellas himself composed additional stanzas, it is also likely that during the *Slander*'s history of transmission and reception, readers

I have based my transcription and translation of *Grisel y Mi-rabella* upon the first known printed edition of 1495. The present transcription is not offered as a complete critical edition. Rather, recognizing that all textual criticism is an interpretive act, I have sought to provide a text that is legible for non-specialists but that also conserves some of the characteristics and linguistic fluctuations of late fifteenth-century Castilian textual culture. In the interests of readability and to eliminate confusion among readers who are not accustomed to late-medieval language and printing, I have modernized certain elements of the text. Abbreviations are expanded and word separation follows modern norms, except in the case of contractions, which I have noted with an apostrophe (del → d'él; della → d'ella). Capitalization and accentuation also follow modern norms. I have regularized the vocalic and consonantal usages of *h*, *i* and *j*, *i* and *y*, and *u* and *v*, with the exception of their use in proper names.

Punctuation, like language itself in the late fifteenth-century, was a fluid affair. The printer and compositor of the 1495 edition made free and frequent use of colons and full stops, which I have reproduced in the transcription, adding question marks, quotation marks, and exclamation points according to my interpretation of the text. I have also inserted paragraph separation to make reading and tracking between the Spanish and the translation easier, generally following the 1495 edition's usage of capital letters at the beginning of certain sentences that mark transitions in the text.

The printed edition of 1495 became the basis for all subsequent Spanish editions and for the first translations of the romance into other languages. However, this printed text contains errors as well as several textually unstable passages. I have made some silent corrections of typographical errors and, where possible, I have clarified ambiguous passages by reproducing the text from the manuscript versions of *Grisel y Mirabella* and successive editions.[117] In these cases, I have italicized the changes made in the main body of the text and reproduced the ambiguous wording from the 1495 printed edition in

---

added additional complaints against women to the work. It was common for poets to gloss the verses of others in the *cancionero* tradition.

117. For the full texts of the manuscript versions, see *Grisel y Mirabella*, ed. María Ciccarello di Blasi, 210–357.

the endnotes. In this way, readers may see both the text as first trans-
mitted in print and the clearer wording presented in the manuscripts.

A Note on the Cover Image

The image on the cover of this volume is a portrait of Juana of Castile
(1479–1555) by the painter Juan de Flandes (d. 1519). Juana, known
as "la loca" or "the mad," is a legendary figure in Spanish history, literature, and art, who went down in history as a woman driven insane
by love. The third child of Isabel I and Fernando V, Juana became heir
to the throne upon the deaths of her older siblings, but never ruled in
her own right. Her madness was supposedly caused first by jealousy
for her husband the Archduke Phillip "the Fair" of Flanders and then
by her excessive grief after his death in 1506. Juana would likely have
been among the historical readers of Juan de Flores's romance and the
texts with which it is in dialogue. She was also arguably a victim of
the prevailing beliefs associating femininity with feeblemindedness,
outsized sexual appetites, and irrationality that are voiced in many of
the Early Modern texts debating the nature of women.[118]

118. For Juana's life and an assessment of her "madness," see Bethany Aram, *Juana the Mad:
Sovereignty and Dynasty in Renaissance Europe* (Baltimore: Johns Hopkins University Press,
2005). For Juana's portrayal in literature, theater, film, and art, see *Juana of Castile: History
and Myth of the Mad Queen*, ed. María A. Gómez, Santiago Juan-Navarro and Phyllis Zatlin
(Lewisburg: Bucknell University Press, 2008).

PERE TORRELLAS

MALDEZIR DE MUGERES

∾

THE SLANDER AGAINST WOMEN

I

Quien bien amando persigue   1
dona, a sí mesmo destruye,
que siguen a quien las fuye
y fuyen de quien las sigue;
non quieren por ser queridas,   5
nin galardonan servicios,
mas todas, desconoscidas,
por sola tema regidas,
reparten sus beneficios.

II

Donde apeteçen los ojos   10
sin otro conoscimiento
allí va el consentimiento,
acompañado de antojos,
y non es más su bondat
que vana parencería: 15
a quien non han voluntad
muestran que por honestad[1]
contrastan a su porfía.

III

De natura de lobas son
ciertamente en escoger,   20
de anguillas en retener,
en contrastar, de erisón;[2]
no estiman virtud ni abteça,
seso, bondat nin saber,
mas catan abinenteza,   25
talle de obrar e franqueza
do puedan bienes aver.

I

The man in love who courts   1
a woman, destroys himself;
women chase a man who flees
and flee one who pursues;
they love not for being loved,   5
nor reward love-service,
yet, ingrates all,
ruled by a single fixation,
dole out their favors.

II

Wherever their eyes are pleased,   10
there, without a thought,
goes women's consent
led on by appetite;
and women's goodness is nothing more
than an empty show: 15
when they do not want a man
women act as if virtue[1]
makes them resist his advances.

III

Truly, women are just like she-wolves
when they choose a mate,   20
like eels, when hooked into the bait.
when they resist, like porcupines;[2]
women think nothing of virtue or abilty,
intelligence, kindness, or wisdom
rather, they look for advantage,   25
comely ways, and generosity,
where riches may be had.

IV

Tened aqueste conçepto,
amadores, vos supplico:
con quien riñen en publico   30
fazen la pas en secreto;
dissimulan el entender,
denuestan lo que desean;
fingen de enojo plaser,
lo que quieren non querer   35
y dubdar quando más crean.

V

Por non ser poco estimadas
de quien mucho las estima,
fasiendo de honesdad rima,
fingen de mucho guardadas,   40
mas con quien las tracta en son
de sentir lo que meresçen,
sin detener galardón,
la persona y el coraçón
abandonan et ofreçen.   45

VI

Muchas por non descobrir
algunas faltas secretas,
a las personas, discretas,
non dexan al fin venir;
bien les demuestran amar   50
y que bondat las detiene;
mas, con aquello trattar,
han sus engaños lugar
lo que en secreto contiene.[3]

IV

Listen, lovers,
to my advice, I beg you:
women will scold in public   30
and then make secret peace;
women feign innocence,
deride what they desire;
they pretend to be pleased when angered,
not to want what they want,   35
and to waver when most certain.

V

So as not to be ill thought of
by a man who thinks much of them,
making a game of virtue,
women pretend to be quite retiring;   40
yet, to a man who flatters,
saying he knows their worth,
without withholding favor,
they abandon themselves,
offering both body and soul.   45

VI

Many women conceal
certain secret defects;
so as not to reveal them,
they do not go all the way;
saying, though they love indeed,   50
virtue holds them back;
yet, with such an artifice
women play their tricks,
hiding their secrets.[3]

VII

Son todas naturalmente   55
malignas et sospechosas,
non secretas et mintrosas
et movibles ciertamente;
buelven como foja al viento,
ponen'l absente en olvido;   60
quieren comportar a çiento,
así que el más contento
es cerca de aborresçido.

VIII

Si las queréis emendar,
las avéis por enemigas,   65
et son grandes amigas
de quien las quier' lisonjar;
por gana de ser loadas
qualquier alabança cogen;
van a las cosas vedadas,   70
desdeñan las sojusgadas,
e las peores escogen.

IX

Sintiendo que son subjectas
e sin nengund poderío,
a fin de aver señorío   75
tienen engañosas sectas;
entienden en afeitar
y en gestos por atraer;
saben mentir sin pensar,
reír sin causa et llorar   80
e aun enbaidoras ser.

VII

All women are by nature   55
malignant and suspicious
indiscreet and lying
and changeable, believe you me;
they turn like leaves on the wind;
women forget an absent man,   60
want to please a hundred more,
and the most contented man,
is all but abhorred.

VIII

If you want to reform them,
women are your enemies   65
and they are great friends
to those who would flatter them;
for the sake of being praised
women accept any adulation;
they go for forbidden things   70
disdain what is decorous,
and choose the worst.

IX

Feeling that they are subjugated
and lacking any power
in order to take control   75
women form shady sects;
they are experts in cosmetics
and in coquetry for attracting men,
they know how to lie without a thought,
laugh without a cause and cry too;   80
women can be such frauds.

X

Provecho et deleite son
el fin de todas sus obras;
en guarda de las soçobras
suplen temor e fección;   85
si por temor detenida
la maldat d'ellas non fuese
o por fección escondida,
non sería hombre que vida
con ellas fazer pudiese.   90

XI

Mujer es un animal
que se diz' hombre imperfecto,
procreado en el defecto
del buen calor natural;[4]
aquí se incluyen sus males   95
e la falta del bien suyo
e pues les son naturales
quando se demuestran tales,
que son sin culpa concluyo.[5]

XII

Aquesta es la condición   100
de las mugeres comuna,
pero virtud las repuna
que les consienta rasón;
así la parte mayor
muchas disponen seguir,   105
et tanto han meyor loor
quando el defecto mayor
ellas merescen venir.

X

Profit and delight are
the ends of all their doings;
women are wary of trouble,
equipped with fear and falsehoods;   85
if women's wickedness
were not reigned in by fear,
or hidden by falsehoods,
not a man in the world
could live with them.   90

XI

Woman is that animal
we call an imperfect man,
procreated by defect
of nature's good heat;[4]
here we find her evil nature   95
and lack of goodness;
and so, it is women's nature
to be as I have said,
it is not their fault, I conclude.[5]

XII

Such is the condition   100
common to women
yet virtue holds them back
from what reason permits;
and if many choose to follow
the better path   105
they deserve so much more
—given their greater defect—
praise to come their way.

XIII
Conclusión

Entre las otras sois vós,
dama de aquesta mi vida,   110
del traste común salida,
una en el mundo de dos;[6]
vós sois la que desfaséis
lo que contienen mis versos;
vós sois la que meresçéis   115
renombre, et loor cobréis
entre las otras, diversos.

XIII
Conclusion

You, Lady of this my life,
are unlike all the others;   110
far from the common lot,
you, alone in a world of two,[6]
are she who undoes
all that my verses contain;
you are she who deserves   115
renown and receives praise
apart from all the rest.

Notes

1. On the fifteenth-century Castilian term *honestad*, see the Volume Editor's Introduction, 48.

2. On the proverb equating women with wolves when they choose a mate, see the Volume Editor's Introduction, 18–19.

3. Torrellas' play on the word "secret" [*secreto*] in this stanza, and perhaps previously in stanza IV as well, implies that women hide something defective within or beneath their skirts. See Volume Editor's Introduction, 20.

4. The idea that women were malformed men, the results of gestational damage to the normative male homunculus, is a medieval commonplace, traceable to Aristotle and Galen. Moreover, the importance of heat and humoral theory, which also derived from ancient medical authority, for medieval and early modern ideas of gender classification cannot be overstated. Women were thought to be of a cold and moist complexion, while men were hot and dry, and therefore superior. See Gail Kern Paster, "The Unbearable Coldness of Female Being: Women's Imperfection and the Humoral Economy," *English Literary Renaissance* 28.3 (1998): 416–40.

5. In some versions of the poem this line can also be interpreted, "So, blameless, I conclude." In either case, the poet's tongue is firmly in cheek at this juncture of the poem.

6. Casas Rigall suggests that Torrellas' description of his lady as "alone in a world of two" is meant as a comparison between the lady praised in the poem and the Virgin Mary (*Agudeza y retórica*, 209). Archer, on the other hand, argues that Torrellas means that his *dama* is so rare, there are only two like her in the world (*Obra completa*, 216). Both meanings could in fact be present in the final stanza.

PERE TORRELLAS

*RAZONAMIENTO DE PERE TORRELLA EN DEFENSIÓN DE
LAS DONAS CONTRA LOS MALDEZIENTES*

THE DEFENSE OF LADIES AGAINST SLANDERERS

Razonamiento de Pere Torrella en defensión de las donas contra los maldezientes, por satisfación de unas coplas qu'en dezir mal de aquellas compuso

Pues el nombre *dona* designa "señora" y aquél de *muger* "mansedumbre," atrayéndome l'uno a la obediençia de demandar perdón y l'otro a la confiança d'alcançar aquél,[1] confiesso yo a vos, las mugeres e mis siempre señoras, que con desatiento d'enamorada passión movido a creençia sin causa e a vengança sin injuria, compuse las coplas aquellas que de mugeres mal dizen.[2] E porque, Señoras, creáis el juizio que tantos bienes de vosotras percibe—si no, obcegado de passión, consintiera a la lengua referir el contrario—vos suplico queráis ver las razones qu'en defensión vuestra contra los maldizientes me occorren. Si me farán digno de perdón, sea do no reciba pena, que no podrá seer tanto grave que a mí no sea plaziente en pensar a qué y a quién satisfaze.

Pregunto yo, pues, maldizientes, si vuestro fablar s'entiende a singular caso o a general ser. Si a singular caso, sin debate quedamos, que yo confiesso, segunt que en los hombres, haver entre las mugeres, malas, comunales e buenas e ninguna, como ninguno, perfecta. Si a general ser, o está en el alma o consiste en el cuerpo. En el alma no es possible, como sean todas en sí propriamente buenas. Qu'el cuerpo suyo sea compuesto de aquellos mesmos quatro humores e calidades que el de los hombres no es dubda ninguna, salvo que la frior e mollez es más apropriada a las donas e más la rudeza e calor a los hombres.[3] En cada uno d'estos extremos distraídos, entre floxedat e rigor, se causan inclinaçiones no buenas. Aquel convenible medio qu'entre éstos se falla ningún natural orden contrasta que en las mugeres segunt que en los hombres no pueda avenir, como vehemos entre ellas algunas por viril conplessión, y en los hombres por femenina, la natural procreación fallecer. E aunque por la parte corporal universalmente todos a más mal que a bien seamos dispuestos, aquellas condiçiones que loables se dizen, assí como piedat, benivolençia, suavidat e vergüença caen en la complesión femenina. La qual aprovando no sólo ser buena más mucho, aquel justo repartidor de las gracias formó Adam del vil limbo de la tierra y a Eva de la más noble parte del hombre. Adam en el campo damaçeno, a Eva

A Treatise by Pere Torrellas in the Defense of Ladies against Slanderers, in Recompense for Some Verses He Composed in Which He Defames the Aforementioned Ladies

Given that the word *lady* means "she who rules" and *woman* means "she who yields," the first leads me to obey and ask for forgiveness and the second to believe that I will be forgiven.[1] I admit to you women, forever my ladies, that I, crazed with the passion of love, moved to belief without cause, and to vengeance without injury, composed those verses that speak ill of women.[2] And so that you, Ladies, will trust in the wisdom of one who sees so many good qualities in you, who only blinded by passion would allow his tongue to utter the contrary, I beg you to deign to read the arguments that I have composed in your defense against slanderers. If my arguments prove me worthy of forgiveness, let it be; if not, let me be condemned. My punishment cannot be so harsh that it will not give me the pleasure of thinking about what and whom it satisfies.

I ask you then, slanderers, if your words are meant to be understood as referring to a single case or as a general rule. If your slander refers to a single case, there is nothing for us to debate. For I admit that, just as among men, there are bad, ordinary, and good women; not a single woman or man is perfect. If you propose a general rule concerning women, your words must refer either to the soul or the body. You certainly cannot mean the soul, because all souls are in themselves good. As for the female body, there is no question that it is composed of those same four humors and qualities as male bodies, although coldness and softness are found more in ladies while toughness and heat are more often found in men.[3] When these opposing humors, weak and hard, are unbalanced, harmful inclinations are created. Nothing in nature forbids a fitting balance between extremes to occur in women, just as it may in men; yet, when natural procreation fails, we also see women with masculine complexions or men with feminine ones. And although we all may be equally disposed more to evil than to good because of our corporeal side, those conditions that are deemed praiseworthy, such as piety, benevolence, gentleness, and shame, occur in the feminine complexion. Seeing that feminine nature was not only good, but very good, God, that just dispenser of graces, formed Adam from the lowly limbo of the earth and Eve from the noblest part of man; Adam in the Damascene field, Eve in the earthly paradise; Adam rustic, fierce, and

en el terrenal paraíso, Adam rústico, feroce y peloso, a la naturaleza de los animales brutos pareçiendo, a Eva blanqua, suave, delicada e lisa, más angélica idea que forma humana representando.[4] E pues de pasta más apurada, en lugar más noble y de forma más bella qu' el hombre fue la muger creada, de su más perfecto ser argumentar se puede (e mayormente que tienen los sabios las carnes muelles) ser ábiles a sçiencia, e si a sçienca, a discrecion, e si a discrecion, a virtut, a bienaventurança.

Pero, maldiziente, como quiere que estas e muchas otras singularidades al natural femenino sean conoçidas, yo confiesso que ni alabança ni vituperio a ningunos por naturaleza deve ser dado, salvo por aquellos hábitos que juzgando adquirimos o por aquellas obras que practicando mostramos. E si tú, que bien dezir non sabes, en denuesto de las femeniles costumbres me alegares dichos de letrados, reportes d'estoriadores e práticas presentes, digo que estos letrados o han scripto las mugeres ser malas en sí, o en sguarde de vida perfecta, o en respecto de los hombres, o voluntariamente han querido fablar. A lo primero bastan, me paresçe, las razones ya dichas. A lo segundo, ¿qué más responder se deve salvo ninguno ser bueno? A lo tercero satisfarán mis dichos siguientes. E a lo çaguero respondo que algunos dissolutos e afeminados sçientes assí como Salamón, Ovidio, Johan de Mena, e Vocacio, praticando no donas mas fembras, quales a su viciosa dissolución conferían,[5] por ser d'ellas trocados o refusados, movidos a furiosa vengança, en escrivir mal de mugeres su saber aviltaron.[6] Mas, ¿qué os diré, señoras? Pues assí fablando publicaron la injuria suya, séales perdonada la vuestra.

Algunos sanctos doctores e sabios philósophos, conociendo las mugeres ser tanto amables e plazibles a los hombres que, por las haver, postposada temor, razón e vergüença, a qualesquiere peligros e crímines se ofreçen, a fin d'esquivar un tan dañoso inconveniente, quisieron so el denuesto de las mugeres procurar el común bien de todos, aderiendo, pero, todavía sus dichos a singulares intentos, e si a generales, como sean muchas scriptas e conoçidas por buenas, deven freturar d'auctoritat los dichos de aquél a quien mentira comprehende. Los istoriadores no niego yo, maldizientes, que assí d'ombres como de mugeres viçios e virtudes no hayan recitado. De los hombres, pero, ¿quáles sino muy pocos virtuosos se scriven? Malos sí, tantos qu'

hairy, much like the brute animals in his nature; Eve white, soft, delicate, and smooth, seeming more like an angelic idea than a human form.[4] Thus, woman was created from a purer material, in a nobler place, and in a more beautiful form than man; from her more perfect being it can be argued (and all the more so because wise men have soft flesh) that women are capable of wisdom, and if they are capable of wisdom, of discrimination, and, if capable of discrimination, then they are also capable of virtue and blessedness.

But, slanderer, even though these and many other characteristics of feminine nature be known, I admit that no one should be either praised or vituperated for their nature, rather only for such habits which by reason we have acquired or for such deeds as we have performed. And if you, not knowing how to speak well, quote me the sayings of learned men, the writings of historians, and current authors in order to decry feminine behavior, I reply that those learned men have written either that women are evil in and of themselves, or that they are evil with respect to the perfect life, or with respect to men, or else that they have spoken willfully. In response to the first point, it seems to me that all my previous arguments are sufficient. To the second point, what more must one respond other than that no one is good? My following responses will deal with the third point. But to the final point I respond that a few dissolute and effeminate learned men, such as Solomon, Ovid, Juan de Mena, and Boccaccio, speak of not ladies, but of females—those females who had joined them in their immoral dissolution.[5] These sages besmirched their wisdom by writing evil things about women because they had been cheated or rejected by them, and driven to enraged vengeance.[6] Well, Ladies, what can I tell you? By speaking thus, they broadcast their own villainy; let them be pardoned for insulting you.

Some doctors of the Church and wise philosophers, who acknowledge that women are so kind and pleasing that men will put aside fear, reason, and shame, indeed risk any present danger or crimes, in order to have them, attempted to ensure the common good of all with the aim of evading such harmful disturbances by denigrating women; while their sayings about individual cases are still useful, those arguing the general case, as happens in many well known and respected works, should be discredited by those who understand lies. I do not deny, slanderers, that historians have recounted the vices and virtues of both men and women.

en muy extenso volumen cundirán solamente sus nombres. Lo qual por contrario pareçe de las mugeres, ca d'aquellas que dezir malas se pueden puedes tú solamente nombrar Mirra, Clitamnestra, Venus, Medea, Leena, Flora, Senpronia, Agrepina, Sabina, Cirçes e por ventura otras pocas algunas;[7] mas yo muchas a ti, por insignes, virtuosas, no sin castedat dignas de gloriosa fama. E dexemos en caridat, piedat, benignidat e vergüença, virtudes tanto naturales e conformes a las mugeres qu' en las scripturas passadas e costumbres de las presentes son falladas sin cuento. Más fallamos singulares en sabieza Eritea, Isis, Aragne, Nicostrata, Almatea, Cassandra, Manto, Nicaula, Irine, María, Senpronia, Sapho, Corniphicia, Medusa, Prona, Dannes, Angeronia, Astrea, Lapita,[8] Thetis, Ceres, Turburtina,[9] Othea,[10] Crestina, Deliora e Minerva; en magnanimidat Europa, Libia, Niobe, Tamaris, Atalia, Cloelia, Artemisa, Claudia, Armonia, Busa, Trosena, Ameta, Diripetua, Porçia, Agripina, Cenobia, Irene, Johanna, Bannes,[11] Cornelia, Hian,[12] Machavea,[13] Beleguela,[14] María[15] e Senpronia. En justicia, Gaya, Ipermestra, Isiphile, Hécuba, Venturia, Virgínea, Emilia, Julia, Rebeca, Curia, Ortensia, Suplicia, Ester, Antonia, Pompeya, Sara, Camiola, dona Anna, Eletra, Antigona, Judich e Creusa; en temprança Argia, Penélope, Dido, Labina, Ipo, Virgínea, Lucreçia, Marçia, Sipora, Suplicia, Orgiagonta, Claudia, Engaldrada, Diana, Pira, Britona, Cicilia, Atalanta, Vesta, Efigenia, María Coronel, Fauna e Susana. E no passemos sin recordar la insigne honestat de las tudescas, el virtuoso amor de las menias,[16] la conjugal fe de las indianas, l'animoso denuedo de las cantabrias,[17] l'apaziguada igualdat de las sabinas, la conservada virginidat de las seis mil israeleticas, la tanta santedat de las innumerables cristianas, sin muchas otras ebreas, bárbaras, latinas e griegas. De las quales, por no dilatar e callando sus nombres, basta que, en las nombradas, qualquiere exemplo de virtut haviendo complido lugar en reprovación de los maldizientes, animosidat, bondat e discreçión en lo femenino s'aprueva.

Mas ¿qué digo yo quando en el batalloso exerçiçio e arte sus ánimos e delicadas personas tanto contrario, se han virtuosamente mostrado, segunt se lee de Lampeto, Oricia, Menalipe, Camila, Pantasilea, Ipólita, Laodice y Sicratea, Calixta, Triaria, Arpaliçe, Marposia e Johanna la françesa con todas las amazonas? ¿Qué es de pensar de las

Yet, of men, how many more than a very few virtuous ones have been written of? The names alone of all the wicked ones would fill an extensive book. Of women the opposite is true. Of those who can be called wicked, you can only name Myrrha, Clytemnestra, Venus, Medea, Leana, Flora, Sempronia, Agrippina, Sabina, Circe, and perhaps a few more.[7] However, I can name for you many illustrious, virtuous, not unchaste women worthy of glorious renown. Let us leave charity, mercy, goodness, and shame aside, as they are virtues both so natural and normal to women that there are innumerable examples in histories of the past and in the comportment of women in the present day. There are many examples of women of singular wisdom: Eritrea, Isis, Arachne, Nicostrata, Almathea, Cassandra, Manto, Nicaula, Irene, María, Sempronia, Sappho, Cornificia, Medusa, Petronia Proba, Danae, Angerona, Astrea, Lapitha,[8] Thetis, Ceres, Tiburtina,[9] Othea,[10] Christina, Deborah, and Minerva; for their magnanimity, Europa, Libya, Niobe, Tamyris, Athaliah, Cloelia, Artemisia, Claudia, Harmonia, Busa, Theoxena, Amata, Dripetua, Portia, Agrippina, Zenobia, Irene, Johanna, Evadne,[11] Cornelia, Hian,[12] Macabea,[13] Berenguela,[14] María,[15] and Sempronia; for justice, Gaia, Hypermnestra, Hypsipyle, Hecuba, Veturia, Virginia, Aemilia, Julia, Rebecca, Curia, Hortensia, Sulpicia, Esther, Antonia, Pompeia Paulina, Sarah, Camiola, St. Anne, Electra, Antigone, Judith, and Creusa; for temperance, Argia, Penelope, Dido, Lavinia, Hippo, Virginia, Lucretia, Marcia, Zipporah, Sulpicia, the wife of Origago, Claudia, Gualdrada, Diana, Pyrrha, Britomartis, Cecilia, Atalanta, Vesta, Iphigenia, María Coronel, Fauna, and Susanna. And let us not continue without recalling the notable virtue of the Wives of the Cimbrians, the pure love of the Wives of the Minyans,[16] the conjugal constancy of Indian women, the spirited valor of the Cantabrian women,[17] the peaceable equanimity of the Sabine women, the preserved virginity of the six thousand Israelite women, the great sanctity of innumerable Christian women, not to mention other Hebrew, Barbarian, Roman, and Greek women. For the sake of brevity I pass over the names of these women in silence, but any one of the above named women of exemplary virtue is sufficient cause for reproving the slanderers: these women are proof of the spirit, goodness, and discretion in female nature.

Moreover, what can I say about those women who, contrary to their nature and physical fragility, have demonstrated their virtuosity in the craft of war, as we read of Lampedo, Orithya, Melanippe, Camilla,

otras más conforme virtudes sino ser tantas e tales qu' en las scrivir antes papel que verdadera relación falleçiesse?

E veniendo a las prátiquas presentes, vos quiero primeramente dezir que en el conduzimiento d'aquesta mísera vida es ninguno perfecto. Antes, qual más o menos, ellas e nosotros erramos y falleçemos. E si tú, maldizientes, dizes: "Fulana yerra", en esto responderé yo "e Fulano en aquesto", por manera que sería processo confuso e infinito. E soy cierto que, fecha la cuenta, tú quedarías deudor aunque ciento te rendiesse por una. Et quanto más que los hombres, como más robustos, de sus febles personas usurpada la preheminencia e senyoria, más obligados al bien del contrario, caemos en mayor culpa. E d'otra parte, teniendo a ellas, non poco apremiadas e retraídas, queremos mostrar que no en su voluntat mas en nuestra guarda la bondat suya consiste, que d'apeteçer el mal e desdeñar el bien es ocasión mucho grande.

E aun si verdat es lo que los hombres pretendemos—convenir más a la perfección de naturaleza—, tanto más en ellas el bien y menos el mal, y en nosotros más el mal y menos el bien, deven ser estimadas. Assimesmo, o por no conoçer los hombres ellas tener mayor disposición en la más noble parte, que es l'entendimiento, movidos a invidia, o por el señorear a suberbia, les havemos quitado prática y sçiencia. Las quales dos nodriças del entender es sin aquellas quasi ninguno, de lo qual se sigue que las obras de las mugeres acompañando ignorancia e aquellas de los hombres sabiduría, en cargo de nosotros son diferentes las culpas. Somos, pues, los hombres no sólo dignos de mayor reprehensión en los yerros humanos, mas de los suyos prinçipal causa. Ca de nuestras premias procede ignorançia, madre de errores, resulta negligençia, nodriça de cargos, apareçe desconfiança, promovedora de males, e naçe apetito de lo contrario. Sobre lo qual si la soltez a de las francesas o tártaras e la premia de las ciçilianas o africanas se mira, no freturara çiertamente aprobaçión a mis dichos. E veemos aun que las cosas do las mugeres son libertadas, assí como en oír missas, en escuchar sermones, en visitar dolientes, en confessiones, ayunos, limosnas e oraçiones, e complidamente en las siete obras de misericordia, con todas las otras cosas que en fe, de caridat y sperança redundan, más santamente que los hombres pratiquan.

Penthesilea, Hippolyta, Berenice and Hypsicratea, Callisto, Triaria, Harpalice, Marpesia and Joan of Arc and all the Amazons? What are we to make of the other, more instinctive virtues, except that they are so numerous and of such a quality that we would run out of paper before we could relate all the true histories?

Turning to contemporary practices, firstly I wish to say to you that no one is perfect in the course of this wretched life. Rather, some more or some less, both women and men, we err and fail. And if you, slanderer, say of a woman, *"doña* so-and-so does wrong," to this I will respond: *"don* so-and-so does too," and so we would continue in a confused and infinite discussion. For I am certain that, tallying them all up, you would be the loser even if one of your examples were worth one hundred of mine.

This is all the more true because we men, who are stronger than women and have usurped preeminence and sovereignty over their frail persons, are more obligated to be good than its opposite, and thus our guilt is greater. What is more, we men, who have kept women confined and secluded, claim that their goodness is the result of our protection and not of their own will, that desiring evil and disdaining good is their compelling motive.

Now, even if our claim that men are more perfect by nature be true, then women's goodness should be counted all the more, and their evil less, while our evil be counted more than our goodness. Moreover—either because men do not know that women have a greater disposition to that most noble faculty, which is understanding, moved by envy, or because command has made us proud—we have withheld practice and knowledge from women. There is almost no man who has gone without these two wet-nurses of understanding, from whence it follows that if the deeds of women are accompanied by ignorance and those of men by wisdom, we are guilty of different charges. Consequently, we men are not only deserving of greater blame in human wrongdoing; we are more its principal cause. For it is all from our tyrannies that ignorance—the mother of misdeeds—stems, and negligence—wet-nurse of guilt—occurs, and distrust—promoter of evils—appears, and the appetite for harmful things is born. Concerning all this, if the freedom of French and Tartar women and the oppression of Sicilian and African women are considered, my conclusions will not lack proofs. And we see as well how women excel in the activities that they can engage in freely, such as going to hear mass, listening to sermons, visiting the sick, going to confession, fasting, almsgiving and prayers, and duly fulfilling the seven works of mercy,

Si en esta parte, pues, maldizientes, que sola en sabieza prevaleçen, ¿en quál se devrían llamar falleçidas? ¿Querréis por ventura dezir que, a ellas principalmente assignada la virtut de castidat, siguiendo al veneroso amor ofenden aquella? No niego yo, maldeziente, qu'en esto no yerren mugeres, pero ni vosotros a mí que unos por desalte o por honestat refusados, por naturales defectos e por ançiana hedat indispuestos, malenconiosos quedando, intituláis vuestro nombre e, surtiendo cada uno do passión le puñe, blasmáis aquellas, unos de poco amar, otros d' engañosas artes, algunos de mal escoger e muchos porque curen d'amar. Ora, pues, no vos engañés, ignorantes. Ca su delicada naturaleza, su amigable condiçión e su descansado bevir causan en qualquiere amor muy más perfectamente que los hombres amar, e no sin testimonio del virtuoso.

Ameta, Artemisa, Julia, Marçia, Pompeya, la Çamorana spañola e otras, con las muchas indianas ensemble, en poder de amor dexaron sus vidas. Veo las presentes mucho mejor amar a maridos, padres, hermanos, e qualesquiere personas devidas que son d'ellos amadas. E otras conozco, las quales, trayendo l'enamorada passión figurada en sus gestos, muestran, pues la fin del deseo con su querer confereçen, qu'entre verdadero amor y honesta defensión son apassionadas, en tal extremo presumiendo de muchas que secretamente embían sus spiritos a amor, segunt públicamente fizieron Félix, Rocelina, Gismonda, Tisve, la donzella de Huesca e la dama del Castell de Rosellón, con algunas otras enamoradas que de los hombres oviera sido Píramus comienço e fin si el nuestro Oliver no lo oviera seguido.[18] De quáles los d' agora en esta parte les somos, no aya yo descubrir el secreto.

Basta ya sepan las donas nos gloriamos no bien de amar, e en verdat de tan engañosamente tratarlas. Que ni presentes les guardamos lealtat ni absentes firmeza ni verdat en cosa ninguna. Antes alabamos entre nosotros aquél que, sin ninguna amar, de muchas se faze querer. E si de las quexas de que nosotros abusamos pudiessen usar líçitamente las donas, no serían de creer las maldades que de nosotros a ellas se descubrirían. Pero por el silencio no se quitó el conoçimiento, e veyendo las mugeres que do nosotros bistraemos trabajos e palabras, ellas aventuran horores e vidas, si temen, sospechan, fingen, bariegan e dissimulen, ninguno se maraville. Ca entre sus evidentes peligros e

along with all the other works of faith, charity, and hope; and they do it all with more saintliness than men.

If in these things, then, slanderers, as everyone knows, women prevail, in what way should they be called defective? Do you perhaps wish to say that, since chastity is a virtue principally assigned to women, that by pursuing venereal love they offend chastity? I do not deny, slanderer, that women sin in this way, but nor can you deny to me that some of you, when rejected by women—some because you are not pleasing, some for the sake of chastity, some because of physical defects, or the indisposition of old age—become melancholic and rail against women, impugning yourselves. Each and every one of you, according to the measure of his own passions, blasphemes women: some of you accuse women of loving too little, others of being wily tricksters, some say that women choose the worst men, and many of you do this as a cure for love. Therefore, do not be fooled, ignoramuses. For women's delicate natures, open hearts, and pleasant ways make them better at loving and inspire more perfect love than men, even virtuous love.

Amata, Artemisia, Julia, Marcia, Pompeia, the Spanish Zamorana and others, along with all the many Indian women, gave up their lives for love. I see how women today love their husbands, fathers, brothers, and whomever else they should love, even better. And I know other women who, showing with passionate gestures that the satisfaction of desire goes along with their love, are caught impassioned between true love and defense of virtue. Such women, driven to extremes, secretly devote their spirits to love, just as other women in love did publically, such as Phyllis, Rocelina, Ghismonda, Thisbe, the Maiden of Huesca and the Lady of Castell de Rosellón, while among men Pyramus would have been the first and the last, if our Oliver had not followed him.[18] If there are men among us today who do the same, let me not reveal their secret.

Enough. Let the ladies know that we boast not about loving, but rather about deceiving them. That we are neither loyal when near nor faithful when absent, nor true in anything. Rather, among us, we praise the man who, loving no woman, makes himself beloved of many. And, concerning the false accusations we make, if the ladies were allowed to level the same accusations at us, the wickedness they would discover about us would be unbelievable. But silence does not preclude knowledge and no one should be surprised if women fear, suspect, lie, prevaricate and dissimulate, seeing that men stake only love-service and

nuestras conoçidas maliçias no fallan ninguna cosa segura. Et caso que algunas correspondiessen a nuestros engaños e otras catassen más a la salvaçión de la fama que a la disposiçión del amante, me pareçe que no malas, mas las unas avisadas e las otras discretas se deviessen dezir. De la otra, las quales mediante buen grado vienen amar, ¿por qué te quexas, di, hombre refusado? Ellas siguen amor, el qual, ningún otro costreñimiento queriendo sino aquel que de sí a sí mesmo se faze, sin catar serviçios ni otros mereçimientos, do bien le paresçe reparte los bienes suyos. Si en el repartimiento no te cupo la suerte, callando de las mugeres blasma la desaventura tuya, e piensa que en el caso de la injuria nunca el injuriado es convenible juez. Aqueste amor que Cupido se llama, ¡o maldizientes!, en el ser humano incluso y de celeste impressión, ayudando las naturales fuerças, fechas con las suyas una mesma cosa, ha tanto poder en nosotros que ni arte ni animosidat ni sciençia ni otra fuerça ninguna contra d'él prevaleçe. Y aquesto se vee no sólo por continuas experiençias mas por exemplo de César, d'Ércules, de Aristótil, de Salamón, de Virgilio, de Samsón, d'Achilles, David, Octoviano.

Mas ¿por qué emprendo yo de numerar el número que es infinito? ¿Quáles personas passan por el pelegrinage humano que no combata amor, e quando les combate que no se riendan, e quando les se rienden que no cometan erradas? Por çierto pocas o no ningunas. E si de los hombres los muy solíçitos, los sçientes e los mucho feroces por propria inducçión amando fallecen, ¿las ociosas, simples e febles mugeres continuamente requeridas es maravilla errar? Yo veo que quando con humildes ruegos, quando con esforçadas juras, quando con piadosas lágrimas, quando con ricas dádivas, quando con appassionados gestos, quando con mañosas terçeras, quando con virtuosas aparenças, por tantas maneras e artes, las tentamos e requerimos, que no a la amable muger de carne humana vestida mas a la imagen de dura piedra escolpida deviéramos mover. E con todo se fallan assaz las quales, no por vicioso apetito mas por agradable juizio atraídas, e otras que, no de vana inclinaçión mas de humana compassión movidas, vienen a la obediençia d'amor. Lo qual devidamente considerado faze la culpa del tal consentimiento quasi ninguna.

words, whereas they risk honor and their very lives. For between the clear dangers women face and our well-known wickedness, there is nothing safe for them. The fact that some women reciprocate our seductions and others care more about saving their reputations than the desires of their lovers, seems to me not proof of their wickedness, but rather proves that some women should be called prudent and others discreet. As for those other women who love willingly, what do you have to complain about? Tell me, rejected man. Such women follow Love, who governs by his own law, without a care for service or any other worthiness; Love doles out his gifts where he sees fit. If you have had no luck with Love, cease to talk about women and blaspheme Fortune's onslaughts; remember that in a case of injury, the victim is never a fit judge. This Love, who is called Cupid—O slanderers!—in human and celestial form, joins his own powers to natural forces, and thus has so much power over us that neither cunning nor animosity, nor knowledge, nor any other force can prevail against him. We see this not only in our ongoing experiences, but also in the example of Caesar, Hercules, Aristotle, Solomon, Virgil, Samson, Achilles, David, and Octavian.

Yet, why do I endeavor to enumerate an infinite number? How many people travel along the pilgrimage of human life without battling love, and when love attacks, do not surrender themselves, and in surrendering do not commit evils? Surely, few or none. And if among men, those who are very diligent, those who are learned, and those who are very fierce, allow themselves to die of love, is it any wonder that unoccupied, naïve, and feeble women, who are continually courted, go astray? It seems to me that when we tempt and woo them, be it with our humble begging, strident declarations, and pious tears, or with our extravagant gifts, passionate gestures, or by using cunning go-betweens, with our virtuous play-acting, and with all sorts of methods and skill, that we have the power to persuade statues carved of stone rather than merely kindhearted women dressed in human flesh. And moreover, there are many women who come to obey Love, attracted not because of their sinful appetites, but rather by pleasing judgment, and others who are moved, not by careless inclination, but rather by human compassion. Taking all this into consideration, it is clear that there is little or no guilt in such consent to love.

E si yo presumiesse, sin prejuizio de aquellas, intitular las presentes, yo mostraría no pocas las quales, no abastante todos los sobredichos combates, acompañadas de muchas virtudes, la fortaleza d'onestat defienden e guardan. Oy reconozcámosnos y veamos quál de nosotros, tentado por tantas vías, so confiança de secreto, no pecaría en cosa naturalmente inclinado e siempre dispuesto. Por çierto yo conozco muchos los quales con muy menores ocasiones han vendido castillos, deçebido amigos, derogada justiçia, traído señores, perpetrado crueles muertes e cometidas muchas otras públicas maldades a las quales no natural inclinaçión mas maliçiosa intençión solamente los induzía.

Digo, pues, concluyendo, que mis razones consideradas, e visto los principales yerros e quasi todos aquellos de las mugeres de la mayor fuerça de la naturaleza proçeyen e de viril astuçia sean conduzidos, e aquellos de los hombres de sola malicia e proprio movimiento resulten, quiere razón que los hombres perversos y las mugeres de non malas, ante en su respecto muy buenas, devan ser llamadas. Que ellas veyéndose sobjectas, maltractadas et menospreçiadas de los hombres, se trabajen con polidos afeites, con atractivos gestos e con muchos abillamentos fazerse plazer a quien las señorea, digo que es bien.[19] Ca ningunas otras armas quedan a su vençida delicadez para redreçar su libertat e defenderse de los viriles denuestos sino aquellas que les ha dexado amor. Loable astuçia es por agradables complazimientos atraher a ssí la voluntat de aquél que a mandar indevidamente se dispone.

Mas di, hombre no hombre,[20] si cargo de mugeres te plaze, puesto que verdaderos fuessen quantos crímines de donas podrías pensar, ¿es nunguno de igualar aquél por el qual dixo Dios: "Yo m'arepiento d'aver fecho l'ombre"?[21] Por cierto no. Mas nosotros, de malicia consejado, en son que olvidamos nuestros defectos, los suyos pequeños fazemos muy grandes, los dudosos ciertos y los encubiertos públicos. No nos basta que de compañeras las hayamos tornado siervas. Non nos basta que, sin consentimiento suyo casadas, demos tales por señores a muchas que de vassallos suyos apenas serían dignos. No nos basta que, como fazedores de las leyes, a nosotros favoresçiendo e aquellas menguando, nuestros yerros criminales por sibiles, e los suyos civiles sean criminales havidos. No nos basta que unas por çelosos

Now, if I were to presume, without prejudice concerning them, to name ladies of our own day, I would show not a few who, notwithstanding all the aforesaid battles, armed with many virtues, protect and defend the fortress of chastity. Today let us acknowledge them and consider which of us, tempted in so many ways, under the cover of secrecy, would not give in to sin, when we are so naturally inclined and always willing? Truly, I know many men who have with much less cause sold castles, deceived friends, miscarried justice, betrayed lords, perpetrated cruel deaths, and committed many other public evils, induced not by natural inclination, but only by wicked intentions.

I say then, in conclusion, if we take all my arguments into account and acknowledge that most—indeed almost all—of women's wrongdoing stems from the great force of nature and is provoked by masculine cunning, while the wrongdoing of men is the result of wickedness and will, we see that, by rights, men should be called perverse and that women, rather than evil, should be called very good, in their way. If women, seeing themselves subjugated, mistreated, and looked down upon by men, contrive to be pleasing to those who have power over them by using sophisticated cosmetics, attractive gestures, and many garments, I say it is good.[19] For they have no other arms left to them in their abject frailty for the restoration of their freedom and for defense against masculine insult, but those that Love has given them. Theirs is a praiseworthy cunning, which by pleasing pandering sways the will of men who are undeservedly in command.

But tell me, you unmanly man,[20] if accusing women pleases you, if all the crimes that you impute to women were true, could any one equal that crime for which God said, "It repenteth me that I have made man"?[21] Of course not. But we men, taking counsel from malice, as if forgetting our own defects, make women's little flaws out to be huge, their doubtful defects certain, and their hidden ones public. We are not satisfied by having turned women from companions into slaves. It is not enough for us that we marry them off without their consent, that we give many women to lords and masters who would hardly be worthy of being their vassals. It is not enough for us that, as lawmakers, favoring ourselves and putting women at a disadvantage, we define our own criminal offenses as civil ones, and women's civil offenses as criminal. No, it is not enough for us that—some by jealous husbands, others by malicious mothers-in-law,

maridos, otras por maliciosas suegras, otras por renzillosas madres, otras de quienquiere, nunqua les fallesçiendo señores, sean continuamente maltratadas. No nos bastan mil otros daños, sinrazones e cargos que de nosotros reçiben, mas aun con levantamiento de nuevas maliçias les buscamos infamia.

En verdat, de maravillar no sería, aquestas cosas consideradas con la reprovada manera de nuestro señorear, que las mugeres, en son de desesperadas, desasiendo del bien, a nuestro mal pretendiessen. Mas su muy dulçe condiçión, a paciençia, a benignidat aderiendo, causa que, non obstante los tantos ultrages, sean conduzidoras de nuestros plazeres, consoladoras de nuestras tristezas, lamentadoras de nuestros infortunios, curadoras de nuestras dolencias, descanso e reparo de todo nuestro bevir.

Quisiera yo, maldiziente, la presente invençión consentiera bolumen de libro a fin que más complidamente tus falsas opinones e mis verdaderas razones podieran ser conoçidas. Pero para creençia de los buenos e percepçión de los entendidos assaz cumplen las dichas, que a los ignorantes ¿quáles razones podrían ser tan complidas que no viniessen escassas? Ellos, comúnmente maliçiosos, ni quieren descreer el mal ni saben conoçer el bien. Los viles, naturalmente enemigos de gentileza, e por consiguiente d'onor, d'amor e de donas, en cargo de sus costumbres sean libertadas sus lenguas. Ruégovos pues, maldizientes, visto que bondat vos contrasta e razón nos ayuda, con aquestas leales de gentiles ánimos quedéis assí apaziguados que, con salvoconduto de vuestras lenguas, el fuible tiempo traspassen.

E vos, las señoras, si bien amadas de aquellos dispuestos a ser amados vos véis, suplico sean no en tal manera tratados que de servidores tornen enemigos.

E a vos, dona de cuya disposición e costumbres he traslatado los bienes qu'en la presente se ecriven, pido de graçia con aquellas de vuestra escuadra ayuntada comuniquéis las presentes razones e con aquellas a quien mi mal dezir ofendió, por manera que en la graçia de todas y en el servicio de vos más plaziblemente se despienda mi vida.

others by spiteful mothers, others by whomever, for they are never lacking in superiors—women be continually abused. We are not satisfied by
the thousands of other injuries, injustices, accusations, and even more
attacks on women, so now we seek their dishonor with an onslaught of
new insults.

Truly, it would not be surprising if women—upon consideration
of these things along with our reprehensible way of ruling over them—in
desperation, turned away from good and sought to harm us. Still, their
very sweet natures, their propensity for patience and kindness—despite
so many betrayals—make women the source of our pleasures, the com-
forters of our sadness, the bewailers of our misfortunes, the curers of our
sicknesses, the rest and remedy of all our lives.

Oh, slanderer, how I wish that this composition could fill an entire
book so that your false opinions and my true reasoning would be known
all the more fully! But what I have said here is sufficient for convincing
good men and for persuading intelligent ones. As for the ignorant, what
arguments could be so consummate that they would not fall short? Ignorant men, who are generally wicked, neither want to disbelieve evil nor
do they know how to discern good. Low men are by nature the enemies
of gentility, and consequently of honor, of love, and of women; let their
tongues be loosed according to their character. So I beg you, slanderers, given that goodness is against you and reason supports us, to make
peace with these loyal and gentle souls, so that women may live out their
fleeting days with safe-conduct from your tongues.

And you, Ladies, if you see yourselves truly loved by those willing
to be loved, I beseech you, let them not be treated in such a way that they
turn from servants into enemies.

And of you, my Lady, from whose character and habits I have
translated the virtues that are written here, I ask that you, together with
those ladies of your retinue, communicate my arguments to those who
were offended by my slander, so that I might more happily spend my life
in the favor of all ladies and in your service.

Notes

1. Torrellas is clearly referring to the definition of woman given in Isidore of Seville's *Etymologies*. See Volume Editor's Introduction, 24–25. However, while he refers to Isidore's authority, Torrellas is playing upon the terms *woman* and *lady*, and their interpretation, by implying that to be a *dona* or lady is to be *unwomanly*. Moreover, from his opening words on, and throughout the *Defense*, Torrellas refers back to his own slanderous verses, alerting readers to the tongue-in-cheek quality of his arguments.

2. Torrellas implies that the *Slander* was composed in reaction to his being rejected by a woman.

3. As in the *Slander*, Torrellas refers to commonly held beliefs about the humors (cold or hot, and moist or dry), gender and temperament.

4. Here, Torrellas rehearses standard profeminine arguments regarding the superiority of both place and material in the creation of Eve.

5. As Rodríguez Risquete observes, it is possible that Torrellas meant to refer not to the Spanish writer Juan de Mena, but rather to Jean de Meun, the continuator of the *Romance of the Rose* and consequently a subject of the *Debate of the* Romance of the Rose. *Obra completa*, 2: 178 and 190.

6. Stories of wise men laid low by love are commonplaces of misogynist writing. For example, in the first book of his *Corbacho*, Alfonso Martínez de Toledo devotes an entire chapter to "how wise men lose their wisdom to love" of women.

7. Most of the women named in the *Defense* would have been familiar to Torrellas's contemporaries because many of their legends were standard entries in catalogs of women and others derive from well-known biblical and classical narratives, such as Ovid's *Metamorphoses*. Torrellas draws heavily upon Boccaccio's *Famous Women* for his lists of exemplary and infamous women. The lists given in the *Defense* also share many examples with the catalogs of his close contemporaries Diego de Valera and Álvaro de Luna. In the translation presented here, I follow Virginia Brown's rendering of the names in Boccaccio's catalog. *Famous Women*, ed. and trans. Virginia Brown (Cambridge MA: Harvard University Press, 2001).

8. Lapitha was the daughter of Apollo, according to Isidore of Seville. *Etymologies*, IX.ii.70, 195.

9. Tiburtina is another name for Nicostrata.

10. Rodríguez Risquete suggests that "Othea" refers to Huldah, a prophetess, in 2 Kings 22.14. *Obra completa*, 2: 191. However, Torrellas may refer here to the Amazon queen

Orithya, to whom Boccaccio devotes a chapter in his *Famous Women* (41). Moreover, Torrellas may have heard of or known Christine de Pizan's *Letter of Othea to Hector* (1400), in which Othea (a goddess of wisdom) writes to the young Trojan hero Hector. The following reference to "Cristina" in the Spanish original may thus refer to Christine herself or to St. Christine.

11. Rodríguez Risquete identifies "Bannes" as Evadne, whose story of suicide at her husband's death was recorded by Ovid. *Obra completa*, 2:192

12. Rodríguez Risquete notes that the name "Hian" may reflect a textual corruption in the Spanish manuscripts. *Obra completa*, 2:192. Given his reliance upon Boccaccio, Torrellas may refer here to Pope Joan. "Joan, an Englishwoman and Pope" in *Famous Women*, 215–17.

13. Rodríguez Risquete suggests that the reference to "Machavea" is to the mother of the seven brothers in 2 Maccabees 7. *Obra completa*, 2:192.

14. Torrellas includes some specifically Spanish examples, such as Berenguela and María Coronel. "Berenguela" may refer to Berengaria, a thirteenth century Queen of Castile and Leon. As mentioned in the Editor's Introduction, according to legend, María Coronel protected her chastity by self-mutilation (26).

15. Torrellas mentions various "Marias," each of which could refer to the Virgin Mary. Since this second María is included among the magnanimous queens, she may be a reference to a historical Iberian queen, such as María of Aragón, or perhaps to Boccaccio's Mariamme, Queen of Judaea. *Famous Women*, 175–77.

16. The *Cancionero de Herberay*, fol 20r, contains marginal glosses on the *Defense of Ladies against Slanderers*, which explain the stories of the Wives of the Cimbrians (a Germanic group from what is now Northern Italy) and the Minyans (a group from Greek mythology), the Indian practice of *sati*, and the suicidal battle fought by the Cantabrian women during Roman invasion. The legends of the Minyan and Cimbrian women are found in Boccaccio's *Famous Women*. Upon the retreat of their husbands from the Romans, the Cimbrian women chose to kill their children and themselves rather than become war booty. *Famous Women*, 165–66. The Minyan women rescued their captive husbands from the Spartans by exchanging clothes with them and allowing their escape. *Famous Women* 61–63.

17. The gloss in the *Cancionero de Herberay* explains that the Cantabrian women defended their city against Roman invasion when their husbands' strength had given out. Then, when the *cantabrias* no longer had weapons to fight against the Romans, they bombarded their enemies by throwing the bodies of their children from the city walls and, finally, by throwing themselves from the walls.

18. The maiden of Huesca and the Lady of Castell Rosellón are two specifically Iberian examples of women devoted to love. The "maiden of Huesca" may be a reference to the Aragonese legend of the "Lovers of Teruel," dramatized in the nineteenth century by Juan Eugenio Hartzenbusch. According to legend, the Lady of Castell Roselló or Serimonda was lover of the troubadour Guillem de Cabestany (1162–1212). Her husband, Raimon of Castel Rossillon, upon finding out about the love affair, fed the poet's heart to his wife. The story may have served as Boccaccio's inspiration for the story of Ghismonda. *The Vidas of the Troubadours*, trans. Margarita Egan (New York: Garland, 1984), 53–5. "Our Oliver" is cited by various fifteenth century writers as a man who committed suicide for love. Rodríguez Risquete, *Obra completa*, 2:197.

19. Here Torrellas praises women for the same behavior he decries in stanza nine of the *Slander*.

20. Cantavella suggests that this is a reference to sodomy, 113. Archer, on the other hand, argues that it is an allusion to Matthew 26:24, where Jesus prophesies his betrayal. *Obras completas*, 239.

21. Genesis 6: 6–7.

JUAN DE FLORES

GRISEL Y MIRABELLA

❧

GRISEL AND MIRABELLA

Tratado compuesto por Johan de Flores a su amiga.[1]

Como el fin de mis pensamientos concluye en que mejor serviros pueda mi voluntad *busca* en que trabaje con desseo de más fazerme vuestro.[2] Y no me contento en serviros sólo en las cosas más a mí convenibles mas aun en aquellas que más agenas que mías puedo lamar. Esto porque si con autoridat de sciencia de que carezco: presumía hazer cosa a mí bien scusada: no miré que dava causa de publicar mis yerros: y que el que no sabe la falta de mi flaco juizio la sepa.

Y assí sin más determinar en ello salvo senyora que vuestro favor puede dispensar en mi ozadía: por ser yo tanto vuestro: con lo qual me harré de vuestro esfuerço: sin más temor y vergüença puse en obra esta mal compuesta letra. Y no curé de buscar aquella gracia de hablar como por a tal caso convenía. Y si ello no stá tal que de oír sea: vos senyora merezcáis la pena de mi culpa. Pues stá claro que sin esfuerço vuestro yo no ozara atreverme a tan loco ensayo. Que si por ventura lo que no creo: algo de bien habrá en ello: a vos que se ha de dar la pena: den las gracias. Pues yo d'esto solamente soy scrivano. Que por la comunicación de vuestra *causa*[3] he trabajado por fazer alguna parte de las obras de vuestra discreción: para me aprovechar en esta necessidad d'ellas.[4]

Por lo qual aunque non quepa en el número de las loadas: yo pienso que aun no tan buena se crea de mí. Y si alguno lo dexare passar siendo a mí favorable en dissimulación sin loar ni rehutar: bien pareçe que sin esfuerço de vuestra ayuda no podiera hazer cosa que razonable fuesse. Que si vuestro favor en ello no me ayudara: diera grande occasión a la riza y malicia de los oyentes. Y por esto lo envío a vos senyora: como persona que lo malo encobrirá: y lo comunal será por más de bueno tovido. Y si del todo fuesse inútil: que le daríades la pena que mereçen mis simples trabajos. Porque non más de vos fuessen públicos mis defectos. Pues es razón: que así como havéis seido causa de me dar soberbia: que seáis reparo para la culpa d'ello.

A Romance Written by Juan de Flores for his Lady.[1]

All my thoughts turn to how I might best serve you; I seek to labor in my desire to make myself all the more yours.[2] For I am not content to serve you only in the ways that are fitting to my station, but also in ways that may be expected of others, but not of me. I say this because, lacking the authority of wisdom, I have dared to do something well beyond my talents; I paid no mind to making my own faults public, nor did it concern me that the feebleness of my poor mind will now be known to those who did not already know of it.

And so, my lady, without further ado and with the confidence that your favor will forgive my impudence—I being entirely yours, will arm my-self with your strength—I wrote this poorly composed text without further fear or shame and without endeavoring to write with the graceful elo-quence that such a story calls for. If it is not worth reading, then you, my lady, deserve to be punished for my crime, for it is clear that without your urging I should never have been so bold as to dare compose such a folly as this. Nevertheless, if by chance there is some good in it, which I doubt, let the credit be all yours, since you are also the one to whom punishment must be given. For I am nothing more than the scribe of this text, one who has served you[3] in order to carry out a portion of the works of your will, benefiting from your need for service.[4]

Thus, although this work may not be among your more praise-worthy ones, I believe it is the best yet to come from my pen. Although one of my friends might have circulated it anonymously, neither praising nor criticizing the writing, it surely seems that I should never have written anything worth reading without the fortitude given by your aid. For had your favor not supported me, my work would inspire derision and sharp criticism from its audience. And so I send it to you, my lady, as to one who will conceal what is bad and cause what is made public to be appreciated all the more. But, if this work is completely unworthy, give it the punish-ment that my simple efforts merit. But let my defects be known to you alone. For it is proper that just as you have been the cause of my pride, you should be the remedy for its errors.

Comiença el tractado

En el regno de Scoçia huvo un excellente Rey de todas virtudes amigo.
Y principalmente en ser justiciero. Y era tanto justo: como la misma
justicia. Y este en su postremera edat huvo una hija que después de sus
días succedía en el reino. Y esta llamaron Mirabella.[5] Y fue de tanta
perfectión de gracias acabada: que ninguno tanto loarla pudo: que
el cabo de su mereçer contar podiesse. Y como ella fuesse heredera
de la senyoría del padre: non havía ningún emperador ni poderoso
príncipe que en casamiento no la demandasse. Y aunque ella fuera de
pequenyo stado: sólo por sus beldades y valer la fizieran de las senyoras más grande.

Y el Rey su padre por non tener hijos: y por el grande merec-
imiento que ella tenía: era d'éll tanto amada: que a ninguno de los ya
dichos la quería dar. Y así mismo en su tierra non havía tan grande
senyor a quien la diesse: salvo a grande mengua suya. De manera que
el grande amor suyo era a ella mucho enemigo. Y como ya muchas
vezes acaeçe quando hay dilación en el casamiento de las mujeres: ser
causa de caer en vergüenças y yerros: assí a esta después acaeció.

Pues en aquestos comedios assí como su edat crecía: crecían
y dublavan las gracias de su beldat en tanto grado: que qualquiere
hombre dispuesto a amar: así como la mirasse le era forçado de ser
preso de su amor. Y tan en stremo la amavan: que por su causa venían
a perder las vidas. Tanto que la flor de la cavallería de casa del Rey
su padre feneció sus días en esta tal guerra. De manera que sopido
por el Rey: la hizo meter en un lugar muy secreto: que ningún barón
verla pudiesse: por ser su vista muy peligrosa. Porque el desastre con
buenas guardas se resiste.[6]

Y ella así retraída en lugar apartado: dos cavalleros que havían
quedado de aquellos muchos que ya eran muertos: aquella empresa
tomaron. Estos eran puestos en strecha amistad. Lo qual non dio lugar que'l strecho amor de Mirabella el uno del otro supiesse. Por ser
su caso muy peligroso. Que aun de sí mesmos se encelavan. Pero cada
uno d'ellos buscava maneras cómo verla podiessen. Y el remedio d'ellos
era la secreta noche. En la qual con diligente desseo cada uno d'ellos
ensayava de traer consigo una scala: por do sobían a una ret de hierro:
por ver aquella donzella la vista de la qual conservava sus passiones. Y

Here Begins the Romance

Once in the kingdom of Scotland there was a most excellent and virtu-ous King, who was above all righteously just. Indeed, he was as just as justice itself. This King in his old age had a daughter, who would, at the end of his days, succeed him to the throne. She was called Mirabella.[5] So well endowed with grace and beauty was she, that no one could pos-sibly praise her sufficiently to recount the sum of all her perfections. Now, since she was to inherit her father's crown, there was no emperor or pow-erful prince that did not ask for her hand in marriage. Even if she had been of lowly estate, she would have been thought the greatest of ladies for her beauty and character alone.

Since the King her father had no sons—and because of her great merit—Mirabella was so beloved by him that he refused to give her to any foreign suitor. Nor was there so great a man in his own lands that the King could give her to him without causing great suffering to himself; thus the King's great love was a dire enemy to his daughter. And, as is so often the case when women's marriages are delayed—delay leads to shame and error—so it befell Mirabella.

This being the state of things, as Mirabella grew, so did her grace and beauty, which flourished to such a degree, in fact, that when any man disposed to love laid eyes on her, he was taken by force as a prisoner of love. Men loved her to such extremes that they came to lose their lives for her; indeed, so many men were killed that the flower of chivalry in the King's retinue perished in the struggle. When the King learned of the bloodshed, he imprisoned Mirabella in a secret place where no man might see her, since the sight of her was so perilous, for disaster may be averted by a strong defense.[6]

While Mirabella was thus hidden away, two knights, who had sur-vived when so many others lay dead, took up the banner of love. The two were intimate friends, but even so, neither one knew of the other's deep love for Mirabella; since loving her was so perilous, they concealed it from one another. The knights found ways to see her, taking refuge in the cover of night: filled with desire, each one would bring a ladder to climb up to an iron grate through which they might see the maiden, whose visage kept their passions aflame. Now, because the two knights both insisted upon their perilous gazing, it so happened that when one was gazing at Mirabella

así como cada uno d'ellos continuava: aquella peligrosa vista: acaeció que stando el uno contentando su voluntad en la vista de Mirabella: el otro venía por se reparar con la misma consolación. Y como allegasse: firiéronse el uno al otro muy fieramente. Y los mantos enbraçados y las spadas sacadas conbatiéronse hasta que en las aquexadas y secretas vozes se conocieron. Y acordándose de su amistat strecha: y aún por no ser de la casa conocidos: stuvieron quedos. Retrayéndose en un lugar apartado donde el uno al otro tales razones se dizen:

No hallo causa yo que tan justa sea: para que yo de vos y vos de mí quexarnos devamos. Porque cada uno por sí es más obligado al amor de Mirabella: que a ninguna strecha amistad. Y por esto no me pareçe que yo por respecto vuestro: ni aun vos por el mío: apartássemos de seguir la famosa enpresa ya por cada uno de nos comiençada. Ni así mismo sería virtud que amos en un lugar amassemos. Ca sería grande mengua a tan amigable hermandat como la nuestra. De manera que en este caso yo no sé más de un sólo remedio y es que echando suertes entre amos: se aparte nuestra contienda. Y al que por dicha copiere el seguimiento d'esta donzella: sigua sus amores. Y el otro se retraya d'ellos.

Respuesta de Grisel[7]

Vuestras palabras traen consigo prueva del poco amor que con Mirabella tenéis. Porque quien verdaderamente ama: non se porná al peligro de non le caer la suerte. Mas vos que os offrecéis: parece que non temistes la contraria ventura. Y el que non teme: non ama. Mas yo que verdaderamente amo: no me plaze poner mi vida en ventura de las suertes. Porque puesto que me copiesse: el apartarme de amar no sería en mi mano. Porque ya en mi voluntad di lugar a mi libertad que ageno senyorío la possea:[8] mas vos que ozáis tomar a ventura: ligero vos sería quedar sin ella. Y esta es verdadera suerte y prueva por donde vos merecéis perder aquella que vos ahora fingidamente seguís. Y non quiero con vos ninguno pleito. Sino que pues que más amo: más dignamente la merezco.

to his heart's content, the other arrived in order to treat himself to the same consolation. When they met, the two knights exchanged fierce blows, gravely wounding each other. Then, with their mantles wrapped about their arms as shields and their swords drawn, the two fought on until they recognized one another by the sounds of their dolorous but stifled cries. Recalling their intimate friendship, and not wanting to be discovered by the household, they quietly withdrew far from Mirabella's prison and then one said to the other:

"I cannot find just cause to blame you for my plight, nor can you fault me for yours, for each of us is compelled more by love for Mirabella than by any bond of friendship between us. Therefore it seems that neither I, out of respect for you, nor you, out of respect for me, should relinquish the heroic venture we each have undertaken. Still less would it be honorable for us both to love the same lady, for it should be a great harm to our brotherhood of friendship. Consequently, in this case, I know of only one remedy: we may resolve our dispute by drawing lots. And he to whom Fortune grants the courting of this maiden may continue in his passions, while the other must retreat."

The Knight Grisel[7]

Your words themselves prove your lack of love for Mirabella, for a man who loves truly would never gamble at such stakes. What is more, by proposing a game of chance, you appear not to fear adverse Fortune, and he who does not fear does not love. But I, a true lover, do not wish to leave my life up to chance. If I were to lose, it would not be in my power to cease loving her, as I have already willingly surrendered my freedom to the rule of another.[8] But it would be easy for you, you who dare to gamble your love, to lose her. For this is truly your fortune and proof that you deserve to lose the woman you now pretend to desire. I have no grievance with you, for I love her more than you and so I am more worthy and deserving of her.

Respuesta de Grisamón

Non creáis ser yo tan poco constante que si no me conociesse por más dichoso: y tener mejor drecho: que otro lo dexasse a la suerte. Mas como en las batallas y suertes se muestra Dios más favorable a la verdad: teniendo por cierto que assí como otro alguno conmigo en amar no se podía igualar: que tan poco en las suertes se igualaría. Porque cierto daría el drecho a cuyo fuere: y por esto conocía de mí quedar con ello. Y ninguna cosa dudava. Porque de mi dicha tengo tal seguredat: que nunqua la hallé contraria. Porque muchas vezes la he hallada cierta: quando con drecho y verdad la sperimentava. Assí que bien sé cierto: mayormente fuera en ésta: en que tanto me va. Y porque tan conocida avantaja tengo: pedía las suertes como quien la mejor tenía de su mano. Y este spediente saqué por aquell deudo que a la amistad devía. Y por scusaros la prueva por el trançe de la batalla: haziéndoos seguro de mayor mal: donde no se scusava vuestra muerte: por el menor que solamente era la suerte. Y si esto no quisiéredes: sea por la manera que a vos mejor paraciere según la fuerça de vuestro coraçon. Y a lo que dixéredes me obligo.

Respuesta de Grisel

Pues aun la razón que agora ponéis por scusa de vuestro yerro: os faze más condennado. Porque es cierto: que todo hombre que bien ama: es desdichado. Y todas venturas contrarias l'empeescen. Mas siempre a los menos dignos amor les es favorable que non lo sopiendo dezir amar nin seguir: sus fechos se hazen mejor que lo piden. Mas los que verdaderamente mueren amando: el padecer d'ellos por vida lievan y por gualardón. Y porque amor no tiene a cada uno de los que le siguen en más de lo que pueden soffrir: los que son de vuestra qualidat: non consiente que penen mucho. Porque presto se retraen de seguir a lugar que caro se venda. Porque ellos no podrían seguir ni disponerse a las passiones que otros semejantes que yo se ponen. Y por esto conviene que sean dichosos. Que aun no pidiéndolo: les digan "plázeme": mas a los que éll conosce por muy constantes: y tanto que adonde aman mueren o vençen: a estos desdichadas venturas los prueva penando.

The Knight Grisamon

Do not think me so inconstant; for were I not sure of my greater fortune and rights, I would not leave it to chance. God always favors the truth in the outcome of battles and games of chance; just as no one can equal me in loving, no one can equal me in the luck of the draw. God will surely favor the rightful winner, thus I know without a doubt He will choose me. I have great confidence in Fortune, because she has never yet turned against me; many times have I found favor with her, when I tested her rightfully and truthfully. Thus I am sure that she will favor me all the more in this endeavor, since she has always been on my side. Knowing my obvious advantage, I suggested casting lots, as would a man who knows he has already won the toss. What is more, I suggested this course of action because of my duty to you as a friend and to spare you from the danger of combat, which would surely have been the greater evil for you, because your death would have been inevitable, whereas leaving it to chance would have been the lesser evil. If you do not agree, let us come to a decision in the manner that seems best to you, according to your heart's desire, and I shall do whatever you say.

The Knight Grisel

The very reason you offer as an excuse for your offense condemns you all the more. For it is rightly said: the man who loves truly is unfortunate and all adverse fortunes befall him. Love always favors the least worthy, for they, knowing not love nor how to pursue it, succeed beyond their hopes, while those who truly die for love embrace their suffering as life itself and Love's reward. Love metes out to his followers only as much suffering as each can withstand: He does not allow lovers of your quality to feel much pain, for your kind would sooner flee than persevere when the price is high. Your kind cannot feel nor dedicate themselves to passion in the way that lovers of my kind do. So it is fitting that your kind be happy in love. For even without courting, women say to them, "You are pleasing to me." Yet Love puts his most constant followers—those so constant that in loving they either die or conquer—to the test by sending them misfortunes and pain, so that when their glory at long last comes, the rewards are redou-

Porque con el grande padeçer merezcan quando les viniere la gloria que sea dublada. Y por trabajos disfavores y males se conoçe quanto hasta la fuerça de su virtud. Y a los que sin pena aman: no es menester pruevar su poca paciencia. Que con la menor fatiga que en los tales trances oviessen: luego se retraerían del campo. Y tan sin vergüença fuyen. Y tan alegres vencidos como vencedores.

Así que yo lo que por caro precio he comprado: no quiero ponerlo en aventura de suertes sino de batalla. Pues al bien amar nunqua se le apartan desdichas. Porque con la merced de Dios lo entiendo de hazer comprar más caro que lo yo compré. Y en esto creo es más cierto Dios mostrarse: que no en suertes como vuestro flaco coraçón y menos verdad pedía: por scusarse de la affruenta que hará enganyoso vuestro amor y flaquas las fuerças que nunqua fueron fuertes.[9] Y entonces conoceréis: como en las fortunas y males crecen las fuerças de la afección. Y que al buen mártil de amor con la passión de las muchas muertes se la dubla la fe.[10] La qual pues está agora conmigo: no creáis podáis scusaros por otras intricadas razones ni spedientes salvo por batalla. Y pues esto es de fuerça: mostrad fuerça de flaquesa: o dad vantaja del seguimiento a quien d'ello es digno.

El auctor

Estos dos cavalleros después de haver mucho questionado quién más dignamente la merecía: vinieron en tan grandes rompimientos de palabras: que el que no consentió en las suertes: mató al otro. Y tan secreta fue la question entre ellos. Que jamás el Rey pudo saber quién lo havía muerto. Aquell cavallero vencedor llamavan Grisel. El qual prosiguiendo sus amores: Mirabella en pena de quantos por su causa eran muertos: viendo la grande requesta d'este: de su amor fue presa. Y aunque en grande ençerramiento la toviesse el Rey su padre: ella por sí sola sin terçero buscó manera a la *no* más plaziente que peligrosa batalla:[11] donde los desseos de Grisel y suyos vinieron a efecto. Y después que algunos días muy ocultos en grandes plazeres conservaron sus amores: ella no pudo encobrirlo a una grande y antigua sierva suya. Porque en su cámara más communicava. Y esta camarera suya amava mucho a un maestresala[12] del Rey y como supo el secreto de

bled and through their labors, trials, and torments the strength of their virtue is known. As for those who love without pain, it is not necessary to test what little patience they have, for they retreat from the field when faced with the slightest obstacle and shamelessly flee, equally content to be conquered as to be conquerors.

And so, I refuse to leave to chance that for which I have already paid such a high price; rather I will fight for it. Adversity is never far from true love, for by the grace of God, I intend to put an even higher price on my love than I have yet paid. I am sure that God will protect me. He will not be on the side of chance, as you wrongly and faint-heartedly have claimed in order to avoid our duel; now your love shall be discovered to be false, and your strengths—which never were forceful—frail.[9] Then you will see that Love's force grows in fortune and misfortune; the martyr of true love doubles his vows with the passions of many deaths.[10] I will live up to my vow now: do not think that you can save yourself with more intricate reasoning or tactics; you must perforce do battle: show now the strength of your frailty or cede the right to love Mirabella to the man worthy of it.

The Author

After the two knights had debated at length over which of the two was more worthy of Mirabella, their words became so increasingly violent that the one who had refused to draw lots killed the other. The victor, called Grisel, persevered in his love. Mirabella, repenting the number of deaths she had caused, and seeing the strength of Grisel's suit, fell captive to his love. And, despite her imprisonment by her father the King, without the help of a go-between, Mirabella found a way for a no less pleasing than perilous battle[11] to occur, in which Grisel's desires as well as her own were realized. And after they had spent several days of great pleasure hidden away in love, Mirabella could no longer conceal it from her most loyal and constant maidservant who was often present in her room. Now, this servant was in love with the King's taster,[12] and when she found out about her mistress's secret, her loyalty was not strong enough to keep her from telling her lover what was afoot between Mirabella and Grisel. The steward,

su senyora: no pudo su lealtad tanto soffrir: que no lo descobriesse al su amante lo que Mirabella y Grisel passavan. Y éll viendo tan grande error: doliéndose mucho de la honra de su senyor: o por ventura de invidia movido: no pudo callar lo que al rey no publicasse la maldad que en su casa Grisel cometía.

El qual como oyó tan feo caso: con grande discreción buscó manera como amos los tomassen en uno. Y una noche stando Grisel en la cama con Mirabella: el Rey mandó sercar la casa.[13] Y aunque grande rato se defendió: pero a la fin tomados en strechos cárçeres por fuerça fueron puestos.

Y como el Rey fuesse el más justificado príncipe que a la sazón se hallasse en el mundo: aun en aquell caso no quizo usar de rigor ni de enojoso accidente. Mas como si fuessen sus iguales: con ellos se puso a justicia. Y las leyes de su reino mandavan: que qualquiere que en tal yerro cayesse: el que más causa fuesse al otro de haver amado: que padeciesse muerte: y el otro destierro para toda su vida. Y como acayesse quando dos personas se aman: el uno tener más culpa que el otro en la requesta: por esto las leyes no disponían las penas fuessen iguales. Y luego por el Rey spressamente fue mandado la pezquisa se hisiesse: porque la verdad fuesse sabida: qual de aquellos dos fuesse más digno de culpa. Y los juezes fazen luego las diligencias que por el caso convenían. Pero tan secreto fue el trato de sus amores: que no podieron saber quién havía más trabajado en la requesta y siguimiento del otro. Salvo quanto la camarera dezía no haverlo ella sopido: hasta que ya entre ellos concertado estava. Y como por la pezquiza no hoviesse lugar en condemnar a uno más que a otro. Fueron los juezes por mandado del Rey donde Mirabella y Grisel estavan. A los quales tomaron juntamente. Y les demandaron dixiessen quién fue más causa al otro de tal error. Y ellos como ya sabían que el más culpado havía de padecer muerte: fue preguntado y en tal modo.[14]

upon hearing of such a great crime, and pained by the threat to his lord's honor—or perhaps moved by envy—was unable to hold his tongue and keep from the King the crime committed by Grisel in his house.

When the King heard the ugly truth, with great discretion he devised a plan to catch the lovers together. And so one night, while Grisel lay in bed with Mirabella,[13] the King ordered that the house be surrounded. Although Grisel fought off the King's men for a long time, in the end, the two lovers were taken by force and cruelly imprisoned.

Now, this King being in those days the most just of all the princes the world over, he refused to respond with severity or impassioned anger, even in such a case as this. Rather, since the lovers were nobles of his land, he would apply the rules of justice. For the laws of his realm decreed that when any pair of lovers was caught in such an offense, the lover who had led the other into sin would be put to death; and the less guilty lover, banished for life. As often happens when two people are in love, one is more to blame than the other for seduction, and that is why the laws do not mete out equal punishment. Straightaway the King himself ordered an investigation so that the truth of the matter might be known concerning which of the two lovers was more blameworthy. The judges then acted with the diligence that the case required. However, the love between Grisel and Mirabella had been kept so secret that it was impossible to ascertain which one had endeavored to pursue and seduce the other. All the maidservant would say was that she had known nothing until the lovers were of one will. Since the investigation resulted in no proof for the sentencing of one lover over the other, the King ordered the judges to go where Mirabella and Grisel were held, and question them together, asking who was more to blame than the other for the crime. The lovers knew that the guilty party would be put to death; Grisel was questioned and responded in the following manner.[14]

Responde Grisel

Esto es sin más apurar la verdad: que yo el comienço medio y fin fue del cometido error. Y según las demasiadas cautelas que yo busqué par haver tan grande victoria: lo que nunqua se hizo ni dixo: yo lo supe dezir y hazer. Y açí como la presa era preciosa y cara de haver: ansí las diligencias se requerían. Mas como yo cativo me viesse: cosas ya más non pensadas por mi libertad pensé. Y como esta senyora fue el cabo de todas las excellencias del mundo: y los qui eran en edad floresciente de virtuosos ánimos: en esta demanda siguiessen la estrecha senda de la muerte: yo con temor de aquella huve de hazer cosas: que en pensamiento presedían a las que Iason hiso en la victoria del velleçino de oro. Y como Mirabella fuesse tan peligrosa: y mas de haver: yo me armé de tales pertrechos: como quien pensasse combatir de las baxuras de la tierra a las alturas del cielo. Pues manifiesto está que yo tan alta persona vencí: que ella no se venció con las civiles requestas de las communas gentes. Mas assí como a grandes requiere: grandes cosas le convenió hazer y con mis aquexadas congoxas tales y tantas artes obré: que castidad y vergüença non queriendo vencí. Ni otra cosa a ella fuera possible hazer. Porque es cierto: que quien con affección sigue amor: tan bien vençe las cosas altas como las baxas. Por donde yo con amor y paçión ninguna cosa temía: que postpuesto todo temor y desechado de mí el empacho: como quien en tales cosas se antepone: tan bien las seguí: que por fuerça la traxe vencida: assí que la culpa mía no la hagáis agena. Y dexando a ella libre: a mí que la muerte merezco la deis. Pues yo gozé de la gloria ligera me será la pena.

Dize Mirabella

Grisel non penséis que por hermosas razones ni saber lo bien decir: vuestras palabras puedan más que la verdad. Pues conocido es: ser más desonesto el oír a las mujeres: que el requestar a los hombres. Y puesto que vos lo acometiérades: lo qual yo niego: si yo lugar no diera a las hablas de vuestros desseos: non consideraran en el cumplimiento d'ellos. Y mi deshonesto mirar y favorecer vuestra demanda: era más deshonesto a mí: que el requestar a vos ¡O quán ligero es de conocer

Grisel

This is the whole truth: I was the beginning, middle, and end of the crime committed, thanks to the many schemes I used to win such a great victory. I knew just how to do and say everything necessary: things never before done or said. And as my quarry was precious and costly to obtain, so my pursuit required diligence. What is more, since I was already her prisoner, I was able to contemplate things that never would have occurred to me when I was a free man. This lady was the most excellent to be found under the sun, and, if those who had pursued her with the virtuous spirit of flowering youth trod the narrow path to death, I, fearing death, was compelled to feats even greater than those realized by Jason in his capture of the Golden Fleece, for Mirabella was just as dangerous to pursue and even more so to win. I armed myself with the weapons of a man preparing to battle from the depths of the earth to the heights of heaven. It is clear to see that I conquered a most noble personage; the base sort of seduction used by lowly common folk could not have won her. No, she was pursued as befits a great person: great feats were required and I, with much artifice and such anguished complaints of how I suffered for her, seduced her; even though her chastity and shame were unwilling, there was nothing else she could possibly do. For it is true that he who pursues love with fervor conquers noble things as easily as lowly ones. So I, with love and passion, feared nothing. All fear put off and qualms cast aside, like a champion lover, I went after her and I forced her to surrender. So, do not attribute my guilt to another; set her free and give me the death I deserve. Since I took pleasure in glory, the punishment will be nothing to me.

Mirabella

Do not think, Grisel, that your pretty speeches and rhetorical savvy can trump the truth. For it is well known that women's ears are more shame-less than men's seductive words of love. Even if you had committed the crime, which I deny, had I not given you the opportunity to speak of your desires, you would not have seen them fulfilled. My shameless glances and favoring of your suit were more shameless for me than your seduc-

en las mujeres quando aman que sin condeçender en lo que es demandado: dan senyales de consentir en ello![15]

Pues de aquestos tales y desonestos actos en mí muchos
conocistes. Y ante que vos pensastes quererme: mi voluntad quereros
pensó. Y con cautela desonesta os declaré lo que mis desseos querían.
Pues ¿quál persona fuera por mí requestada como vos fuestes: que
non hiziera lo que vos? Y puesto que de lealtad presumiérades en casa
de vuestro senyor: mi merecer y beldad vençe a todas las cosas: pues
¿con quál scusa y vergüença podiérades fuir de mi requestada porfía:
en no fazer lo que a vos da tan grande loor? Pues par Dios Grisel confessar devéis la verdad. Porque aunque yo tenga la culpa: no dudo el
Rey mi padre haverse conmigo piadosamente. Lo que con vos segund
su grande enemiga ligera echaque tomara por culpa principal. Assí
pues que el yerro es mío no hagáis vuestra la pena. Y muera la triste
que lo ha merecido. Y no padeza el igoscente la muerte de mi peccado.

Dize Grisel

¡O enemiga Fortuna assí como me fuese favorable en el vencimiento
de Mirabella: sé me agora buena para que la scondida verdad sea pú-
blica! Y vos senyora en lo que me pensáis que me sóis piadosa: me sois
cruel. Porque vos moriendo: queda mi vida muy peligrosa. Y más por
vos dezir: que aunque sea vuestra la culpa: el Rey vuestro padre no pro-
cederá contra vos. Pero aunque del crimen *non* quisiere enpeeçeros: y
relieve a vos de pena:[16] ¡O quán grande infamia sería a vos: si tal fuesse
como lo dezís: en haver a mí requestado! Y por sólo esso más quiero
yo consentir en mi muerte: que dar lugar a vuestra vergüença. Y pues
sabéis cierto ser yo occasión de todo vuestro mal: no me seáis storvo
de la pena d'éll. Mayormente sopiendo que mi maldad y porfiosos
enganyos: sabrían vençer a toda virtud. Que tan atribulado triste y
lloroso ante vos me ponía continuo: y de vos misma quexándome tanto: que sin haverme amor: me oviérades piadad. Y según las cosas que
yo hize y dixe: creo non ser yerro lo que vos hizísteis. Pues era deuda
conocida. Porque yo de muy largos tiempos con trabajos muchos vos
he comprado. Y vos no seríades fija del rey tan justo si non diérades
mi merecido premio. Y con otra ninguna cosa salvo con vos misma:

tion. Oh, how easy it is to tell when women are in love! Without openly consenting to what is sought, they give signs of willingness.[15]

Truly, you saw me do such things and act shamelessly many times. Even before you thought of loving me, my heart was set on loving you, and I declared my desires with shameless tricks. For how could anyone pursued by me, as you were, do any differently? Loyalty to your lord was expected in his house, but my worth and beauty conquered all; with what excuse and shame could you have fled from my insistent pursuit? How could you not do what would grant you great fame? For God's sake, Grisel, you must confess the truth. For even if I am found guilty, I am sure that the King my father will be merciful to me. Yet it will be easy for him to find you guilty because of his great enmity toward you. Since the crime is mine, do not make the punishment your own; let the miserable woman who deserves it die. Do not let an innocent man die for my sin.

Grisel

Oh, cruel Fortune, you who favored me in the conquest of Mirabella, aid me now, so that the hidden truth be made known! And you, Lady, thinking you are merciful to me, are cruel, because upon your death, my life will be in great danger. As you have said, even if you are guilty, your father will not punish you. But even if the King wanted to absolve you of the crime and spare you from the death sentence,[16] what a great infamy it would be to you if, as you say, you had in fact seduced me! For that alone I would rather consent to my own death than allow your shame. And since you know well that I am the cause of all the evil that has befallen you, do not stand in the way of my receiving the greater sentence, knowing that my depravity and insistent wiles were able to conquer all virtue; time and again I came to you so overcome by tribulations, melancholy, and weeping, blaming my suffering on you, that you, without loving me, took pity on me. And given the things that I did and said, I do not believe that what you did was a crime, but rather your duty: because I had bought you with my constant and many efforts. As the daughter of so just a king, of course you gave me my well-earned prize. Nothing less than your very person could have satisfied my passion and service, for nobles are obliged to give

non podiérades satisfazer a mi passión y servicios: pues la condición de los grandes es fazer mayores las pagas que los trabajos mereçen. Y si vos senyora seguistes la costumbre y naturaleza de vuestro stado en remunerar mis grandes servicios: a ninguno no agravastes. Y pues quien tan altas merçedes de vos recebió: non sea scasso de offreçer la vida. Y aunque el cuerpo muera: consoláos. Pues que l'alma nunqua muere. Y seréis cierta de mi fe que siempre jamás vos viva.

El auctor

Poniendo contra sí Mirabella grandes culpas: que parecía ella haver seído entera causa del amor y yerro entre ellos cometido: mostrando infinitas razones como Grisel fue d'ella quasi forçado: y que éll ninguna culpa ni falta tenía: más ella sola era merecedora de todo aquell mal: pero Grisel negava todo lo que contra sí misma dezía: y éll por la salvar de la muerte: dezía éll ser principal causa de todo yerro que ella consentiesse. Y ya visto por el Rey que estos no querían confessar la verdad: mandólos muy cruelmente atormentar. Tanto que las llagas que soffrían eran de mayor dolor que la misma muerte que speravan. Pero ni por aquello ninguno pudo tanto dolerse de sí mismo: que mayor temor non oviesse del peligro del otro. Y quanto más los tormentavan: tanto más cada uno hazía las culpas suyas. Y ansí como aquella donzella vido tormentar a su amante: con muchas lágrimas de grande piadad comiença a dezir.

Mirabella dize

Grisel si de ti no has compassión: hávela agora de mí: que las tus penas y las mías padezco. Pues ¿por qué quieres que muera por tantas maneras? Y una muerte pues la merezco: ligera pena me será. Mas tú piensas me ser piadoso: y éresme cruel en negar la verdad. Tú no sabes cómo yo ansí por fuerça te traxe vencido. Más de mis ruegos muy disolutos que de tu querer: pues ¿quál hombre fuera tan ozado a me dezir cosa tan grave: si en mí no viera senyales de grande aparejo? Y

rewards greater than the service received, and if you, my Lady, followed the custom and nature of your estate by remunerating my great efforts, you offended no one. Now, let the man who has received such great favors from you be not unwilling to offer his life. And, although my body may die, take consolation in the knowledge that the soul never dies, and in my faithfulness to you, which too will live forever.

The Author

When Mirabella thus accused herself of great crimes, it seemed that she had been the sole cause of the love and misdeeds committed between the two. She gave infinite proofs of how she had all but taken Grisel by force and, thus, he was neither guilty nor negligent in any way. Rather, she alone was deserving of all punishment. But Grisel denied everything that Mirabella said against herself. Now, Grisel, in order to save her life, said that he was to blame for every misdeed to which she had consented. When the King saw that the two lovers refused to confess the truth, he ordered that they be tortured with such cruelty that the wounds they suffered be more painful than the very death that awaited them. Yet not even such great torture was capable of making either lover forget the danger the other faced. And the more the King's men tortured them, the more each lover claimed all the guilt. When the maiden saw her lover being tortured, crying from the great pity she felt, she began to speak.

Mirabella

Grisel, even if you have no compassion for yourself, have some for me now, for I suffer your pain as well as my own. Why do you desire so many deaths for me? For I deserve only one, which will be an easy punishment for me to bear. You think yourself merciful, yet you are cruel to me by denying the truth. Do you not see how I took you by force? It was my lustful entreaties, not your desire. For what man would ever be so bold as to speak to me of such a dangerous thing, if he had not seen in me the signs

porque yo era cierta que según mi stado: que aunque tú me amaras: la vergüença te causara non me lo ozar dezir. Mas yo como senyora ansí como quien te puede mandar: te mandé que fuesses mío. Lo qual tu contradezir no podiste. Y ante te diera la muerte: si rehusaras mi ruego. Por ende ansí como en aquello me fueste obediente: en descobrir la verdad no me seas enemigo y da lugar a mi muerte: y non a los tormentos d'ella: pues ellos al fin te lo harán conoçer. Y en el tu negar mala sperança tiene mi vida. Y tú quedándome bivo que yo tu muerte no vea: mi vida aunque se muera ninguna cosa me duele.

Respuesta de Grisel

Por cierto senyora si más no me doliesse la vergüença y tormentos que por mí padecéis: que el miedo de mi muerte: ningún dolor me sería. Pues soy seguro que al fin vos verníais en conocimiento de la verdad. Y no se gana aquí salvo dar dilación a mi vida. Pero al fin aquella pereçoza de *mi* muerte no se scusa. Y pues que es mía: y mis merecimientos la han ganado: no la me quitéis. Que si bien conociéssedes quántos tormentos me dan los vuestros: diríades que la muerte no me es pena en comparación de lo que siento por la vuestra. Mayormente conociendo tener yo la culpa. Y que vos padezcáis la pena: esto me es incomportable passión. Y que yo quiera dezir quál y quántas cosas hize en el complimento vuestro: seríame tan grave de recontar: como amor áspero de padeçer. Y tanbién si dixiesse con quántas cosas y servicios vos he comprado: y los trabajos que me costáis: loándome d'ello sería merecedor de perderos. Y por esto me es mejor callar. Y a Dios a quien es el entero saber de nuestra causa: a éll plega de os traer a conocimiento de la verdad y entre las mercedes muchas ésta no se me niegue queriendo ya conoçer yo ser causa de todo este mal. Y en perder yo la vida por vos: no me sería pena más acabado plazer.

of great willingness? I was sure that because of my great estate, even though you loved me, shame would keep you from daring to tell me about it. But I, being your Lady, and thus one who commands you, insisted that you be mine. You could not refuse me, for I would have killed you if you had shunned my entreaties. Therefore, just as you were obedient to me then, do not go against me now: tell the truth and let them kill me and put an end to this deathly torture, for you will admit the truth in the end. Your denials are evil omens for my life. I cannot bear living if you die: even though I lose my life, I will feel no pain.

Grisel

Truly, my Lady, were I not pained by the shame and torture that you are suffering for my sake, I would feel no pain at all. I am sure that you will come to see the truth. All this talk only delays my death. Yet, belated Death cannot escape me, for she is mine, and I have earned her with my merits; you cannot take her from me. If only you knew how your suffering torments me, you would say that death would cause me no pain at all compared to what I would feel at your death. Above all, knowing that I am guilty, your death would be an insufferable ordeal to me. To tell of all I did and how I seduced you would be as grievous to me as the pains of love itself. For if I boasted of all I did and the services with which I bought you and the labors you cost me, I would deserve to lose you. That is why it is better for me to keep silent and pray to God, who knows everything about our love, to show you the truth. I pray that among his many mercies He not deny me this, since He knows that I was the cause of this great afflic-tion. Losing my life for you shall not pain me, but rather be my greatest pleasure.

Habla el auctor

Muy atormentados fueron estos dos amantes. Mas ninguna crueldat les pudo tanto enpeesçer: que conociessen la verdad del más culpado entre ellos. Porque cada uno dezía todas las culpas esser suyas. Y como el Rey viesse que no havía ningún remedio para saber la claridat d'este secreto: demandó consejo a sus letrados. ¿Qué era lo que sobre este caso se debía hazer? A lo qual respondieron: que en ninguna manera podían conoçer la differencia entre estos amadores. Mas ante creían: que ellos juntamente se amavan. E igualmente trabajaron por traer a efecto sus desseados desseos. E iguales merecían la pena.

Mas como las leyes de su tierra antigamente ordenaron: el que más causa o principio fuesse al otro de haver amado mereciesse muerte: y el que menos destierro. Pero que en este caso de su hija no conocían differencia salvo una: que examinasse si los hombres o las mujeres o ellas o ellos quál d'estos era más occasión del yerro al otro. Que si las mujeres fuessen mayor causa de amar los hombres: que moriesse Mirabella. Y si los hombres a ellas: que padeciesse Grisel. Y aquellos letrados y oidores del consejo real determinadamente concluyeron diziendo: que no havía otra mayor razón para saber la verdad.

Entonçes dixo el Rey que lo determinassen ellos en su consejo. A lo qual ellos respondieron: que como fuessen personas más dadas al studio de las leyes que de los amores: que no sabían en aquella causa determinar la verdad. Pero que se buscassen por todo el mundo una dama y un cavallero: los quales más pudiessen saber en amores: y más sperimentados fuessen en tales casos. Y que ella tomasse la voz de las mujeres: y éll de los varones. Y quien mejor causa y razón mostrasse en defensión de su drecho: que aquell venciesse aqueste pleito començado. Y pues que jamás el tal caso nunqua era acaecido: que dende en adelante fuesse determinado y scripto por ley. Y a este consejo vino el Rey: y luego mandó que se buscassen personas que fuessen de tal qualidat: qual en aquell caso se convenían.

Y en aquell tiempo havía una dama de las más prudentes del mundo en saber y en desemboltura[17] y en las otras cosas a graciosidat conformes. La qual por su grande merecer se havía visto en muchas batallas de amor y casos dignos de grande memoria que le havían acaecido con grandes personas que la amavan y pensavan vençer. Pero

The Author

The two lovers were most cruelly tortured. Yet no pain was great enough to break them and reveal who was in truth more to blame, for each one claimed all the guilt as their own. When the King saw that there was no way to uncover the truth of this secret, he turned to his learned counselors for advice. What should he do in this case? To which question they responded that there was no way to find any difference between these two lovers. Rather, the counselors believed that the two loved one another equally, and that the two had both labored together to satisfy their desired desires, and, thus, deserved equal punishment.

Nevertheless, the ancient laws of the land stated that the lover who was the greater cause or motivation for the other to have loved deserved death, while the other, less guilty lover, deserved banishment. Yet in this case of the King's daughter, the counselors could find no difference between the two lovers save one, and so proposed that it be determined whether men or women, females or males, which of the two is more at fault for the sin of the other. If women were the greater cause of men's loving, then Mirabella should die. And if men caused women to love, then Grisel should suffer death. Thus the wise men and ministers of the royal council decisively concluded, saying there was no better way of learning the truth.

The King then asked them to resolve the question in their council, but the counselors responded that, though they were authorities in matters of the law, they understood little of love, and knew not how to find the truth in this case. Rather, they advised, the whole world over should be searched for a lady and a gentleman who were most learned in love, and most experienced in such cases; the lady should speak on behalf of all women, and the gentleman for men. Whichever of the two could prove guilt of one party and argue better in defense of the other should prevail in the trial. Then, whenever such a case arose in the future, written legal precedent would already have decided it. The King was convinced by his counselors' advice and without delay ordered that such persons as the case required be found.

Now, in those days there lived a lady who was among the most wise in the world, so learned and so graced with open, easy courtesy and elegance[17] was she. Due to her great merits, this lady had seen many

no menos le ayudava discreción: que saber. Y esta senyora havía por nombre Braçayda. E ansí mesmo fue buscado en los regnos d'Espanya un cavallero que para tal pleito pertenecía. Al qual llamavan Torrellas. Un special hombre en el conocimiento de las mugeres. Y muy ozado en los tratos de amor. Y mucho gracioso como por sus obras bien se pruevava. Este fue elegido por defensión y parte de los hombres.

Pero en este caso Torrellas y Braçayda fueron a ruego del Rey a examinar la dicha questión. Los quales fueron más caros de haver: de lo que aquí se encareçe. Pero después que en el Regno de Scocia llegaron: fueron magníficamente recebidos. Principalmente la Reina madre de Mirabella fizo tan grandes fiestas a Braçayda: que ellas por sí fueron dignas de scripturas memoradas. Y esto fazía la Reina por la tener más contenta. Y porque más en cargo tuviesse la offiensa de su fija. La qual ansí con ruegos: como con lágrimas affectuosamente la encargava que trebajasse como Mirabella non padieciesse. Faziendo al Rey tan sin clemencia en lo que tocava a justicia. A lo qual Braçayda respondió: que ninguna necesidad le era encargárgelo ni mandárgelo: que ella mucho en cargo lo tenía: y aunque la compassión y peligro de Mirabella no la moviesse a piadad: la movería el general amor de las mugeres todas. Y sólo aquell desseo de salvarlas de quantas malicias los hombres contra ellas dezían. Por lo qual se quizo poner al cargado camino. Y con esta seguridad y otras cosas bien dichas: que la Reina oyó de a Braçayda sin temor de la muerte y danyo de su fija se consolava.

Y ansí mesmo el Rey fizo gran recogimiento a Torrellas. Pero porque no se mostrasse parte o de los hombres o de su fija: non le fazía fiestas tan sobradas como la Reina a Braçayda. Pero muchos cavalleros que para ver aquell acto fueron allí ajuntados: muy magníficos se mostraron en el recebimiento de Torrellas. Al qual con muchas dádivas y valerosas joyas le recibían. Y dávanle grande cargo que en la honra de los hombres mucho mirasse. Que si de allí quedassen condemnados: para siempre con las mugeres quedavan perdidos. Principalmente algunos cavalleros de aquella tierra a quien continuo crecía enemiga con Mirabella. Porque su grande beldad havía sido causa: como muchos se havían perdido en la requesta y seguimiento famoso de aquella amorosa batalla. Por esto rogavan a Torrellas: que defendiesse su partido. Lo qual supo bien contentar: y

love-battles and other adventures worthy of long memory, which had befallen her with great personages who loved her and thought to conquer
her. Yet she was no less aided by her discretion than by her learning. This
lady was named Braçayda. Likewise, a gentleman well equipped for the
case was found in the realms of Spain. Called Torrellas, he was renowned
for his knowledge of women. He was quite daring in the business of love
and a great wit, as his writings amply demonstrated. This was the man
chosen for the defense and representation of men.

Torrellas and Braçayda were called by the King to argue the aforementioned case. No expense was spared in bringing them to court—far
more than can be described here—and once they had arrived they were
received magnificently. The Queen, Mirabella's mother, held such great
celebrations in honor of Braçayda, that they were themselves worthy of
memory. Now, the Queen did this because she wished to please Braçayda
and also to make the lady dedicate herself all the more to her daughter's defense. With tearful entreaties, filled with feeling, the Queen urged
Braçayda to make every effort so that Mirabella not receive the death
sentence, since her father was so pitiless in matters of justice. To which
Braçayda responded that there was no need to entreat or order her, because this was a case close to her heart, and even if compassion and the
danger Mirabella faced had not moved her to take pity, she would have
been moved by her general love for all women and by her desire to save
them from all men's slander. For all these reasons, she wanted to take
on the difficult task. When the Queen heard Braçayda's assurance and
her other well-spoken words she no longer feared her daughter's death or
injury and was comforted.

The King welcomed Torrellas honorably as well. However, since
he did not wish to appear partial to either the side of men or his daughter,
the King did not hold such great celebrations as those the Queen held for
Braçayda. Nonetheless, many knights came to receive Torrellas, welcom-
ing him with many gifts and costly jewels, and gravely charged him with
the protection of men's honor, for if they were found guilty in the suit, they
would have lost everything to women forever more. Hostility toward Mirabella mounted among some of the Scottish knights in particular, for her
great beauty had led so many men of the land to lose their lives wooing
her and bravely fighting for her love. For this reason they begged Torrellas
to defend them. He knew well how to assuage and satisfy the appetites

satisfazer a los apetitos de cada uno d'ellos. Y ansí andavan la Reina y sus damas con Braçayda. Y los cavalleros con Torrellas favoreciendo cada uno su partido.

El auctor

Después que el día del plazo fue allegado par al examen del pleito: en una muy grande y maravillosa sala fueron unas muy riquas gradas compuestas: do los juezes en juizio se asentaron. Los quales fueron elegidos por personas de mucha consciencia y sin suspecha: con solennes juramentos que fizieron de juzgar según fuesse su más claro pareçer. Y a la una parte de la sala estavan la Reina con infantas y damas y otras donzellas: que para ver y oir fueron juntadas allí. Y a la otra parte el Rey con grande multitud de gentes: y a la postremera grada estava Mirabella que veía a Braçayda por su avocada: y Torrellas con Grisel. Y lugo dexaron de tanyer un alto son de trompetas. Y todos guardando y dando silencio: en tal manera comiença Braçayda su razón contra Torrellas.

Braçayda contra Torrellas

A gran ventura lo he Torrellas: que sóis venido a tiempo de satisfazer y pagar a las damas las de vos recebidas injurias. Que soy cierta que ganaréis aquí dos cosas: la una que muera Grisel de quien parte y defensión vos mostráis: y la otra como la scondida malicia de los hombres se publique. Ansí que creet que venistes a fazer emienda de las cosas por vos contra las mugeres compuestas. Por ende en remuneración del trebajo de vuestro camino: bien se os emplea que llevéis tal gualardón en pago del vuestro malicioso propósito. Y por comienço de mis demandas diré de vuestros más civiles yerros: porque si contradezís o negáis para el fin se guarden los más criminiosos.

Digo pues Torrellas: como a todos sea manifiesto la vuestra solicitud ser grande en el seguimiento nuestro: y si algunas con sano consejo se apartan de oir vuestras enganyosas fablas: non puede apartarse de oír en las calladas noches el dulçor de los instrumentos

of each man. Thus were the Queen and her ladies with Braçayda, and the knights with Torrellas, each one favoring his or her own side.

The Author

On the day set for the trial, richly decorated platforms were set up in a large and marvelous hall, where the judges sat in judgment. They had been selected as persons of good conscience, free from suspicion, and they had sworn solemnly to judge according to their most enlightened opinions. The Queen was on one side of the hall with princesses, ladies, and other maidens who had gathered there to watch and listen. On the other side of the hall stood the King with a great multitude of people. Mirabella, with Braçayda acting as her advocate, and Torrellas with Grisel, stood upon the highest platform. And when a loud trumpeting sounded, all fell and kept silent, turning to look as Braçayda began her argument against Torrellas.

Braçayda against Torrellas

It is my great good fortune, Torrellas, that you have now come to satisfy and to make reparation to women, whom you have wronged. For I am certain that you will achieve two things here: the first is the death of Grisel, whose side and defense you take, and the second is the revelation of men's secret malice. Know well that you have come to make amends for the things that you have written against women. It is fitting, therefore, that in return for your efforts you be rewarded for your labor with such favor as your malicious intent deserves. Now, to begin my accusations, I will speak of your most lowly sins, for though you might contradict or deny these, I reserve your most criminal deeds for last.

I say then, Torrellas, that men's persistence in the pursuit of women is obvious to all. Even if any well-advised ladies avoid hearing your false words, in the quiet of the night they cannot avoid hearing the sweet sounds of your instruments and the strains of soft music, which

y cantos de la suave música. La qual par al enganyo nuestro fue por vosotros inventada. Y bien se conosce ser una sobtil ret para las erradas nuestras. Y si algunas d'esto refuyen: de las danças justas torneos toros y canyas y otros muchos sin cuenta deportes todos para nos atraer a veros enganyosamente fuir no pueden: porque los castos ojos occupados en vuestras deleitosas obras: de alguna d'ellas sean presos. Y por ventura algunas que por grande virtud se retraen de los tales deportes: otras mil maneras buscáis: que con las sobtiles embaxadas y muy enamoradas letras por fuerça las conqueréis. Por donde aun en las ençerradas cámaras do se sconden por no veros: con sotiles motes de sus siervas y cartas entráis. Y si ellas castigan las mensageras: y rehúsan en no leer las cartas: quando ya veis que con las cosas dichas y otras infinitas no las podéis empeescer: porque puede más vuestra maldad y porfía: que nuestra virtud: buscáis rodeos para danyar nuestras famas.

Y contra nuestras moradas sin ver aquella a quien mostráis querer: a las paredes o finestras enamoráis con stranyas senyales y enganyos y remiramientos. Por donde aunque allí no esté persona alguna: fingís que la veis. Y como que responde a vuestros auctos y malicias. A fin de dar lugar a los que lo vieren de sospechas y presumpciones. Por vía que de fuerça o de grado la más fuerte es contra vuestra malicia muy flaca. Pues ¿quál puede ser tan grande defensora de sí misma: que contra tantas cosas refrenarse pueda? Pues ansí del que más trabaja en las obras de bien o mal: más merece el gualardón o pena. Por donde pruevo vosotros ser causa y merecedores de todo mal. Ansí que mi sano consejo vos conseja conozcáis la culpa: y no deis lugar que más de vuestras scondidas malicias publique. Las quales por honestad me callo y aun vos es partido se callen. Y mucho seríais dichoso Torrellas: si la muerte vuestra passassen las innocentes de vuestros enganyos vencidas. Y pues en tierra tan justa stamos: spero de vos justicia.

you invented for seducing us. It is well known that your music is a clever net for trapping those of us who stray. And even though some ladies flee from this music, there is no escaping from the dances, jousts, tourneys, bullfights, mock-battles, and other innumerable sports, all cunningly designed to attract our gaze, since even the chaste eyes that behold your delectable deeds will be captivated by them. When ladies of great virtue shun such sports, you find a thousand other ways of seducing them: you take them by force with your clever embassies and love poems. By sending clever notes and letters with ladies' servants you find ways to enter even the locked rooms where women hide from you. And even if they punish the messengers and refuse to read your letters, when you see that you cannot assault ladies with the aforesaid and other infinite ploys, you invent schemes to defile our good names, for your depravity and tenacity are stronger than our virtue.

You come to our doors and, without even catching sight of the woman you pretend to love, you speak of love to the walls and windows, extravagantly going through the motions, and feigning an exchange of glances. Although no one is there, you pretend to see the lady and act as if she were responding to your gestures and wicked intentions, giving anyone who sees you reason to suspect her and presume she loves you. Thus, by force or by will, even women of the greatest fortitude are quite frail in the face of your wickedness. What woman could ever be so skilled in self-defense that she would be able to protect herself from all these tricks? Therefore, I conclude that, just as he who strives most in good or evil works is more deserving of the prize or punishment, you men are the root of all evil and deserve to be treated as such. So, my good counsel counsels you to acknowledge your guilt now, and in so doing, not give me reason to reveal your secret maliciousness, which I have kept silent for the sake of my honor and which is in your interests to keep silent. You would be most happy, Torrellas, if your death sufficed to satisfy the innocent women who were vanquished by your beguiling tricks. In this most just of lands, I await justice from you.

Respuesta de Torrellas a Braçayda

Si mi venida vos faze senyora alegre porque d'ella speréis vengança
y satisfación de la enemiga que conmigo tenéis: lo qual oír cierto me
plaze: porque si algo de vosotras pensava callar: vos me fagáis agora
sin vergüença para que diga algunas cosas secretas de las que de mujeres conozco: la inimistad que me tenéis me haze sin culpa. Aunque
por cierto yo no quisiera: qu'el stremo de vuestros stremos por mí se
pregonasse. Mas pues queréis que nos oyan: oyan par Dios.

A lo que dezís senyora ser nuestras enganyosas palabras y
obras tales: que de fuerça vos vencen: digo ser verdad. Mas nunqua
la vi tan buena: que lo rehusasse porque la más honesta de vosotras
se precia de ser amada. Y la voluntad vuestra sin ser rogada. Luego
querría dezir "plázeme": si el freno de la vergüença no dilatasse y
enfrenasse la desbocada respuesta. Por donde parece a los que poco
conoçen: que de honestad procede.[18] Mas el scondido secreto de
vuestro querer: a vosotras remitto el conocimiento d'éll. Y a Dios el
juizio d'ello: que si alguna haya acaecido por se fingir buena: refuzar
de oír el dulçor de la música que dixestes. ¿Quién vos apremia en las
frías noches el avorrecer el suenyo: y correr a los no lícitos lugares?
Y por luengo tiempo que dure el son de las canciones: vos parece
corto. Y aunque la grande frialdad penetre las delicadas carnes:
el encendimiento del coraçón vos faze sentir por caloroso verano
el destemplado ivierno. Y allí mostráis lo que rehusáis el día: que
deseáis las noches.

Que quando las alegres danças y justas y otros deportes que
dixestes fazemos por a plazeros: acaece que se fazen: los plazeres sana-
mente mirados: ¿quién los faze enemigos a las virtudes? mas ¿quién
me negará: que allí en las tales fiestas justas o torneos no vayan las empresas que distes en los corrientes cavallos y favorecidos cavalleros?[19]
Y allí vuestro favor da occasión a vosotras de encendimiento: y a ellos
de victoria Pues digo: que de qualquiere vencimiento pues favorecéis:
si fuera obra virtuosa: fuera vuestra la gloria: y si es mala. Sea vuestra
la pena.

Quanto a las letras y embaxadas que dezís enviamos: siempre las vi ser bien recebidas. Y si ad alguno desdichado el contrario
acaece: vosotras con honesta discreción sin ver la carta conocéis lo

Torrellas

My lady, it pleases me indeed to hear that my presence here makes you happy because you expect vengeance and satisfaction for the enmity you bear me. For although I had determined to keep quiet before, now you have relieved me of the shame I should feel by speaking of what I know about some of women's secrets: the ill will you bear me absolves me of guilt. Truly, I should not wish to be the one who made the extent of your excesses public knowledge, yet since you want me to be heard, by God, let them be known.

You claim, my Lady, that our beguiling words and tricks take you by force; I say this is all true. Yet I have never seen a woman so virtuous that they displeased her, because even the most chaste of women prides herself on being loved. If the reins of shame did not deter you and hold back your unbridled passions, you would eagerly say, "I desire you," before we men even spoke to you of love. Men who know little about women think that your shame comes from virtue.[18] But I charge you to acknowledge your hidden desires and leave God to judge them. If, by chance, one woman, feigning virtue, refused to listen to the sweet music you mentioned, tell me, who forces you all to leave your beds in the cold of night and run to illicit places? No matter how long our singing lasts it seems too short to you, even when the freezing cold penetrates your delicate flesh; your flaming hearts make you feel as if the depths of winter were the heat of summer. And so you show that what you disdain by day, you desire at night.

As for the merry dances, jousts, and other sports that you accuse us of using to attract you, it happens that this is so. Such pleasures, if gazed upon with prudence, who ever said they are the enemies of virtue? Now then, who will deny that you give your tokens to the knights you favor to wear or display on their horses?[19] Who will deny that your favor in fêtes, jousting, and tourneys sets you aflame and spurs the knights to victory? So, I say that you women favor the victorious: if this were a virtue, you would deserve all the glory; if it is wicked, let the punishment be yours.

As for those verses and messages you say we send you, I have always seen them well received. If some unfortunate man finds his missives are refused, you ladies, refusing—out of supposedly virtuous discretion—to read, know just what the letter seeks without even reading it. Not reading is just as good as reading it, so even if you tear a letter up

que puede pedir. Y vale tanto como leerla. Y aunque allí con furia la fazéis pedaços enjuriando al portador: en aquell mismo enojo se sconde un deleitoso plazer. Mas el gualardón d'esta falsa honestad darlo he más a la vergüença: y non a vuestros desseos. Y las otras cosas que a vuestras finestras dezís fazen: vosotras sóis inventadoras d'ellas. Y aun las monjas lo llevaron aprendiendo del mundo: "quando fiziéremos esto: entiéndese queremos aquello."[20]

De manera que vosotras por non dezir sin infamia vuestros desseos: buscastes senyales más honestos para los necios que a los cuerdos. Y entonçes mejor se descobría lo desonesto a nosotros que menester no nos faze por occultas maneras dezir lo que queremos. Mas vosotras por non poder*nos hablar*[21] las vezes que queréis: nos mostráis las tales senyas: que valen más que palabras. Y las más vezes el temor más que la vergüença vos faze buscar tales senyales.

Pues no me contento aun haver satisfecho a cada una de las cosas por vos allegadas: segúnd lo que de vosotras hay que dezir. Y quiero pediros como bien sabéis la llave de vuestros stados y honras. Y esta stá en la balança de la casta virtud: y sola está como principal vos es defendida: como cosa donde tantos peligros y menguas se vos siguen. Mas vosotras pospuesto todo temor y vergüença: de los encendidos desseos vencidas os vencéis. Ni miráis honor de marido fijos parentes ni amigos ni de vos mismas a quien más obligadas sóis. Ni a reverencia de fama. Ni muy menos al temor de la muerte. Más antes todo aquello de un tibio plazer lo posponéis. Y todo se pone en olvido por sólo que la voluntad se goze. Aunque sepáis que a la postre lo havéis de llorar. Diziendo que más queréis plazer presente: que gozo advenidero. Pues a nosotros el contrario acaeçe. Que el más loado de nos: es el que de vosotras más alcança. Por donde paresce claro: que pues aventuráis perder: más es razón de ganar si fuera obra virtuosa. Más como es torpe y desonesta: más merecéis la pena. Y aun en esto me paresce concluyo. Y si porfiáis negando: sé que daréis causa que más descubra. Que no hay razón con que se cubra. Y de pura lástima de Mirabella no digo quanto podría. Y aun porque vuestros vicios entiéndelos el sezo: y no sabe dezirlos la lengua: mas si los secretos de l'alma se viessen: allí se descobriría lo que mi rudeza esconde.

in a fury, insulting the messenger, your very anger serves as a cover for your delectable pleasure. Yet I attribute this show of false chastity to your shame and not to your desires. As for the other things that you say we do at your windows, you women invented such playacting. Even nuns bring this worldly knowledge into the convent: "When we make such and such a gesture, it means, we want such and such."[20]

In fact, you ladies use gestures in like manner: so that you can tell us your desires without scandal, you have devised gestures that seem more decent to simple men than they do to men of understanding, and thus you communicate unchaste thoughts to us. We men have no need of hidden ways to say what we want, but you ladies, because you cannot speak to us when you want to,[21] signal to us with gestures that are worth more than words. More often than not, it is fear and not shame that makes you resort to such signs.

However, I am not content to have simply answered each of your allegations, for there are accusations that I must make against you. I ask of you, as you well know, the key to your fame and honor, which hangs in the balance of chaste virtue. You claim that you risk great dangers and loss in the defense of chaste virtue alone. Yet you ladies put aside all fear and shame and, overcome by your fiery desires, you vanquish yourselves. You care nothing for the honor of your husbands, sons, families, or friends, much less for your own honor, to which you are most obliged, nor do you revere your reputations, and much less fear death. Rather, you disregard all this for the sake of a vain pleasure, forgetting everything but the satisfaction of your desires, even when you know that all will end in tears, saying that you care more for passing pleasure than future joy. With us men it is the contrary: we praise the man who seduces many women. From whence it seems clear that, since you risk losing more in love than men do, you would rightfully win this trial if loving us were a virtuous deed. Yet, since it is lascivious and indecent, you are all more deserving of the punishment. And so, I believe I will conclude. If you persist in denying your guilt, know that you give me reason to reveal even more—no argument can shield you. I have not said all that I might about women out of sheer pity for Mirabella, and because even though my understanding comprehends your vices, my tongue knows not how to say them. If only the secrets of your souls were seen, all that my lack of eloquence obscures would be revealed.

Responde Braçayda a Torrellas

Aún no era vuestra fama Torrellas como agora parescen las obras. Pero más quiero vençer lo más fuerte malicioso: que no lo simple y flaco. Y quanto vos sepáis mejor defender: será a mí más loor condenarvos. Y lo que dixistes: nosotras pospuesto temor y vergüença por complir desseos: digo que a vuestros sotiles enganyos no hay quien contra ellos se pueda defender ni poner. Y si algunas presumen ponerse en defença: vuestra porfiosa maldad usa de tales y tantas artes: que donde hay mayor castidad y nobleza: aquella menos resestir puede. Y aunque como sea cosa cierta las mujeres ser de menos discreción que los hombres: fízolo nuestra generación ser subjeta a la vuestra. Pues ¿quién merece mayor pena del error: el que más conoce de la culpa: o el que menos? Ansí que concluyo vosotros ser mejores conocedores del mal: y mayores ocasiones d'ello. Pues quien la mayor pena meresca: set juez de vos mismo.

Y aún dexando esto. Ya vemos ser cosa común las animalias ser los machos que las fembras más bellos. Y quiero traer en exemplo el pavón. Que aún no contento con la beldad de su plumage: pone en rueda las sus doradas plumas: por más aplazer a una sin comparación tan fea ave como es la pava. Y aún esta quiere ser muy rogada. Y en pago de quanto se trabaja por la plazer: tanto más ella desvía de mirarle. Y por semejante la mayor parte de las fembras animales quieren ser rogadas. Pues aquellas por ningún temor ni vergüença lo dexan: mas porque naturaleza los ensenya ser suyo el encareçer: y de los machos el requestar. Pues los hombres d'aquella qualidad misma sois encitores de todos aquestos males desseos non menos que los animales brutos. Pues por aquí pareçe arto abiertamente y cierto: ser nuestro el defender y vuestro el requestar.

Y las muchas fatigas ansias tribulaciones que por nosotras dezís que fingidamente mostráis: ya pareçe mayor error: dar *indicios* al mal non amando.[22] Que nosotras quando nos vencemos: es por amor. Y así está claro segunt las grandes menguas y peligros que nosotras tenemos: que si l'amor no nos forçasse: sin querer no sería possible vencernos. Mas vosotros que non amando mostráis amor: mirad quánto sois dignos de penitencia en consentir en el peccado sin deleitaros en éll.

Braçayda

Your arguments now surpass your well-earned reputation, Torrellas. But I much prefer defeating a most forceful, evil man, rather than just a simple and weak one, so the better you know how to defend yourself, the more will it be to my credit to condemn you. You accuse us of shunning fear and shame in order to act upon our desires; I say that there is no woman alive who can defend herself against you men or oppose your subtle beguilements. And even if some women do try to defend themselves, you men, in your relentless depravity, make use of so many and such extraordinary tricks that women of great chastity and nobility are those who can least resist you. Even though it may be true that women have less discretion than men, it is because we were created subordinate to men. So, who deserves the greater punishment for sin? He who knows more about evil or she who knows less? Thus, I conclude that you men are more knowledgeable about evil and the greater causes of it, and so you deserve the greater punishment: be your own judge.

All this aside, as we know, it is common among animals for the males to be more beautiful than the females. I shall take as an example the male peacock, who, not content with the beauty of his plumage, fans out his golden feathers to better please the peahen, a bird so ugly as to be beyond compare. Yet even she demands to be courted, and the more he tries to please her, the more she shows her disdain in return. The greater part of all female animals similarly want to be pursued, for they, without any fear or shame, let the males pay court, because nature teaches them that theirs is to resist and males must pursue. You men, sharing this quality, are thus the instigators of all sinful desires, no less than brute animals, hence it follows quite clearly and truly that our role is to defend ourselves, and yours to pursue us.

And as for all the many labors, anxieties, and tribulations of love, which you say men feign to suffer for us, well, sinful scheming without being in love[22] surely seems to be a greater crime than ours. When we are vanquished it is by love. It is clear that if were we not forced by love, we could not be ravished against our wills because of the great risks and dangers that threaten us. So, consider how you, who fake being in love, must do penance. For you consent to sin without taking love's pleasure in the sinning.

Mas aquellas que forçadas se vencen: digo no ser error. Porque en cosa tan flaca como las mujeres cargar tan grande peso: doblar o quebrar las conviene. Y ninguna puede oír vuestros enganyosos consejos: que tomando alguno por bueno: no le sea empecible. Pues ¡maldicha sea generación: que todos sus propósitos contra nos se endreçan a las peores partes! Y que aquellos que nos son dados para administración nuestra aquellos mismos nos sean más danyosos y enemigos para nuestras honras. Y mirad quánto puede vuestra maldad: que si alguna con sobra de virtud de vosotros sabe guardarse de vuestras maliciosas lenguas: no se podrá defender porque en la companya de vuestras amistades por loaros traéis en prática: que havéis ovido más de lo que pedir quesistes: pues contra esto ¿qué faremos? Ningún remedio contra lo tal conozco. Que sin pecar nos culpáis. Aunque no se faga. Se dize por donde todas o de fama o de obra recebimos manzilla y somos enpeescidas. Y creo que los atormentadores del infierno no podrían más hazer en su officio: que vosotros fazéis en el vuestro. Que aun las castas monjas de quien ya dezís de todas temptaciones se guardan. Y de las vuestras no pueden. Y creen ante vuestras maldades por buenas: que los exemplos santos. De manera que los ayunos abstinencias y rezar contra vosotros non bastan. Que más vale una enganyosa palabra vuestra: que muchos provechosos sermones. Mas ¿cómo se guardarán las que entre sus enemigos conversan y tractan? Pues ya esto no lieva razón ninguna. Salvo si los juezes por ser varones non cieguan de la afeción de vosotros. Mas si la verdad me vale: vos iréis de aquí menguado y condenado. Por donde vuestro porfiar sessará de más dezir. Y como Dios padeçió por los buenos. Vos venistes a padeçer y pagar por los malos.

Moreover, I say of those women who are overcome by force, that they commit no sin, because when a great weight is applied to something as frail as a woman, it is only natural that she bend or break. For no woman hearing your beguiling counsel, and thinking it good, could believe it would be harmful to her. Oh, damnable creation, all of your intentions towards us are directed in the worst ways! The very men who rule us are most dangerous and harmful to our honor. Consider the power of your depravity. Even if a woman of outstanding virtue manages to resist you, she cannot defend herself against your evil tongues. For, in the company of friends, you will boastfully claim that you have gotten much more from her than you ever asked for. How can we defend ourselves against this? I know of no remedy. You accuse us when we are without sin. Although we do nothing, you accuse us, and so all women are harmed and defamed, either by your slander or your deeds. I believe that Hell's torturers cannot be better in their profession than you are in yours. For even chaste nuns, you will say, can resist every temptation but you; even they find your evildoings better than saintly examples. You claim that nuns cannot protect themselves from you with their fasting, abstinence, and prayer, that one beguiling word from you is worth more than many instructive sermons. How then, can women who speak with and live among men resist them? Your arguments are not valid. Unless the judges, being men, are blinded by their partiality for you, if the truth be served, you will leave here dishonored and condemned. From this day forward, your depravity will no longer be celebrated. Just as God suffered for the sake of the good, you came here to suffer and pay for evildoers.

Responde Torrellas a Braçayda

Si dezís que por ser yo malo y saber más que otro a vos será mayor loor de condemnarme: pues sabed que yo non lo habré por mucho venceros. Y como en los casos de amor sois ligeras de vencer: así creo lo seréis en las otras cosas. ¡Quánto más en ésta: que tan grande causa de verdat se me ofrece! Y parece que dixistes por traer a vuestro propuesto un exemplo en el pavón. En vosotras es el contrario. Que de graciosa beldad sois naturalmente compuestas más que los varones.

Este loor quiero daros: porque faze a mi caso. Y allende de la fermosura que naturaleza vos dio: buscáis ricos vestidos joyas y afeites. Por más dorar lo dorado. Pues esto al fin que se faze: bien claro es. Que por cierto el vuestro pomposo atavío: es a nosotros más deleitosa rueda: que la del pavón a la pava. Y aun por esto se suele dezir: "la cosa del mundo más bella es ver damas de rico aparato." Lo que a nuestro propósito traigo. Pues nuestra quistión es quál más causa da al otro del amor. Y esto agora manifiesto se prueva: que la más y meyor guarnida más ocasión trae del amar. Y a esto no es razón que contradiga.

Y cerca de las otras cosas que de nos quexáis: todas concluyen en nuestro pensar que es buscar nueva manera como mejor enganyaros podamos. Y esto non lo salvo. Nin lo quito. Nin lo condemno. Porque como ya dixe: el que de vos más puede alcançar: es de mayor loor. Mas si ya a Dios pluguiesse ordenar un uso nuevo: que todos los hombres fuessen de un acuerdo: de estar algún tiempo sin requestaros: porque se provasse vuestra virtud: tan poco y menos que digo confío d'ella: y soy cierto: que como viéssedes que non érades rogadas: necessidad os haría herederas de nuestro officio. Y juraré yo que con mayor diligencia seríamos de vosotras importunados rogándonos en mayor grado que agora nosotros lo fazemos. Mas como sabéis que nuestro es el seguimiento: en cordura cabe que nos lo vendáis caro. Mayormente porque conocéis tanto de la condición vuestra: que la que más lo encareçe tenemos en mayor stima. Mas si la oviéssemos por buena la que más presto lo atorgasse: muy scusados serían nuestros trebajos. Mas sabéis qu'el mucho encareçer lo havemos por mejor. Y esto os da loor que parescáis honestas. Mas yo que os conozco: non creáis en lo tal reciba enganyo. Que quanto más os defendéis: mas me dais lugar

Torrellas

You may say that yours will be the greater glory for condemning me because I am evil and wiser than other men, but know well that it is no great deed for me to defeat you. For, just as you women are easy to conquer in love, so I think that you will be easy in other ways: it will be all the more easy to win in this trial, since I defend a great truth! You said, it seems, that the example of the peacock would serve your defense, but among women the contrary is true, for you are naturally endowed with more graceful beauty than are men.

I wish to praise women in this way because it supports my argument. For in addition to the loveliness Nature gave you, you wear rich dresses, jewels and cosmetics to gild the golden all the more. Yes, in the end it is clear that you do this because your splendid clothes are to us what the peacock's attractive plumage is to the peahen. That is why it is said, "The most beautiful thing in the world is to see ladies arrayed in rich attire," which I cite for our defense, for the question at hand is who makes the other fall in love, and it is now manifestly clear that whoever is more attractive is the greater cause of love. This cannot be refuted.

Now, concerning all the other accusations you make against us, they all amount to our schemes for finding new and better ways to seduce you. I do not exclude these, nor do I discount them, nor do I condemn them, for as I have already said, the greatest glory goes to the man who seduces the most women. However, if it were to please God to order new customs, and all men decided to leave off pursuing you women for a while in order to put your virtue to the test, I have so little faith—less even than I say—in your virtue, that I am sure that as soon as you saw that you were not courted by men, necessity would make you take up our profession. I am willing to swear that you would pursue us with even greater zeal and persistence than we now court you. Nevertheless, as you know, it is our role to pursue you, and it is wise of you to make it difficult for us, for you know well that men prize and admire those women who are most scornful of our advances. Surely, we should never take such pains to seduce if we thought a good woman was one who readily gave in to us. However, as you know, we prize as best what is most costly, and this is what gives you an excuse to appear chaste. Yet, do not think that I am deceived by this ruse, I who know about you women. The more you resist, the more I suspect you, for I know that your

de suspechar. Pues que sé lo deseáis quanto más lo encarecéis. Pero si viniesse a caso que la libertad nuestra tuviéssedes: sé que sin ninguna vergüença nos rogaríades: assí como nosotros fazemos: ¿y quién se fallaría tan guarnecido de fortaleza: que de vosotras defenderse pudiesse? Y tanto confío en vuestro sobrado saber: que si lo tal acaeciesse: nos haríades buscar en los montes y silvas.[23] Y aun agora con tanto peligro y vergüença se lo fazéis. Y por mí digo: que cosas terribles en este caso son passadas. Y me son acaecidas. Las quales callaré si de vos no soy seguido a las dezir.

Así que agora podéis ver que luego *estando enfrenadas* os váis de boqua:[24] ¡quánto más haríades: si os soltassen la rienda! Y lo sé cierto que la tribulación vuestra no es sino que este mal a vosotras deleitoso non lo havemos por *santo y bueno*.[25] Y por esto vos siempre combate la vergüença: porque non quiere lo que vosotras queréis. Y también acaece cada día: damas de grande stado irse a perder con sus menores siervos. Y si yo quisiera quatar quántas se me han proferido no una vez mas muchas: havría ovido lugar mi perdimiento. Mas miré razonablemente lo que me pudo bastar dexando carga danyable. Y no quiero dar lugar más a mis razones. Sperando que como vos doléis de nosotros ansí os dolréis de vuestras honras. Non dando lugar que por el mundo las culpas que stán secretas se publiquen.

Responde Braçayda a Torrellas

Yo os veo lastimero Torrellas y más enemigo: que parece que para maldezir de nosotras si en el altar fallássedes malicias de que os podiéssedes aprovechar sin fazer d'ello consciencia de allí las tomaríades. Mas si vuestro sotil razonar en este pleito me vence: por aquí pruevo que *quando* nos requestáis y tan graciosamente allegáis de vuestro drecho: que es de fuerça seamos vencidas.[26] Y vuestra cautela como tenga poder de ganar de nos las mejores *partes*: que lo tenga agora de ganar de nos lo mejor de nuestra contienda:[27] no lo havré por mucho. Porque nuestra innocencia y vuestro sobrado saber fazen de lo falso bueno. Y aunque otra cosa no nos fiziesse sin culpa sino la simplicidat que es subjeta a la prudencia: y el que menos sabe: se

desire grows the more you scorn us. If it indeed came about that you had men's liberty, I know that you would court us shamelessly, just as we now court you. And what man could ever be so richly endowed with strength that he could resist you? I have such confidence in your incomparable cunning, that, if it were to happen, I know you would chase us into the wilderness and forests.[23] Even now, with all the danger you face and your shame, you go after us. I will tell you that in my experience of love, tremendous things have happened to me, which I shall keep silent, unless you force me to tell of them.

Thus you see that even now, held back by the bridle of shame, you strain at the bit.[24] What would you not do if the reins were loosened! For certainly your travails are nothing more than this delectable affliction of shame, which we men do not consider good or healthy.[25] You are always struggling against your shame, for it does not allow you to do what you desire. Every day noble ladies ruin themselves with lowly servants. What is more, if I had given in to the many ladies who have offered themselves to me—not only once but many times—it would have been my ruin; but I took care and considered what I would gain instead by avoiding harmful accusations. Now, I do not wish to extend my arguments further, in the hopes that, just as you have compassion for us, you will also be concerned for your own honor, and so not give me the opportunity to make public knowledge of women's secret guilt.

Braçayda

You are so hurtful, Torrellas, and so hostile to women, that you would not scruple to defame even the woman you see upon the holy altar, in order to slander us all. Should your subtle arguments defeat me in this trial, I will nevertheless prove here that when you men court us and so artfully demand your rights, we are perforce vanquished.[26] You claim that your cunning, which has the power to win the best of women, has the power to win this battle now.[27] I take this into little account. For our innocence and your incomparable cunning turn lies into truth. And even if nothing other than our simplicity, which is subject to prudence, made us blameless—just as the ignoramus is advised by the discerning man—we sin in ignorance because we take counsel from men, who know best how to

aconseja con el más discreto. Como nosotras que simplamente pec-
cando: tomamos consejo con el que más sabe lo qual nos danya. Ansí
que nosotras por vosotros de lo lícito y honesto muy *desviadas*: sois
causadores de nuestros innocentes yerros.[28] Y ansí a quien nos sigue:
se deve atribuir doble culpa. Y aun en esto hay una grande differencia
entre afición y razón.

   ¿Y qué nos cumple questionear contra los que por sí tienen
auctoridades *y* leyes y toda ordinación de la universidad de las cosas?
Porque la infamia y mengua nuestra nos desdoráis: no como lo pide
la razón: mas como mejor la voluntad vos da aparencia. Mayormente
sin tener contradicción alguna. Porque en nuestra simplicidad no hay
quién scriva en favor nuestro. Y vosotros que tenéis la pluma en la
mano: pintáis como queréis.[29] Por donde no es mengua sino fuerça el
sofrir a más no poder. Mas non se sigue: que en la maldad de vuestro
saber stén las virtudes o maldades en la pintura de vuestras palabras.
Y Dios no nos puede más demandar de aquello: de quanto el sezo nos
basta. Que si con vosotros iguales nos fiziera en saber: estava dudoso
el debate. Mas vuestra malicia puede tanto: que las innocentes mujeres
pagan la penitencia de vuestro peccado. ¡O quientos venís ante nos tan
mortales y tristes: que sin amor era razón de os haver piedad! Y por
daros la vida: buscáisnos agora la muerte. Pues si os dexamos morir:
dezís que por más encareçer se faze. Y quexáisos con los males. Y no
queréis luego los bienes. Venís por escapar la vida: y pésaos porque
quitan la muerte. Aunque es más cierto: que quando más os fináis: es-
táis más vivos.[30] Y como nuestra innocencia non vos entienda: simple-
mente se enganya. Y todos nuestros yerros y enganyos sallen de la mar
de vuestros enganyos. Que ni defender ni amenazar no aprovecha.
Que de fuerça o de grado a quien queréis sojuzgáis. Y muchas vezes
por temor de vuestras lenguas e difamias: complimos vuestros desseos. Y más queremos errar secreto y contentaros: que ser publicadas
por malas aunque no lo sean. Y unas por amor: y otras por temor:
como fortalezas conbatidas: que por fuerça de los pertrechos a manos
de los enemigos se venden: somos vencidas aziendo del vicio virtud.
Demostrando que más no pueden fazer por amor: lo que fuerça en la
verdad las tenía ya apremiadas.

harm us. Thus are we steered far away from all that is right and honorable: you are the causes of our innocent crimes.[28] Consequently, the men
who pursue us should be found doubly guilty. Here too there is a great
difference between love and reason.

What good does it do us to argue against those who have authority, have made all the laws, and have ordered all things in their own favor?
You lavishly describe our infamy and faults, not according to the truth, but
rather, any way you please, generally without finding anyone to contradict
you. For, in our ignorance, we have no one to write in our favor, while you
men, who hold pen in hand, can say whatever you want.[29] Therefore, it
is not our defect but rather our strength that we withstand you until we
can hold out no longer. It does not thus follow that our virtue lies in your
wicked knowledge, or our wickedness in the rhetoric of your words. God
cannot ask more from us than the capability of our minds, for if He had
made us equals in wisdom, we would lose this debate. But your wickedness is so strong that it makes innocent women do penance for your sins.

Oh, how many of you men come before us complaining that you
are at death's door, so melancholy and lovesick, that we must take pity on
you even if we do not love you! You, by begging us for your lives, condemn
us to death. But if we let you die, you say we do it in feigned scornfulness.
You complain of your affliction, yet do not love the cure. You come to us
to save your lives and then are aggrieved because death is taken from
you, although it is clear that the more you "die" the more you live.[30] In our
innocence we do not understand you; we are easily deceived, and all our
misdeeds and deceits flow from the sea of your deception, against which
neither defense nor threat is of any use, for you overcome whomever you
want either by force or by consent. We often give in to your desires out of
fear of your tongues and defamation, preferring to sin in secret and pla-
cate you, than be denounced publicly as bad women, even though we are
not. Some by love, others by fear—like besieged fortresses that surrender
to well-armed enemies—we women are vanquished and make a virtue of
vice. Thus, we cannot do any more for love than—truly—we are already
compelled to do by force.

Responde Torrellas a Braçayda

Si en el principio de vuestra fabla fallara en vos abaxaros el sinyuelo de razón: como agora vuestras palabras lo muestran: merced fuera que me hiziérades. Porque non oviérades causa de fazerme más inimistar. Ca bien pensastes en el *denuedo* primero: fazer torpe mi lengua.[31] Mas ya veo de vosotras que publicáis el temor de mis palabras: a lo que ya tiempo no da lugar. Mayormente donde hay tan magnífico Rey y Reina y notables cavalleros y damas que conclusión speran. Y buelvo al propuesto de vuestra fabla.

Dezís senyora que la innocencia vuestra vos salva. Ésta sería buena scusa: si por tales vos conociéssemos: que en toda maldad fuéssedes innocentes. Mas d'esto soy bien seguro: que tal scusa non vos relieva las danyadas penas. Porque muy claro es: que los mayores males que por el mundo acaeçen: por vosotras naçen. Si poner quisiesse *exemplo en quántas muertes, guerras, distruiciones de pueblos* vosotras havéis causado: sería cosa de nunqua acabar.[32] Donde muy claro es: que todos sotiles enganyos de vosotras procedan. Y esto veo: que la más discreta: y mayor sabida essa viene mas aína a la conclusión del yerro. Y toda su desemboltura assí en reír: como en burlar y motear se endreça a lo más desonesto.

Y todo vuestro mucho saber os pareçería ninguno: si por al hablar y cortear no aprovechasse. Así que la más aguda y savia par al mal se aprovecha del saber. Ya he yo visto por experiencia: que las mujeres más simples son en alguna manera más castas. Donde consiste que la simplesa os es salud. Y el saber danyoso. Como claro lo veis. Pues que todas las más agudas siguen la carrera de nuestros desseos: y la que más sabe yerra. Assí que bien claro stá: que innorancia no ha lugar de os scusar de culpa. Y es tanto danyosa por vuestro resaber: que a vuestro más crecido sezo pensáis no haver letrado que lo emiende. Y cierto en vosotras hay mil propriadades: que en nosotros no hay de aquellas una. Que a los tiempos que necessidad os constrinye: aparencias y mudamientos de palabras fingís. En las quales luego coloráis con las non tenyidas lágrimas. Y aun ad algunos mostráis amar desamando: y a otros amando los desdenyáis. Mas el arenga d'esto a mis trobados renglones lo refiero.[33] Pues agora me podéis dezir: ¿de quál necessidat de saber os falláis menguadas? Por mí digo: que si tan ventagoso me hallase en tales

Torrellas

You would have done me a great service and I would have had no reason to further my enmity with you if only you had begun your speech by
deigning to argue with a semblance of the truth, as you do now. For you
must have meant to make me tongue-tied from the first with the flair of
your performance.[31] Yet you have proclaimed the power of my words. Time
does not permit me to say more, for a great King and Queen, notable
knights, and ladies await the conclusion of our debate. So, I will return to
the matter of your argument.

You say, my Lady, that women's innocence saves them from guilt.
This would be a good excuse if women were in fact so, if you were the
innocent parties in all evildoing. Yet I am sure that such an excuse does
not absolve you from punishment, because it is very clear that the worst
evils that befall the world are born of women. If I began to offer examples
of all the evils that women have caused, I should never conclude.[32] It is
clear that all cunning deceits come from women. I submit that the more
discerning and learned a woman, the more she is apt to commit a sin; all
her graceful airs are devoted to laughter, teasing, and doing what is least
virtuous.

All of your great cunning would seem as nothing to you if it were
not used in conversing and courting; in this way does the cleverest and
wisest among you make use of her intelligence. I have often seen from
experience that simpleminded women are somehow more chaste; hence
ignorance is good for you and knowledge harmful, as you can clearly see,
since all the clever women follow the course of our desires: "She who
knows most, sins most." Therefore it is quite clear that ignorance does
not excuse you from guilt. Your knowingness is so harmful that you think
no learned man capable of instructing your fully-fledged intellect. Truly,
there are a thousand qualities in you women of which not a one is in
men. When necessary, you keep up appearances, use double *entendres*,
then blush with unfelt tears; you pretend to love men you hate, while you
disdain others, whom you love; for the rest of my discourse on this subject, I refer you to my composed verses.[33] Tell me pray, what wisdom are
women deprived of? As for me, were I so fortunate to be in your place,
I should not care to dedicate myself to the study of letters. Since you
are so knowledgeable in evil ways, you must know good things as well,

casos: ternía en poca mengua al desvelado studio de las letras. Ansí que pues tanto sabéis en el mal: ansí se faría en el bien. Si los desseos no se inclinassen a lo peor. Por donde es cierto: que por innorancia tenéis muy flaca scusa. Y lo que a mí parece: porque del todo no me fagáis enemigo vuestro: hayáis conocimiento del yerro. Y con esto os dexo por culpadas. Y digáis assí: "senyor pequé. Y a ti sólo digo mi culpa;" y más vale pedir perdón: que al yerro público poner scusa. Porque mejor creamos lo que vemos de vuestras obras. Que a la desculpa de vuestras palabras.

Responde Braçayda a Torrellas

Segund yo agora veo Torrellas: tanto mostráis tener nuestra opinión vencida: que aun pareçe no rendríades gracias a los juezes. Pues tenet creído: que si mucho me aquexáis a perder el velo de la vergüença: que diré lo que ya paciencia no puede callarlo. Y si vos presomís vençer con palabras: es porque sin empacho me sobráis en desonestaros. Mas como yo sea muger: aunque lo mejor de vuestro mal bevir para este caso me aprovechava: es fuerça lo calle. Porque más quiero ser por simple tovida: que por desonesta. Pues que de allí nos enjuriáis. Pero non se sigue que los juezes sí lo conoçen. Que por vergüença de vuestra vergüença lo callo: que menos deva valer que si lo dixiesse.

Y respondiendo al mal que dezís sabemos: paréceme que aquellas que muy aquexadas vienen a querer quanto pedís: mejor es el mal obrando con discreción: que no las simples que no sepan las mercedes que dan. Porque quien en poco se stima: poco gualardón merece. Y esto digo: porque sería yerro si negasse en el número de las mugeres que no haya muchas que ansí como lo dezís: lo sepan fazer. Pero yo por las muy dissolutas no vengo en la *defensa* de tan flaco partido:[34] mas tomo la mayor parte de las virtuosas lo que no podéis negar. Y si quisiesse poner en exemplo quantas son muertas por la defensión de la limpia castidad: las historias son llenas de la su noble y imortal memoria. Pues como la muerte sea la más fuerte cosa de soffrir. Quien aquella desprecia y quiere ante morir que ser caída en torpeza: bien menospreciará todas otras temptaciones por fuertes que sean. E pues dadme sólo un hombre: que por la defensión de su

if only your appetites did not incline you to evildoing. Thus it is clear that ignorance is a very weak excuse. As far as I am concerned—do not make of me an enemy entire—you must acknowledge your crimes; I find women guilty. You must say: "Lord, I have sinned and I tell you of my guilt," for it is better to ask for forgiveness than to try to give an excuse for a manifest crime, since we will sooner believe that which we see in your acts than that which we hear in your excuses.

Braçayda

I see, Torrellas, that you are ready now to thank the judges, so confident are you of your victory over women. But believe you me; since you accuse us of throwing off the veil of shame, I will now say what I can no longer suffer to keep silent. You may presume to win with your words, but it is because you have outdone me in unrestrainedly dishonoring yourself. Since I am a woman I am forced to keep silent—though even the most innocent part of your evildoing would serve my case—for I should rather be considered simple than unchaste. That is precisely how you attack us. Yet perhaps the judges do not understand that I refrain from speaking of men's shamefulness out of my own shame, for I would lose honor if I were to speak openly of it.

You say women know evil ways. Well, of those women who—much importuned—come to desire whatever you beg of them, I submit that it is better to act wickedly with discretion, and not as simple women do, who do not understand the favors they give. For he who little esteems himself, deserves little favor. I say this because it would be an error to deny that among women there are many who, as you say, know how to act in this way. Yet I have not come here to defend the weak case of dissolute women.[34] Rather, I take the side of virtuous women, who are the greater in number; this you cannot deny. For if I wanted to give as examples all those who have died in the defense of their spotless chastity, history is full of their noble and immortal memory. Death is the most terrible thing to suffer; she who does not fear death and would rather die than fall into sin, will also surely scorn all other temptations, however strong they may be. Now, show me just one man who in the defense of his chastity

castidad haya de alguna muger recebida muerte. De nosotras sabéis bien puedo deziros infinitos millares.

Pues ¿qué mejor experiencia que ésta: que quando no podéis más: nos tentáis hasta la muerte? Y dexemos las antigas de quien hoy sus famas biven. Más aún vivas yo conozco algunas: ver los punyales desnudos ante sus pechos: y querer ante la muerte: que no condecender en el vicio. Y vosotros queréis: que las maldades vuestras puedan más que nuestras noblezas. Pues ya no queráis en todo ser senyores. Que por esto venimos aquí: porque a lo menos en la justicia seamos iguales. Pues es cierto: que si alguna maldad hay en alguna de nosotras: es por ser de varón engendradas. Y aquello es malo en que vos parecemos. Y pues nos fizistes: condemnad la mala parte que de vosotros heredamos. O muera ya nuestra vida ante que bevir con herencia de generación tan mala sufframos.

Respuesta de Torrellas a Braçayda

¡Quán bien havéis fablado senyora en favor de las mugeres: si muerto fuesse Torrellas! Mas pues que yo bivo: non aprovecha vuestro dezir: sino en dar lugar quanto lo sepan. Y a lo que dezís: ser todas forçadas y seguidas hasta la muerte: si las antigas historias alguna loaron: cada día se usan cosas nuevas. Y si en aquell tiempo usaron nobleza las damas: del contrario os preciáis agora. Y aun pude acaecer: que ninguna cosa de aquellos loores de Lucrecia y Atalante no fuesse verdad.

Y lo que agora de vosotras se conoçe: son cosas que cada día por vosotras passan. Pues mayor fe daremos a lo que la vista nos certifica: que a lo que oímos. Yo no sabría juzgar de virtudes passadas que non vi: salvo de vicios presentes que agora veo. Y puesto que assí fuesse: que algunas de las ya passadas loores mereciessen: para en pago de aquellas hay infinitas más: que sus males scondieron al pequenyo loor de las buenas. Y las scripturas stán llenas de vuestras perversas obras. Y entre tan grande número de mugeres malas: si huvo alguna buena: no haze verano.[35] Si dezís que el mayor mal que hay en vosotras: es por ser de varón engendradas: si más

received death at the hands of a woman. You know well that I can give you many thousands of examples from our ranks.

So, what better evidence is there than this? When all your seductions fail, you put us to the test of death. In addition to all those women from ancient times whose fame lives on, among those living today, I know some who—when threatened by naked daggers at their breasts—desired death before submitting to vice. You have argued that your wickedness can indeed overcome our virtue. Well, now it seems you do not want to be lords over us in everything. Indeed, that is why we have come here, so that at least in the eyes of justice we will be equals. In any case, it is true that if some wickedness is found in a few of us women, it is because we are engendered by men, and what is evil in us is how we resemble you. Since you made us, condemn the evil part that we inherit from you, or let our line die out rather than suffer living with the inheritance of such an evil engendering.

Torrellas

How well you have spoken, my Lady, in favor of women! If only Torrellas were dead! Yet since I still live, your speech can do you no good, rather, it proves just how much women know. You claim that women are assaulted and pursued unto death by men. Although ancient stories may praise some women, every age has its ways, and if back in those days women acted nobly, now you pride yourselves by doing the contrary. Moreover, it may well be the case that those stories praising Lucretia and Atalanta hold not an ounce of truth.

For what is known about you ladies of our time are the things that you do every day, and I have more faith in what I see with my own eyes than in stories I hear told. I know not how to judge past virtues that I have not seen, only present vices that I now see. Granting that some women of the past did indeed merit praise, they are countered by the infinite numbers of those who hid their evildoing behind the scant praise for good women. The Scriptures are full of women's perverse deeds; if one good woman ever existed and among such a great number of bad ones, she does not a summer make.[35] You say that the greatest evil in you women comes from your being begotten from men. Well, your greatest evil must

no empeeciesse a los hombres la parte que de vos tenemos: que a vosotras la nuestra: ligero mal os sería. Por a la prueva d'esto: la primera muger creada en toda inocencia: su malicia pudo tanto: que no solamante peccó: y hizo peccar por le fazer participante en el error al varón: mas aun aquell grande mal que entonçes por ella fue cometido: lloramos todos agora. De manera que naturalmente en mala forma creadas: de día en día venistes en successión peores. Porque aquella en tanta innocencia y limpieza creada: no pudo bevir sin peccado. Pues muy menos lo haríades agora aquellas que en tanta corrupción de peccados bevís concebidas. De manera que no se os deve poner ya culpa. Pues del principio hasta agora havéis los vicios tanto comunes usado: que se tornan en naturaleza. Ansí que impossible os sería poder vevir sin ellos. Y pues que tan larga succession os viene de la culpa de la madre: no la fagáis nuestra. ¿Quál hombre es tan savio: que de vuestros enganyos pueda guardarse? Y vuestros pensamientos buscan grandes cautelas. Que de quien merecéis pena: pedís gualardón. Mas si sois poderosas contra quien desamáis: es vuestra crueldad muy sin medida. Y otras vezes quando más no podéis: tan homildes os mostráis con palabras y lágrimas piadosas: que el más cruel fazéis compassible y manso. Y más vencimiento alcançan vuestras cautelas que las armas nuestras. Y en los casos de amor do es más nuestra quistión: quien queréis es vuestro. Y a quien desamáis no le podéis despedir. Y queréis recebir servicios de enemigos y amigos. Y dezir "aquéll se muere por mí." Pues quien se loa en ser amada: bien demuestra que se deleita en ser querida. Pues d'estas ninguna ya veo: que en lo tal no reciba gloria. Y así es *im*possible que alguna vez no quiera ser requerida.[36]

Y ninguno sabe la causa por qué en los vuestros partos amáis los hijos y avorrecéis las hijas. Y la verdad es esta: que como unas a otras sois affecionadas: desseáis parir varones: porque se críen por al plazer de vuestras vezinas. De manera que del nacimiento nos amáis más que a vosotras mismas porque d'ellas como d'ellos no os podríades aprovechar ni servir. Ansí pues quien más a nos ama: más ha de fazer por havernos. Asimismo havéis dicho que nosotros non amamos. Y digo que es verdad. Pues quien no ama no trabaja: y vosotras que tanto os deleitáis en querer: que más hagáis es cosa convenible. Y si havéis gualardón del vicio: que hayáis pena del peccado.

be nothing more than a trifle, for we are damaged more by what we inherit from you than you can be by what you inherit from us. As proof of this, consider the first woman, created in complete innocence: her wickedness was so powerful that not only did she sin, she led man to sin by making him participate in her crime. What is more, we all weep now because of that great evil she committed then. And so, naturally created in an evil form, you women day after day, generation after generation, become worse. If the woman created in such innocence and purity could not live without sin, much less can you, who were conceived in great sinful corruption. Perhaps you should not be blamed, since from the beginning of time you have so commonly acted out of vice, that vice has now become your nature, and it would thus be impossible for you to live without it. Now, since the mother's guilt comes down to you in such a long line of succession, do not make it ours. What man is so wise that he can protect himself against your wiles? Your cunning ensnares us: you beg favors when you deserve punishment, yet when you hold power over a man you hate, your cruelty is truly without measure. In other cases, when you have no other options, you pretend to be so humble, using piteous words and tears to make the cruelest man softhearted and tame. Your scheming achieves more victories than any of our weapons. Now, when it comes to love, which is more to the point of our debate: the man you love is yours, but you do not release the man you disdain. You desire love-service from enemies and lovers alike and say, "That man is dying for me." Well, she who boasts of being loved also shows that she delights in being desired. Never have I seen a woman who does not glory in these things, and it is impossible for a woman who takes pleasure in being loved ever to wish not to be courted.[36]

No one seems to understand why you women love to bear sons and yet abhor daughters. But here is the truth: since you are all so attached to one another, you desire to give birth to men, so that they can be brought up for the pleasure of your lady-friends. In this way, from birth, you love us more than you love yourselves, because you cannot take advantage of or make use of daughters as you can your sons. She who loves men most will do much to have us. Likewise, you have said that we do not love, and I say it is true, for he who does not love, does not labor, and it is fitting that you, who take such pleasure in loving, strive more, and if you receive favor for vice, you must receive punishment for sin.

Y como havéis dicho ser nosotros enemigos vuestros: pues quien a los enemigos que ha de dar pena da plazeres y gloria ¿al amigo al respecto qué le dará? Por ende parece que aunque fuéssemos simples fríos y feos y sin merecer ser amados: vuestro vicio nos amaría. Y por esto como ya otras vezes dixe en alguna obra mía: sois lobas en scojer.[37] Esto lo causa el encendido desseo. Que ninguna difformidad os es fea: a lo menos d'esto puedo yo dar fe: como mejor conocedor en este caso: que ningún hombre de discreción no demandaría a ninguna aquello que no sperasse de haver. Y primero que lo pidamos conocemos: que no nos perderéis vergüença: pues la tenéis perdida. Porque quien viene en tal demanda: aparejos halla en la muger de senyales. Assí en el mirar como en el reír y otras condiciones que quieren tanto dezir: "si queréis queremos." Ansí que non faze menester que lo digáis. Pues havemos por más cierto lo que la voluntad consiente: que lo que la lengua dize.

Y ¿qué más quiero yo: sino ver trasluzir como vidriera: que quando más desamáis al que requesta: más la cara nos descubre los desseos del coraçón? Y en el secreto de vosotras la voluntad atorga lo que la boca niega.[38] Pues más fe daremos al secreto de l'alma: que al finigido contradezir. Sin duda es cierto que ningunos quieren ni se mueven: si non hallan adonde vuestra beldad y ademanes los embíen. Por do pruevo vosotras ser principio: aunque nosotros procuremos el fin. Pues quien comiença merece. Concluyo que pues sin lo dezir lo fazéis: mayor pena merece la obra vuestra: que la culpa de nuestras palabras. Y más desembuelto es vuestro pensamiento que nuestra lengua.

El auctor

Grandes altercaciones passaron entre Torrellas y Braçayda: más de las que ninguno podría scrivir. Y visto por los juezes las razones de amas partes: tomaron determinación para dar la sentencia. Los quales ya después de complidos: vinieron cubiertos de luto. Y unas spadas manzilladas de sangre. En sus diestras manos. Con otras muchas serimonias. Segund en aquella tierra se acostumbra. Y eran dotze juezes:

Now, you have said that we are your enemies; well, she who gives her enemies—whom she should punish—pleasures and glory, what will she not give her lover? From whence it seems that even if we were simpleminded, cold, and ugly, undeserving of being loved, you would nonetheless love us out of vice. That is why, as I have said before in a certain poem of mine, you are she-wolves when you choose mates.[37] This is caused by your enflamed desire. Not a single deformity is ugly in your eyes. Of this, at least, I can speak from experience, as the most knowledgeable of men: no discerning man would ask any woman for something he had no hope of getting, and before we ask, we know that you will be shameless with us, for you have lost your shame already. A man who decides to seduce a woman has seen willingness in her gestures, in the way that she looks, laughs, and in all of her other actions, which mean, "If you wish it, I am willing." Thus, it is not necessary for you to say anything, for your desire speaks more clearly than your tongues.

What more can I ask than to let the truth shine as clearly as though through glass? The less a woman loves the man who courts her, the more her face belies her heart's desire. In secret, women's hearts admit what their mouths deny, and so I have more faith in the secrets of your souls than in your feigned refusals.[38] Without a doubt no man would love or be moved to act if he did not go where your beauty and behavior lead; therefore I prove that you women are the principal causes of seduction, and although we men may procure the end, it is the one who begins who deserves the punishment. I conclude thus, that—without saying a word—you seduce us; your acts deserve greater punishment than our words. Your thoughts are more daring than our tongues.

The Author

The great debate that continued between Torrellas and Braçayda is beyond the powers of any writer to describe. The judges, having heard the arguments of both parties, determined to pass sentence. After their deliberation, the judges entered with great ceremony, dressed in mourning and brandishing bloodied swords in their right hands, as was the custom in that land. The twelve judges pronounced the sentence: Mirabella must die. They found her at greater fault than Grisel on many counts.

los quales dieron sentencia: que Mirabella muriesse. Y fundaron por muchas razones ser ella en mayor culpa que Grisel.

Y como en presencia de la Reina delante sus damas fuesse condemnada a muerte: las vozes que s'començaron a dar: ponían tal tristeza en los ánimos: que parecía el sol scurecerse. Y el cielo querer d'ello tomar sentimiento. Y ansí como Braçayda vio baxo su partido: movida de piadad por la muerte de Mirabella: en tal manera appellando ante la majestad de Dios: como suberano juez de los hombres clama y quexa.

Appellación de Braçayda

¡O quánto fue mal acuerdo el nuestro senyoras: en poner nuestras honras y famas en poder de los enemigos nuestros! Porque seyendo ellos alcaldes y parte: conocida stava la sentencia que agora oímos. ¡O malditas mujeres! ¿Por qué con tantos affanes de partos y fatigas queréis aquellos que en muertes y menguas vos dan el gualardón? ¡O si consejo tomássedes en el nacimiento del hijo: daríades fin a sus días! Porque non quedasen sojetas a sus enemigos. Y alegre vida viviessen.

¿Mas qué aprovechan mis palabras: quando nos mismas criamos aquellos: que de tantas muertes nos matan? Y si hasta aquí non havíamos conocimiento de sus maldades: no es maravilla que hayamos recebidos enganyos: mas ya de aquí adelante que por muy malos los conoçemos: gran yerro nos sería: si en tener parte en nosotras se loassen. Y si en los pasados tiempos de nosotras han recebido merçedes: de aquí adelante: aunque los veamos morir: demos a sus pasiones disfavores por gualardón. Porque el malo por la pena es bueno.[39]

¡O maldita tanta piadad como en nosotras mora! Que ponemos a nos a la muerte: por salvar a nuestros enemigos las vidas. Y después de complido su querer: se rían de nuestras lágrimas. Pues ¿cuál çeguedad o mengua de juizio tal consiente: que non busquemos vengança de quántas ellos cada día se vengan? Pues ¿qué vale contra ellos nuestro pequenyo poder? Pues debaxo de su mano bevimos. Y como poderosos nos fuerçan y de todas nuestras honras nos despojan: pues mirad excellente y muy illustre Reina y nobles senyoras so cuyas leyes bevimos: que quieren que muera la que es forçada: y viva el forçador. Y tienen razón.

The Queen and all her ladies cried out in great pain upon hearing Mirabella's death sentence, causing everyone present to feel such sadness that the sun seemed to darken, as if the very heavens reflected their pain. When Braçayda saw her company thus cast down, moved by pity for Mirabella's fate, she appealed before the majesty of God, the sovereign judge of men, crying out and lamenting, saying:

Braçayda's Appeal

Alas, what an ill agreement was ours, ladies! We put our honor and reputations in the power of our enemies, who are both the legal authorities and litigants, so it was easy to conjecture what the sentence we have just heard would be. Alas, accursed women, why do you love and desire so to bear sons and to suffer thus for the sake of men, who then reward us with death and abuse? Alas, if only you would take my advice and kill your sons on the day they were born! Women would no longer be subject to their enemies and could live happy lives. Yet, what good are my words when we ourselves breed the men who kill us with so many deaths? If, in the past we have had no knowledge of their wickedness, it is no marvel that men have beguiled us; but now, knowing them to be very evil, it would be a great error on our part if they were to boast of having taken advantage of us. If in the past they have received our favors, henceforth let us reward their passion with disdain, inasmuch as punishment makes a bad man good.[39]

Alas, accursed be the great mercifulness within us! It makes us condemn ourselves to death to save the lives of our enemies. And when their desires have been fulfilled, they laugh at our tears. I ask you, what blindness or lack of judgment permits such a thing? Why do we not avenge each woman they take vengeance upon every day? What is the scant power we have worth against them? We live under their rule and, since they are powerful, they ravish us and despoil the honor of us all. Consider then, excellent and most illustrious Queen and noble ladies, under whose laws we live: men's laws that condemn the ravished victim

Pues ellos son juezes y partes y avocados del mismo pleito. Y cierto asaz simple sería: ¿quién cuenta sí diesse sentencia? Y por esto no recebimos injuria. Pues con poder absoluto nos la pueden dar.

Ca si por ventura *ante* mujeres viniera el determinar aqueste pleito:[40] si nos condemnaran: huvieran lugar las quexas. Mas d'ellos que lo hayan así fecho: no son de culpar. Pues cada uno es más obligado a sí mismo que a otri. Pero a Dios como justo juez: ante aquell appello d'este falso juizio. Donde ninguna verdad se sconde. Ni affección ninguna se presume. Mas mujeres ante hombres pleitear: es gran locura. Mas yo sforçándome con alguna virtud y consciencia en ser muy cierta y clara a nosotras tener la justicia y verdad tan conocida: aún de nuestros enemigos era bien fiarlo. Y creyendo que los nobles de sí mismos usen justicia. Mas en esto do no hay virtud: no la pidamos. Pues no puede dar ninguno lo que no tiene. Y quien de sus enemigos fía: bien se emplea que a sus manos muera.

El auctor

Después que Braçayda de los hombres se huvo mucho quexado: la Reina y ella con todas las damas se ponen ante los pies del Rey: humilmente supplicando por la vida de Mirabella. Al qual ningunos ruegos vençer pudieron. Mas como la Reina lo vio de propósito de fazer aquella justicia: en tal manera le supplicó.

Supplicación de la Reina

Non sé con quáles palabras senyor tan alta merçed te pida: que la vida de Mirabella me atorgasses. Y non me hayas por tan ozada segund lo que conozco de tu justicia: que si otros hijos te quedassen: por ella rogasse. Mas no pareçe ser yerro supplicar por la salvaçión suya. Pues ¿qué valen tus grandezas villas y ciudades: quando hijos en que succedan no tuviesses? Y como los padres a los hijos más que a sí mesmo aman: ¿en quál humanidad cabe que de sí mismo faga ninguno justicia? Y pues a sí no ama: ningunos bienes possee. Por donde es mejor:

to death—and long live the rapist! And men are in the right, since they are the judges, litigants, and lawyers in the same case. Surely only a simpleton would sentence himself. We are not wronged in this way; men can condemn us by their absolute power.

For if we had argued this case before women,[40] and if they had condemned us, then the accusations should have some merit. But the judges who have found against us are not to blame, for everyone is more obliged to favor his own kind than others. Thus, I appeal this false verdict before God, as a just judge from whom no truth is hidden and who is impartial. Ah, it is great folly for women to argue this case before men! Yet emboldened by virtue, by the very certain and clear knowledge that we women are in the right, and by the evident truth, I felt that we could trust even our enemies, believing that noble men would be just. But let us not seek men's virtue here, where there is none. For one cannot give what he does not have, and he who trusts his enemies, well deserves to die by their hands.

The Author

After Braçayda had made her full complaint against men, the Queen and all her ladies threw themselves at the King's feet, humbly begging him to spare Mirabella's life, but no pleading could sway him. When the Queen saw that he was prepared to see justice done according to the decision of the judges, she beseeched him in the following manner:

The Queen's Plea

I am at a loss for words to beg you, my Lord, your most high grace, to grant me Mirabella's life. Had you other children, I should not be so bold as to beg for her life, knowing what I know of your justice, yet it does not seem to be wrong to plead for her salvation. For what are your titles, towns and cities worth if you have no children to inherit them? Since parents love their children more than themselves, can it be human for anyone to wreak such justice upon himself? For he who does not love himself, possesses nothing. Therefore it is better to be less just than overly cruel.

menguar en la justicia: que sobrar tanto en la crueza. Y si Mirabella por el sobredicho yerro es de ti avorrecida: que ninguna piedad le hayas hávela senyor de mí. Que mi vida por la suya vive. Y el plazo de su muerte es el mío. Y a esto ninguna duda pongas. Y pues yo ningún yerro te conozco haver cometido: ¿por qué quieres que muera sin mereçer? Pues en virtud y nobleza consiste: perdonar a quien yerra: ante que dar pena a quien no la mereçe.

Respuesta del Rey a la Reina

Bien pareçe el consejo que tú me das ser más affeccionado que justo. Y si tú grande amor tuviesses conmigo como lo has con Mirabella más dolor habrías de mi honra: que de su muerte. Yo quisiera que consideraras: cómo la persona del Rey es spejo en que todas miran. Y sus obras convienen ser tales: que resplandezcan entre todas las otras gentes. Principalmente en la justicia. Como sea a todos más menesterosa. Ansí que es razón: que ella le dé corona de noble. Y el Rey piadoso: aquell es cruel. Y fasta aquí yo nunqua recebí en tal caso: ni por ruegos ni por affección mengua ninguna. Y aquello que desde mi primera edad me he trabajado por guardar: non sería bien que agora en mis postremeros días lo perdiesse.

Pues en el fin de la vida está el loor.[41] Y si yo fasta aquí he administrado justicia: quando en mi hija non la fiziesse: non me podrían loar de justo. Que quien de sí mismo non faze justicia: non le debe fazer de otro. Mas primero deven los nobles punir a sí mismos: que a sus siervos. Y yo segund el mucho amor que con Mirabella tengo: ante querría soffrir la muerte: que darla a ella. Pero como quien de sí mismo faze justicia: assí me es fuerça fazerla d'ella. Porque mis súbditos no hayan lugar de se quexar: diziendo ser más affeccionado a mí que a ellos. Y viendo mis gentes que de una sola hija sin sperança de haver otra fago padecer: ¿qué sperança terná ninguno en la piadad mía: que yerro cometa? Y quando a mí no la hove ¿quién me ozará supplicar por otro? Y por cierto siempre vi ser de virtuosos ante ozar morir: que caer en vergüença. Pues yo más quiero tener loor de virtuoso y justo: que de poderoso.

And if you hate Mirabella so much for the aforesaid crime that you cannot feel any pity for her, have some pity for me. For I live for her, and her dying day will also be mine; do not doubt it. I have never yet known you to be in the wrong; why now do you want me to die an undeserved death? Virtue and nobility consist in forgiving those who offend rather than in punishing the innocent.

The King

Truly, it seems that the counsel you offer me is more emotional than just, and if you loved me as much as you do Mirabella, my dishonor should pain you more than her death. I would have you now consider how the King's person is a mirror held up to all, and his deeds should be resplendent among those of all other people, especially in works of justice, which are the most necessary to all, for it is justice that rightly crowns the king with his nobility. A merciful king is indeed cruel. Never have I failed to be just, neither in response to pleas, nor out of affection. It would not behoove me to lose now, at the end of my days, that which I have striven to safeguard since my youth. Indeed, "the examination of all is in the end."[41] If heretofore I have administered justice to all, were I not to do so in the case of my daughter, no one could praise me as just. For he who does not apply the laws to himself, should not judge others. Rather, noblemen should punish their own kind before their servants. Now I, in my great love for Mirabella, should rather be killed than condemn her to death, but just as one must apply the law to oneself, so am I forced to judge her. My subjects must have no cause to complain that I care more for myself than I do for them. When they see that I make my only daughter suffer, even when all hope of having another child is lost, what hope will anyone else who commits crime have for my mercy? When I have no mercy for myself, who will dare to beg mercy for another? And truly, I have always seen that virtuous men should rather die than fall into disgrace; well, I want to be praised as a virtuous and just man rather than a powerful one.

I will tell you why. My ancestors won all my realms and seigniorial lands; I cannot boast of conquering them, only what I have kept of their inheritance. Yet if there is any virtue in me, I pride myself on it, thus justice

Y la razón es ésta: que todos mis reinos y senyoríos mis anteces-
sores los ganaron. Y yo non me puedo loar haver ganado: salvo lo que
d'ellos me quedó. Mas si en mí alguna virtud hay: de aquella me precio.
Ansí que pues sola justicia es mi victoria: y lo más loable en mi stado: no
quiero perder aquello: que con tan grande studio y trabajo he ganado. Y
en tal caso no creas ninguna piadad me mueva: y de paciencia te guar-
nece en las cosas do sperança no se spera. Y mi muerte si la quieres: yo
la atorgo. Mas bivo que ella viva es impossible.

El auctor

Despúes que la Reina vio: que la vida de su hija non havía remedio: ella
y sus damas se fueron a lugar secreto: donde palabras con grande compassión con muchas lágrimas sparçen. Y el mucho dolor y angustias por
la muerte de la hija lançando la derribó muerta en el suelo: mas el Rey
non pensava sino cómo a la vida de Mirabella diesse fin. Y aunque en
stremo la amava: pero la justicia era más poderosa que el amor.

El qual lugo mandó dar forma sin dilación: que aquello se fiziesse: y depúes que el día fue llegado que Mirabella moriesse: ¿quién
podría scrivir las cosas de gran magnificencia que para su muerte
stavan ordenadas? Y todas muy conformes a tristeza segund que el
caso lo requería. Ansí fiestas tan tristes: como el día de sus bodas se le
pensaban fazer alegres. Que entre las cosas de piedad que allí fueron
juntadas: eran quinze mil doncellas vestidas de luto. Las quales con
llantos diversos y mucha tristeza ayudavan a las tristes lágrimas de la
madre y desconsolada Reina que con ella y con todas las otras damas
ninguna consolación fallavan a sus dolores. Y enpúes d'esto traían un
carro: en el qual iva Mirabella con quatro obispos qu'el cargo de su
alma tomavan. Y luego allí a Grisel: que por más creçer y dublar en
su pena: demandaron que viesse la muerte de Mirabella. Y el Rey con
infinitas gentes cubiertas de lluto iva al fin de todas: segund costumbre
de aquell reino. Y sallieron fuera de la ciudad donde Mirabella havía
de morir quemada. Porque las leyes de la tierra eran: quien por fuego
de amor se vençe: en fuego muera.

Y desque ya todos fueron ajuntados hombres y mujeres: rogavan al Rey que de la vida de Mirabella se doliesse. El qual ningún

is the only victory I can claim and what is most praiseworthy in my estate; I do not want to lose what I have earned with assiduous labor. Such being the case, do not think that I can be moved by pity, and arm yourself with patience where there is no hope. If you so wish, I will grant you my own death, yet it is impossible for me to remain alive if Mirabella lives.

The Author

When the Queen saw that her daughter's life could not be saved, she and her ladies went to a secret chamber where they spoke piteous words and many tears were shed, and the outpouring of great pain and anguish the Queen felt for the death of her daughter cast her to the floor in a dead faint. The King, on the other hand, thought of nothing but how to end Mirabella's life. Even though he loved her utterly, justice was stronger than love.

Therewith, the King ordered it be done without delay. Now, on the day Mirabella was to die—who could ever find the words to describe all the magnificent preparations that were made for her execution?—all was prepared in accordance with the mournful ceremony that the occasion required; it was to be a day as dolorous as they had thought to make her wedding-day joyous. In addition to all the solemnities prepared, there were gathered there fifteen thousand damsels dressed in mourning, whose many laments and great sadness joined with the sad tears of the mother and despondent Queen, who could find no consolation for her pain, neither in her own spirit nor among her ladies. Mirabella followed them, pulled in a cart and accompanied by four bishops charged with the care of her soul. Then came Grisel, who was commanded to watch Mirabella's death so that his suffering would be increased twofold. And the King, with an infinite entourage, dressed in mourning, came at the end of the procession, as is the custom in that kingdom. All went out of the city to the place where Mirabella was to die, burned at the stake, for the laws of the land commanded: "He who is conquered by the flames of love, in flames must die."

ruego concedía: y puesto que la Reina y muchos duques y condes y grandes senyores ge le supplicassen: en aquell caso a todos perdía vergüença: antes gesto muy irado y sanyoso les mostrava. Y esto visto por la Reina tan grande crueza como el Rey havía: con desenfrenada ravia ansí comiença.

La Reina contra el Rey

Tú non padre más enemigo te puedes dezir. Quando delante de ti mandas quemar tu fija. Y que ninguna piadad d'ella hayas: esto es cosa muy inorme y injusta. Y como non basta para satisfazer al mundo lo que ya contra tu fija has obrado sino que quieres ser stremo. Y por una arrebatada fama que de ti por el mundo se pregone: la qual non dirán justicia mas muy enemiga crueldad: quieres a mí de dolor perpetua ser causa. El primero día que te conocí fue la mi muerte. Pues eres causa que quando reparo sperava: días muertos en vida por descanso me traías. Los quales yo de ti spero recebir.

Ca mis ojos de la su alegría privados: dan al coraçón nueva causa de dolor a ningún otro semblante. ¡O senyores! ¿Qué reparo a mis dolores y a mi mal envejecido? ¿Qué día tan plazentero puede ser? pues que muere la vida de aquella por quien vivía la mía. Si con ella me mandaras matar: usaras de aquella piadad y amor que devías. Mas déxasme morir viviendo: por más creçer mi pena. Plázeme que tu crueza pueda tanto: que en un día sin fijos y mujer quedes solo.

El auctor

Cosas de grande compassión mas por la voluntad que por palabras dezía la Reina. Mas ninguna cosa podía aprovechar. Porque éll ya importunado: mandava más presto dar fin a los días de Mirabella. A la

When at last all were gathered there, both men and women begged the King to take pity on Mirabella. The King did not wish to hear any entreaties. Rather, when the Queen, and many Dukes, Counts, and Noble Lords all beseeched him, the King lost self-control and turned to the people in a show of ire and rage. Now, the Queen, seeing the King's great cruelty, began to speak with unbridled anger, thusly:

The Queen

Well may you be called "enemy" rather than "father," you, who order your daughter to be burned before your eyes and have no pity at all for her— this is an atrocity of injustice. As if what you have already done to her were not enough to satisfy the public, you wish to go to extremes, all in the interests of the exalted fame you want to be proclaimed throughout the world. You will not be renowned for your justice, but rather for your pitiless cruelty. You seek to be the cause of my perpetual sorrow. The day I met you was my death sentence. For you, from whom I expected comfort, now offer me a living death instead of tranquility; such is all I can expect from you.

My eyes, now bereft of their joy, give my heart cause for sorrow like none ever felt before. Alas, noble ladies and gentlemen! What remedy for my sorrow and my increased pain will I find? What joyful day will I ever see? For the life that I lived for now dies. If only you would order my death along with Mirabella's, then you would be treating me with the mercy and love that you owe me, yet you let me die by living, so that my pain will be all the greater. Nevertheless, it pleases me that your cruelty has the power to take from you—in the space of a single day—your lineage and your wife, leaving you all alone.

The Author

The Queen said things worthy of great compassion, speaking more from the heart than by words, yet she gained nothing by it. The King, despite having been thus importuned, ordered that Mirabella's days be brought to an immediate end. The Queen went to Mirabella, showering her with

qual la Reina fue a ver infinitas vezes besándola. Y con calientes lágrimas la banyava. Y en esta forma el dolor de su muerte le manifiesta.

La Reina a su fija

¿Quáles fuerças bastan a tan flaca fuerça que yo viviendo amada fija morir te vea? ¿Quál inhumanidad suffre que viesse a ti viva en mis braços: y que dexasse levarte a la muerte? Para lo qual non sé yo triste sfuerço dónde buscar: para que de tan gran dolor me sfuerçe.

¡O Dios! ¿y cómo te plaze que los mis postremeros anyos vivan: y mueran los de aquella que a mí más justo convenía? ¿Qué me aprovechan las muchas merçedes de grande dignidad y stado que me diste? Si quando mayor fue mi sobir en la rueda de Fortuna: mayor es la cuita. Porque en las baxuras del suelo abaxo embuelvo mis hazes.

¡O Fortuna que otro ningún mayor mal darme pudieras! Que la criada en tantos deleites vegedad: me quita plazer. Y muchos deportes para mi alegría buscados: apenas me podrían alegrar. Special agora que lloros y lágrimas me buscan. Y mi gran senyorío me da tormentos: y pobre y miserable condición pues ya sin ti amada Mirabella mi real stado me da pena. ¿Para quién codiciava yo Reino tan noble? Para ti que digna de mayor eres. Tu discreción. Tu mucha nobleza. Tu gran beldad. Que sin ser grandes tus excellencias te fazían grande. Mueran ya pues mis prosperidades con tu muerte. Y pues tú me dexas: todos los bienen me dexan.

El auctor

Luego por mandado del Rey fue por fuerça quitada Mirabella de los braços de su madre. La qual en una riqua camisa spojaron para recibir la muerte viendo arder ante sí las encendidas llamas del fuego que la speravan.[42] Pero ante que en éll fuesse lançada: llamó a su amigo muy amado Grisel. Y con éll stando: olvidando el temor: desechó la vergüença. Y tales palabras mescladas con lágrimas le dixo.

kisses, bathing her in hot tears, and expressing her sorrow at her daughter's death in this way:

The Queen to Her Daughter

What forces can sustain my frail fortitude, my dear daughter, so that I may bear seeing you die while I live? What inhumanity allows me to see you now alive in my arms, and to let you be carried off to die? Oh miserable me, I know not where to find the fortitude to bear such great sorrow!

Oh, God! How can You allow me to live out my last days while she, who more justly deserves to live, dies? What good to me are the gifts of great nobility and estate that You gave me? If once Fortune's wheel raised me to the highest point, now the fall is greater and I am dragged through the filth of the earth.

Oh Fortune, would that you gave me some other woe! I, who was raised in luxury, now face a woeful old age. Any sport designed for my enjoyment can hardly bring me any pleasure. For now weeping and tears seek me. My great nobility torments me and makes me poor and miserable, for without you, beloved Mirabella, my royal estate pains me. For whom did I desire such a noble realm? For you. You, who are worthy of a yet greater one. For your discretion, your high nobility, your great beauty, they alone would have made you a great woman, even without all your other excellences. All my good fortune now dies with your death, for since you abandon me, all I have abandons me.

The Author

The King ordered that Mirabella be torn by force from her mother's arms then and there. She was dressed in nothing but a rich chemise in preparation for death.[42] When she saw the blazing flames of the fire that awaited her, just before she was to be thrown into it, she called to her much beloved Grisel. Beside him, she forgot her fear, thrust aside her shame, and tearfully said the following words to him:

Mirabella a Grisel

¡O vida de mi vida la fatiga y soledad en que te dexo: creçe tanto mi mal: que por tu pena más que por la mía amargosas lágrimas sparzo! Y non sé quáles palabras te diga que a tu grande desconsuelo puedan alegrar ni consolar. Mas sólo este loor te queda: que vees morir aquella: por quien tantos de amor morieron. Y asaz favor es este: para que con la vida te guozes. Y en los tiempos de las adversidades se conozcan y se vean los corazones fuertes. Y ninguno será por sforçado conocido: si en esta strecha batalla non se huviesse visto.

    Pues oy cavallero sois a tiempo: que se conozca en vos: si vuestras fuerças son flaquas o fuertes. Y encobrit el dolor de mi muerte: porque causa de flaco corazón non vos sea. Y aunque yo muera: siempre quiero que vuestro loor y fama bivan. Y puesto que me digáis: que el grande amor que es entre nos: partiéndose non podría negar el ánimo su pena: digo ser verdad. Mas mirad que yo non menos que vos amo. Y busco siendo muger contra la amor y la muerte fuerças para sforçaros. Mayormente siendo vos varón. Y non moriendo os devéis sforçar. Y baste esto para vuestro bevir. Que lo flaco sfuerça sin fuerça lo fuerte.[43]

Responde Grisel a Mirabella

¡O cómo sería senyora quien a vos pierde todo favor y honra ligero de perder! Y porque veáis quanto esto alexado de buscar a mi terrible passión consuelo: no solamente me duele el perder por vos honras y bienes: mas porque más de una sola vida non puedo perder me es incomportable passión. Y no creo que tan sola mi muerte satisfaga tan grande deuda. Y muero porque más de una sola vez morir non puedo. Y este es el remedio que busco para bevir que por cierto non me satisfaze una muerte que con ella nin cumplo nin pago. Pero básteos que aunque la fuerça sea pequenya: los desseos son grandes. Y con una sola vida os sirvo pues más non puedo. Y más sería hombre perdido que sforçado él que sin vos bevir quiziesse que allí podría bien dezir Braçayda quexándose de la poca fe de los hombres. Y aunque yo la muerte *no* desseasse por non dar mengua d'ellos: era deuda que les

Mirabella to Grisel

Oh love of my life! The pain and solitude to which I abandon you increases my woe so much that I shed these bitter tears for your sorrow more than for my own. I am at a loss for words to console or cheer you in your great distress. Yet this sole glory is left to you: you see die for you the woman for whom so many died of love, and this great love-service should suffice for you to take pleasure in outliving me. Forceful hearts show themselves in times of adversity; and not a one should ever be recognized as strong had it not witnessed this desperate battle.

So today, Sir, it is time for you to show if your fortitude is frail or forceful, and hide your sorrow for my death: do not let me be the cause for your heart's frailty. Though I die, I want your glory and fame to live forever. And if you tell me that your soul's pain at the loss of the great love between us cannot be denied, I say it is true. Still, I love no less than you do, and if I, being a woman, seek the fortitude to fortify you against love and death, you, being a man and not about to die, should gird your strength. Let this be enough for you to live: frailty forcelessly gives force to the forceful.[43]

Grisel to Mirabella

Oh, My Lady, how easy it would be for the man who loses you to lose all favor and honor! I am so far from seeking consolation for my terrible suffering, that not only do I suffer the loss of honor and property for your sake, but the fact that I cannot lose more than just one life for you is an unbearable torment. For I do not believe that my one death can satisfy my great debt. Yet I shall die, for I may die only once. Such is the remedy that I seek for my life, although one death truly does not satisfy me, for with it I neither fulfill nor repay my debt. Yet it must suffice, for although its force is small, my desire is great. I serve you with one sole life since I cannot give more. Were I to prefer living without you to death, well should I be called wretch rather than a worthy man, for I should then give good cause to Braçayda to complain of men's little faithfulness. Thus, even if I did not wish to die, it is a duty I owe men in order not to sully their honor.[44]

devía.[44] Special que ninguna cosa d'aquéllas me mueve. Mas amor que vuestro me hizo tan próspero y alegre en la vida: ansí agora desesperado y triste me veo en la muerte. Y quien se dispuso a la gloria que se disponga a la pena.

¡O si a todos fuesse tan público como a mí por ser toda la causa de quanto mal vos cometistes! A vos libre y a mí condenado farían. Mas mi ventura *non quiere salvo dar muerte a quien no la mereçe*: y salvar al que la bien mereçe.[45] ¡O qué maldad sería si viesse en vos la pena de mi culpa! Mas pues no vale verdad ni justicia: yo de mí faré justicia. Y según el grande dolor que me da el perderos: es despojo de la vida. Y pues en mí ningún tormento igual a tan grave mal no es: asaz remedio es el que me dais con tan pequenya pena como la muerte. ¡O bien aventurada Muerte que tales angustias y passiones me sana! Ella es verdadera amiga de los coraçones tristes. Con la qual pues el cuerpo non puede el alma vos seguirá.

El auctor

Como Grisel dio fin a sus palabras: procuró de dar fin a su vida. Y en el fuego de bivas llamas se lançó sin ningún temor. Tanto que aunque remediar lo quiziessen non fue cosa possible. Y Mirabella lo quizo seguir. Mas Braçayda y las otras damas y donzellas que con ella stavan: de las llamas del fuego a fuerça la quitaron. Y luego la Reina con otros cavalleros llegaron a supplicar al Rey perdonarla quiziesse. Y pues que del cielo vino por maravilloso milagro dar muerte a quien la mereçía: que contra la voluntad de Dios no diesse pena a quien no la mereçe. A lo qual el Rey no atorgava ni contradezía. Salvo lo remetió a los de su consejo. Con los quales ligero fue de alcançar no diessen la muerte a Mirabella. ¡Si ella despúes no la buscara! La qual como vio sacar muerto del fuego a su amado Grisel: no sé cómo scriva las llástimas que ella dixo.

Yet none of this truly moves me; rather the love that made me yours, so fortunate and happy in life, now makes me desperate and unhappy in death. For he who enjoyed glory, must likewise be ready to bear pain.

Alas! If only everyone knew—as I do—that I was the cause of all your evildoing! You would be free and they would condemn me. Yet my fate decrees nothing other than the death of one who does not deserve it and the salvation of one who truly does.[45] Alas, what an evil it would be to see you bear the punishment for my guilt! Yet, since neither truth nor justice has served us here, I will sentence myself. For so great is my sorrow, that losing you is my destruction, and since no torment could be equal to such a great affliction, in such a small thing as death, you give me a great remedy. Oh, blessed Death, which cures me of such anguish and suffering! She is the true lover of unhappy hearts; in death, although my body cannot remain with you, my soul will.

The Author

No sooner had Grisel ended his speech than he ended his life. He threw himself fearlessly into the blazing flames of the fire so quickly that— though many would have attempted it—it was impossible to save his life. Mirabella tried to follow after him, but Braçayda and the other ladies and damsels who were with her pulled her by force from the flames of the fire. The Queen with other knights went straightaway to beseech the King to pardon Mirabella, since Heaven had sent a marvelous miracle and executed the man who deserved it, and it would be against God's will if the King were to sentence someone who was not guilty. The King neither granted nor refused their entreaty. Rather, he turned to the men of his council, among whom it was readily determined that Mirabella should not die. If only she had not sought death afterwards! When Mirabella saw the dead body of her beloved Grisel taken from the fire, she began to lament with such great sorrow, I know not how to describe it.

Mirabella

¿Cómo es posible que yo sin ti el mi amado Grisel bevir pudiesse? Y tú dando fin a tus males: diste comienço a los míos. ¡O apassionada yo que vosotras senyoras que a fuerça la vida me dais! Si sentiéssedes mi tormento la muerte me scogeriades por buena.

Ca mejor es súbito obrando padeçer: que tristeza y pavor de hazerlo sperar. Y no es piadad la que conmigo usáis: mas muy enemiga crueza. ¡Y cómo no sería mejor con una ligera pena feneçer tantas passiones! Mas vosotras por hazer las más crecidas: queréis que viva días muertos en vida. Y el fin que agora me quitáis en breve no se scusa: ya fueran mis males fenecidos y vosotras no queréis que fenezcan. Pues no creáis que amor sea tan poco poderoso: que quitar pueda tan grande fe. Y ansí que no pienses amado Grisel que no te sigua mas spérame que las strechas sendas me ensenyes. Y entre los muchos muertos no trabaje en buscarte.

¡O Grisel! ¿Es cierto que ya no bives? Ante mis ojos te veo muerto y apenas lo puedo creer. Mas como los suenyos muchas vezes me enganyan: desseo esto sea de aquellos sonyados suenyos. Ya querría tomar alguna sperança con alguna falsa imaginación que vivo te me representasses. Mas ¿qué aprovecha? que el dolor dudozo se cree por cierto. Quanto más el que es verdadero.

¡O atribulada yo que tanta pena me da el desseo de verte! Pues ¿qué es de ti tan alexado de mí sin sperança de jamás verte? ¿Cómo lo soffrirá aquella que una hora sola sin ti *no* podía bevir sabiendo que vivo y alegre stavas?[46] Pues no creas que tú sallido de penas: dexes a mí en la vida d'ellas. Que las fees de entre ti y mí dadas: quieren que te sigua quando poder tenga. Y bien perdonarás mi tardança pues agora más non puedo. Pero yo satisfaré a tus justas quexas: y al dolor de mis sobradas penas. Y pues cierto puedes sperar de nada te desesperes.

¡O qué certenidad del amor que me havías me da tu muerte! Nin sé con qué te pague tan grande cargo. Salvo si cumplo en que muera dos vezes. Una en te ver morir: y otra en matar a mí misma. Y si más te devo: ninguno puede pagar lo que no tiene. Que como te dixe poca cosa es según nuestro querer soffrir una muerte: aunque la

Mirabella

How can I possibly live without you, my beloved Grisel? When you put an end to your suffering you gave a beginning to mine. Alas, woe is me! Ladies, you force me to live! If only you felt my torment you would have seen that death is good for me.

For it is better to make quick work of suffering than to extend it with sadness and fear. You are not merciful to me; no, you are cruelly hostile. It would be so much better to do away with all my suffering with one slight punishment! Yet you increase my suffering, you want me to live a living death. Still, the end that you steal from me now, will soon be inescapable. My sufferings were already ended and you now seek to prolong them. Well, do not believe that love has so little might that such great faithfulness can be broken. So, my beloved Grisel, do not think that I will not follow you, but wait for me, so you may show me death's narrow paths, and I will not have difficulty finding you among the many dead.

Oh Grisel! Is it true that you no longer live? I see you dead before my eyes and can scarce believe it. Rather, since dreams often trick me, I wish that this were one of those dreams I dreamt. Would that I might take some hope from a false image of you as you were when alive. Yet, what good would it do? For, if uncertain sorrow is taken to be true, real sorrow is all the more so.

Alas, I am in torment, the desire to see you pains me so! What has become of you, so far from me, without hope of ever seeing you? How will she who could not live a single hour without you when you lived and were happy bear this pain?[46] Think not, Grisel, that you, relieved of suffering, leave me to a life of suffering, for the promises made between us require me to follow you as far as I can. Surely you will pardon my delay, for now I can do no more, but I will satisfy your just complaint and also satisfy the pain of my immense suffering. Now you may await me with certainty, do not despair.

Oh, your death was the surest proof of your love for me! I know not how I can repay such a great deed, except by dying twice: once, by seeing you die, and once again, by killing myself. Though I owe you more, one cannot pay what one does not have. For, as I have said to you, suffering one death is a little thing in light of our love, for my heart desires

voluntad querría padeçer muchas. Por ende non podría loar el perder una vida: que muchas ternía en poco perderlas por ti.

El Auctor

Estando así Mirabella en pena no conocida fue llevada al palacio de la Reina su madre donde muy consolada la presumía hazer. Pero ella jamás quizo cosa ninguna salvo continuar sus querellas. Y una noche la postremera de sus días non podiendo el amor y muerte de Grisel soffrir: por dar fin a sus congoxas: la dio a su vida. La qual speró tiempo que los que la guardavan dormiessen. Y como ella vio el tiempo dispuesto y en su libertad fuesse en camisa a una ventana que mirava sobre un corral donde el Rey tenía unos leones entre ellos se dexó caer. Los quales non usaron con ella de aquella obediencia: que a la sangre real devían: según en tal caso los suelen loar. Mas antes miraron a su fambre: que a la realeza de Mirabella. A quien ninguna mesura cataron. Y muy presto fue d'ellos spedaçada. Y de las delicadas carnes cada uno contentó al apetito.

Y después que recordaron los que a Mirabella guardavan y vieron que en la cama no stava: temieron aquello que después fallaron verdad. Y como la Reina y las damas vieron la beldad de aquella donzella crudamente feneçer de tan raviosa muerte: sin scrivir está bueno presumir el stremo y grandeza de sus llantos. Pero porque yo non podría tan dolorosas cosas como eran figurar: non quiero sino dexarlo a quien pensarlo podiere.

El auctor

Después de la muerte de Mirabella quedó la Reina tan enemistada con Torrellas: que por maneras secretas le buscava la muerte. Pero por temor que de allí el Rey non hoviesse enojo: cessava de hazer lo que la voluntad quería. Pero la Fortuna que sabe buscar a quien desama desaventura hizo: que Torrellas se enamorasse de Braçayda. El qual acatando sus muchas gracias fue preso de su amor. Y pensando remediar su pena: soffría por non le ozar pedir aquello que tan mal

to suffer many. A single death is not praiseworthy, when I would willingly lose many lives for you.

The Author

Rendered senseless by her sorrow, Mirabella was taken to her mother the Queen's palace, where the Queen hoped to comfort her, but Mirabella wanted nothing more than to continue her lament. Then one night, the last of her days, no longer able to endure her love and Grisel's death, in order to put an end to her anguish, Mirabella put an end to her life. She waited until her guards were asleep and, seeing her opportunity and herself free from vigilance, she went, dressed in a chemise, to a window that opened above a corral where the King kept his lions, and threw herself down among them. The lions did not show her the obedience due to royal blood, for which they are often praised. Rather, with greater observance of hunger than of Mirabella's royalty, showing her no restraint, they quickly dismembered her and each one sated his appetite with her delicate flesh.

When Mirabella's guards awoke and saw she was not in bed, they feared just what they soon found to be true. Now, when the Queen and her ladies saw how the damsel's beauty had been so cruelly extinguished by such a brutal death—well, it is better to imagine the extremity and magnitude of their weeping and leave it unwritten. For, since I cannot put all of their sorrows into words, I shall do nothing more than to give leave for those who can envision them to do so.

The Author

After Mirabella's death, the Queen became Torrellas's most bitter enemy. She sought out secret ways to have him killed, but fearing that his death would anger the King, she refrained from doing what she desired. Yet Fortune, who knows how to bring trouble to those she hates, made Torrellas fall in love with Braçayda. Beholding her many enchantments, Torrellas became a prisoner of love. He suffered at the thought of seeking remedy for his agony, because he did not dare to ask for what he so ill deserved.

merecido havía. Pero sforçándose en su mucho saber: presumía que éll desamando alcançaría mugeres: más que otro sirviendo. Y con esta loca confiança acordóle de scrivir manifestándole sus passiones en la manera que se sigue.

Carta de Torrellas a Braçayda[47]

¿Qué mayor prosperidad puede ninguna persona pedir que vengança de sus enemigos? La qual ya vos senyora tenéis: que mi desdicha y vuestra ventura han querido que mis yerros contra vos cometidos con dublada pena pague. Porque de vos y de vuestras gracias me veo tan sojuzgado: que ninguna parte de mí es mía. Mas ansí como del todo vos fui enemigo: del todo vos sea presionero. Y hombre tan malo contra mujeres: en razón cabe que con las malicias igualen las penas. Mas porque es mayor mi tormento qu'el agravio que de mí recebistes: este da lugar que me quexe: porque más de lo que devo me fagáis pagar. Ya querría otra vez ir a juizio. Porque si de drecho dies muertes os devo: dais mil. Y quando por sclavo me desecháis ¿quién me tomará libre? A lo menos sé que vos suelto o preso me avorrecéis. Mas yo no manifiesto mis males con sperança de remedio d'ellos: mas pensando en qué os servir en pago de lo errado: quize alegraros con mi tribulada vida. Pues mis tormentos os serán deportes. Y creyendo que ninguna otra nueva os sería más alegre que esta: como quien serviros dessea vos embío plazeres con la muerte de sus fatigas. Y mirad la voluntad de mi dessear serviros: que siempre los discretos deven encobrir sus desaventuras a sus enemigos.

Mas yo forçado de amor carezco de buen juizio. Y quiero mis males descobrir a quien me los codicia mayores. Y devía buscar piadad de alguna persona que de mí la huviesse: y pídola a quien mi muerte aun no lo haría contenta. Mas yo no vine a pedir merced pues no la merezco: mas a servir y morir por pagar la deuda que devo a serviros por vuestros grandes merecimientos. Y morir por las cosas passadas en que mostráis de mí ser desserida. Y ansí como contra mujeres pequé por ellas muera. Y principalmente por vos a quién he yo más errado mejor satisfaga. Pues vet de qué manera queréis la vengança de mí: que quántas penitencias quiziéredes darme serán mercedes mere-

But Torrellas was emboldened by his worldly wisdom; he presumptuously thought of how he could seduce more women by hating them than any other man could by offering love-service. And with this foolish confidence, he decided to write to Braçayda, expressing his passion in the following way:

Torrellas's Letter to Braçayda[47]

What greater prosperity can anyone desire than taking revenge upon his enemies? You already have it, my Lady, for my misery and your good fortune have so ordained that I be doubly punished for the offences I committed against you, because I am now so much under the power of your enchantments that nothing of me is mine. Rather, just as I was your absolute enemy, now I am your absolute prisoner. For it stands to reason that a man so evil to women should be punished in equal measure to his wickedness. Yet, I have a right to protest, because my torment is greater than the damage I did you, and you will make me pay more than I owe. How I should like to go back to our trial, for if by rights I owe you ten deaths, you condemn me to a thousand. And when you spurn me as a slave, who will take me as a free man? At the very least I know that, bound or free, you hate me. Yet I do not confess my afflictions in the hopes of remedying them, but rather in my desire to serve you in recompense for my errors; I hope to make you happy with my life of suffering, for my torments will be an amusement for you. And so, as one who wishes to serve, I send you pleasures with my pain, believing that nothing will please you more. Consider the nature of my desire to serve you: for discreet men should always hide their misfortune from enemies.

Nonetheless I, ravished by love, lack good judgment and wish to reveal my affliction to the very person who would have me suffer even more; I should seek mercy from someone who would be merciful to me, and I ask it of someone who would not be content even with my death. I did not come to you to ask for mercy, for I do not deserve it, but rather I came to serve and die in payment of the debt I owe: to serve you because of your great merit, to die for all that has happened to make you feel ill-served by me. And so, just as I sinned against women, I will die for them and mainly for you, against whom I have most sinned and hope to best satisfy. Decide, then, how you would like to take vengeance on me, for no

cidas. Mas lo que claro pareçe quiero que sepáis. Quando alguno en lugares de stado y excellentes personas presumen de amar como yo presumo: con mucho afán y servicios trabajan y nunqua alcançan. Y mueren sin gualardón sperar. Pues ¿cómo speraré yo: que en el contrario siempre he trabajado? Mas quien desdichado ha de ser ansí le está ordenando: que de quien haya de ser mucho suyo: enemigas obras le hagan ageno. Mas ansí convenía que fuesse: que por el mal conozca la virtud: pues con el bien la negava.

¡O maldicha seas Fortuna que ansí mi sentido privaste contra aquellas por quien todas las gentilezas y invenciones se hazen! Yo perverso malo invencionava malicias. ¡O maldita la hora en que tal pensé! Y el punto que por desemboltura tomé dezir mal de aquellas que los virtuosos en las loar se trabajan! ¿Quál locura me hizo a mí tan estremo enemigo de aquellas que todo savio amistad procura? Y quando alguno quiere contra las damas maldezir: con malicias del perverso Torrellas se favoreçe. Y aunque digan lo que yo por ventura no dixe: mi fama me haze digno que se atribuyan a mí todas palabras contra mujeres danyosas. Y esto porque de los yerros agenos y míos: haga agora penitencia. ¡Y en quánta fatiga soy triste venido: que allí do más servido havía de tener haya tanto enojado! Esto mis faltas lo mereçen. Que quanto más alexado de sperança me viere: más presto a la desesperada muerte me allegue. Y mi desventura es tan grande: que yo non le sé remedio. Ni sé con qué justa color piadad os pida. Salvo si vuestra nobleza quiere mirar que quando el errado por el perdón se publica: gentileza no quiere vengança del que se riende vencido. Y sola aquesta confiança que en vuestra virtud spero: me haze no buscar con mis manos aquella que es fin de todos los males. Mas quiero yo darme una poca sperança que usaréis conmigo como Dios con los peccadores. Y no tomo más largo término: de quanto vuestra temerosa respuesta me allegue. Y esto supplico sea con delliberado consejo scripta: porque con la enemistad que me havéis: llena de foriosa ira no venga. Pues mejor es de los enemigos recebir servicios: y viviendo darles continuada pena: que no dexarlos morir. Pues la muerte en los ánimos nobles es la menor parte de la vengança.

matter how much penance you may wish to give me, I will accept it as the favor I have earned. Yet I want you to know what seems to be clear: many men pursue love among high and noble personages, as I do now; they strive and serve with great effort yet without success, and die without any hope of reward. So what hope have I now, I who have always done the contrary? Yet he who must be doomed, such is his fate; those who should be loyal will be turned against him by his enemies. Yet this is fitting: for let him know women's virtue through hardship, since his good fortune obscured it in the past.

A curse upon you Fortune, for taking my sense from me and turning me against women, who inspire all courtliness and poetry! I, evil and perverse, composed wicked verses. Oh, cursed be the hour I thought of it, and cursed be moment of my brazenness, when I decided to slander those women whom virtuous men endeavor to praise! What folly made me the bitter enemy of those ladies whom every wise man befriends? And now, when any man desires to slander women, he quotes the evil words of perverse Torrellas, and even if by chance they say things that I did not, my reputation merits me the attribution of all words insulting to women. This is why I now must do penance for others' offenses as well as for my own. I have become anguished and unhappy for I have caused so much anger where I should have most served! Such are the wages of my errors. The further I am from hope, the faster does desperate death approach me. And my misfortune is so great that I know not how to remedy it, nor do I know how I can ask you for mercy, except that perhaps, in your nobility, you will consider that when a sinner begs for forgiveness, a gentle heart does not wish to be revenged upon a man who surrenders himself. Now, the sole confidence of my faith in your virtue keeps me from seeking to put an end to all my affliction with my own hands. Still yet, I wish to allow myself a little hope that you will treat me as God does sinners. So, I will conclude and await your feared response; I beg you to write it with careful consideration, and let it not come filled with furious ire caused by the enmity you have for me, for it is better to receive service from your enemies, and as you live, punish them continually, than to desire their death, for death in noble spirits is the lesser part of revenge.

El auctor

Braçayda como recibió la letra de Torrellas sin tardança la puso lugo en poder de la Reina. La qual como su desseo era buscarle la muerte: parecióle que por aquella causa lo podría más presto traer a lugar secreto: do sus sanyas huviessen entera vengança. Y rogó a Braçayda una graciosa letra le respondiesse. Concediéndole en ella más de lo que por éll le era demandado. Porque con el enganyo recebiesse d'ellas la muerte. Y lugo por Braçayda fue puesto en obra. Y en tal manera a Torrellas responde.

Respuesta de Braçayda a Torrellas

Si en todas las empresas que vos contra las damas tomáis ventura vos es favorable: ¿cómo os quitaréis la bienaventurança que Dios contra nosotras vos dio? Pues que todas con amor o temor os han de querer. Y puesto que non os amen: de fuerça o de grado les faréis amar. Lo qual veo claro pues que yo jamás a vos en ninguna cosa he enojado: y me fuestes tan impeçible guerrero: mayormente lo seríades si agora contradixiesse vuestro querer. Special pues conocéis tanto de los secretos nuestros. Que si yo hiziesse mucho del honesto: parecería que de enemistad más que de honestad procedía. Y por esto stoy en grande differencia que no sé qué hazer: porque si ya viniesse en el complimiento de vuestros desseos: tan presto daría lugar dixéssedes lo acostumbrado. Juzgando mi presta dissolución. Y de la otra parte si no lo hiziesse: sé que diríais que vuestras malicias y no mis desseos me quitan de ser vuestra.

Pues querría agora teneros conmigo: para ver en tal caso qué me consejaríades. Mas pensando en ello adevino lo que me diríades. Y sería esto que a los malos devemos mucho contentar: porque de sus lenguas no nos lastimen. Ansí yo he acordado de darme por vuestra. Por provar si con el bien venceré el mal. ¿Y qué mayor partido puede haver ninguna: salvo tener tregua con vos? Special la que tenga entera amistad presumirá tanto de grande senyora: que aína *creerá* con el sólo tener a vos mandar la mayor parte del mundo.[48] Y por cierto yo me creo si enteramente quiziéssedes ansí alguna loar: como todas

The Author

When Braçayda received the letter from Torrellas, she immediately turned it over to the Queen, who, desiring to bring about his death, thought she could use it to lure him to a secret chamber where her wrath might seek full vengeance. The Queen at once begged Braçayda to write a gracious response, in which she consented to even more than Torrellas had asked of her, so that by tricking him he would die at their hands. And Braçayda set immediately to work, responding to Torrellas in the following way:

Braçayda's Reply to Torrellas

If Fortune smiles upon you in all of your doings with women, why do you deny the good blessings that God has given you with them? For all women must desire you, either out of fear or love. And, when some do not love you, you either take them by force or seduce them. Thus it seems clear to me that since I never displeased you in any way, and you were a ferocious warrior against me, now you will be even fiercer if I refuse your desire. Indeed, since you know so much about women's secrets, if I were to make much of my chastity it would seem that I acted more from enmity than from virtue. Therefore, I am in great doubt and know not what to do, because were I to give in to your desires without delay, you should have reason to repeat your accustomed slander and think me dissolute. On the other hand, if I were to refuse you, I know you would say that your wickedness, and not my desires, keeps me from being yours.

How I should like to have you now with me, to see how you might counsel me in this situation! Yet when I think upon it, I can foretell what you would say to me. You would say that we must well please evil people so that they will speak no evil of us. So, I have decided to give myself to you. We shall see if I can conquer evil with goodness. And what better terms can any woman be on with you than to declare a truce? Indeed, the woman who has your full friendship will think herself to be such a great lady that she will soon believe that—just by having you—she commands the greater part of the world.[48] Surely, I believe that if you wanted to praise a woman in this way, after having insulted all women, you would

havéis menguado: que la que tal dicha hoviesse con vos: digna de noble fama la haríades. Y como tenéis tan buena gracia affeando: mejor
la terníades loando. Si alguna bienaventurada en su favor os fallasse.
Y tanto desseo yo ser aquella: que no sé qué me pidáis que no lo atorgasse. Siquiera por veros contradezir las cosas ya dichas. Por ver si en
vuestra boca podría caber loor de muger alguna.

Por cierto no hay ninguna cosa tan grave de fazer: que a mí no
fuesse ligera. Si con ella podiesse fazeros amigo nuestro. Entendiendo
qu'el mayor servicio que a las damas podría hazer: es fazeros de nuestra
valía. Porque siendo de nuestra parte: no recebiríamos aquellas menguas y offiensas que quien quiere presume ya de hazernos. En special
después que yo contra vos pensé a ponerme allende de las injurias que
ante recebíamos: después de condemnadas quien no sabe hablar busca
lengua prestada para maldezir de nosotras. Y por esto desseo pues
que por mí las damas hovieron tan grande culpa: que por mi causa
ganando a vos sean exalçadas. Pues bien sé que en vuestra mano está
el favor y vituperio. Y loarme han los que lo supiren: tanto de avisada:
como me culparan de poco honesta.

Ansí que muchas causas me mueven a fazerme vuestra. En lo
qual non entiendo caber en mengua nin yerro que a las mugeres con-
demna. ¿Antes sería mayor si diesse lugar a que vuestras injurias me
offendiessen? ¿Y infamada sin obrar el plazer que amor da a los suyos:
o loada con deleite? Mejor es loada con plazeres: que honestad con
vituperio. Yo entiendo que no es más la virtud en la muger de quanto
vuestras palabras quieren. ¡Cómo sería locura de quien procurasse la
guerra contra tan grande guerrero!

Ansí que senyor mío toda paz quiero con vos. Y si vuestra
condición no quiere conmigo amistad: pues que vos la pedís: a lo
menos seguro quierro me deis la fe si bueno contra mugeres no
podéis ser: en no les ser danyoso habremos por partido. Aunque
según lo que por vuestra letra dezís: ya me parece que os conocéis
en la culpa. Y os arrepentís de lo errado. Y non era menester conmigo tan grande temor: Pues en vuestra mano está el bien o el mal
que en las damas consiste.

¿Cómo a mí pedís que vuestra vida scape? Bien sé que conocéis que al mando vuestro ha de obedeçer quienquiera. Y por esto no
conviene sino que os sirváis de quien os agrade. Pues que tan per-

make the one who had such good fortune with you worthy of noble fame. Now, since you are so eloquent in vilifying, you must be even more so when you praise, if ever a woman were to find favor with you. And I desire so much to be that woman, that I know of nothing you could ask of me that I should deny you, if only for the sake of seeing you refute the slander you have said before, for the sake of seeing if praise for any woman could possibly fit in your mouth.

Indeed, there is no great deed that I should not do willingly if I could make you a friend to women; I know that the greatest service I could do for women is to make you our ally, because, with you supporting us, we would not receive all those insults and attacks that now everyone takes the liberty of making against us. For in truth, ever since I challenged you, we are insulted far more than before. Since women were condemned in the trial, even those men who know not how to speak find borrowed words to slander us. And so, I desire that the ladies who because of me were found guilty of great crimes will now be praised because of my having won you over—for I know well that praise and blame are in your hands—and those who learn of our love will praise me for my cleverness as much as they will fault me for my loss of honor.

Thus, I am moved by many reasons to make myself yours. I do not see my actions as sinful or cause to condemn women. Would it be worse if I allowed your slander to offend me and if I were defamed without feeling the pleasure that Love gives to his followers, or if I were praised while feeling delight? It is better to be praised and feel pleasure, than remain chaste and be maligned. I understand that women's virtue is nothing more than what your words make of it. What folly it would be for anyone to try to declare war against such a great warrior!

Therefore, my lord, I want only peace with you. And although your condition does not allow friendship with me, since you have begged it of me, at the very least I want you to give me your promise that if you cannot be good to women, let us agree that you will not be harmful to them, even though according to what you say in your letter, it seems to me that you recognize your own guilt and feel remorse for your sins. You had no need to fear me, for ladies' honor rests in your hands.

How is it that you ask me to save your life? I know well that you realize that every woman must obey your commands. Thus, it is fitting that you be served by whomever pleases you, since virtue is now so ruined

dida va ya la virtud porque por fuerça y non por amor se sojuzgan. Esto non porque yo forçada venga a ello: mas tampoco non movida de affección de vuestros servicios. Mas *espero* en lo que cada día acaece: que las voluntades más enemigas viniendo a la amistad:[49] con mayor fe se conservan. Y ansí puede acaeçer que vos por satisfacer lo errado: trabajaréis doblado en plazerme. O a lo menos de enemigo tan grande: hazer un amigo pequenyo entiendo qué es ganarlo. Y quiero sobre todos los hombres daros en pago de quantas injurias ya dixestes: lo que alguno verdaderamente amando y mucho sirviendo de mí no pudo haver que vos mal obrando y peor sirviendo lo alcanséis.

Pues que queréis quiero lo que fuerça vençe. Y como publicáis los yerros que no pensamos: quiçá loaréis este que cometemos. Y más quiero tomar a ventura en amaros: que tener tan conocido enemigo en avorreceros.

El Auctor

Venida a poder de Torrellas la respuesta de Braçayda: tan alegre y sobervioso se hizo: que ninguno tan prosperado creía oviesse. Y mirad que tan malicioso era: que non pudo su mal secreto guardar que aquella letra con otros galanes no conmunicasse. Loando a sí y menguando aquella: que más cara de lo que éll pensava era de haver.

Pero el malaventurado non pudo conoçer aquell enganyo de la muerte: que en la presta piedad de Braçayda se scondía. Y éll juzgándola por ligera de vençer: fue éll más ligero simple y neciamente vencido. El qual con solicitud procuró de verse con Braçayda. Pensando cómo más presto sus desseos huviessen fin. Y el triste procurava la cruel muerte que scondida le stava.

Y después que muy oculto por terçera persona concertó de verse con ella en lugar secreto: la postremera noche de su vida ya llegada: se fue a los palacios de la Reina. Y entró en la cámara de Braçayda a do aposentada stava: la qual con una falsa riza en las partes de fuera se mostró alegre por más aplazer a Torrellas. Y éll non conociendo el oculto enganyo: con una graciosa desenboltura: muestra senyales de vertadero amor: y tales palabras comienza.

that women are overcome by force and not by love. This does not mean that I am taken by force; nor am I moved by affection in return for your love-service. Rather, I hope that as each day passes,[49] as hearts that were bitter enemies come to friendship, and thrive on greater faithfulness, so it will be possible that you, in order to make amends for your sins, will labor doubly to please me, or at least turn a great enemy into a slight friend—I understand this is a great gain. Indeed, I want to give you—above all other men—in recompense for all the insults you have uttered, what any other man, though he loved and served me truly, should never have; you who have fought against me and served me even worse will be favored.

Since you so desire, I too desire what is won by force. And since you accuse women of offenses that we do not even imagine, perhaps you will praise this one that we do commit. For I desire to risk more by loving you more than I desire to have you as an outright enemy by hating you.

The Author

When Braçayda's reply came into Torrellas's hands, he became so joyful and swollen with pride that he believed no man had ever been so favored. Now, see how wicked he was: he could not keep his evil secret, nor could he resist sharing the letter with the other men, praising himself and insulting her—she who was to cost him more dearly than he had thought.

But the wretched man had no way of knowing the fatal trick that hid within Braçayda's ready mercy, and he, thinking her easily seduced, was all the more easily, simple-mindedly, and stupidly overpowered. He eagerly sought to see Braçayda, thinking about how soon his desires were to be fulfilled, and so, soon brought about the cruel death that awaited him.

When Torrellas had stealthily, with the help of a third party, arranged to meet Braçayda in a secret chamber, the last night of his life had arrived. Torrellas went to the Queen's palace and entered Braçayda's room, where she was waiting with a false smile and joyful demeanor, the better to please him. He, knowing nothing of the hidden trick, acted with the graceful manners of a true lover, and began to speak in the following way:

Torrellas a Braçayda

Tanto creçe la alegría de mi bienaventurança: que desseo la muerte con temor que non venga tiempo que me quite aqueste plazer que posseo. ¡O quán bueno sería morir ante que Fortuna movible me derribasse de tan alta silla! Y dexando de encareçer mi victoria: a vos que tanto conocéis la stimación d'ella esto quiero de mí sepáis: que si no dixérades como me scrivistes que por fuerça veníades a mi querer: non fuera yo tan poderoso que con tan sobrado deleyte bevir podiesse. Que no podría soffrir tan alta gloria. Pues que non menos amata el demasiado plazer: que la incomportable pena en las voluntades tristes. Mas si yo puedo sostener la vida: que con la fuerça de tan grande gozo no muera: es porque scrivistes más por fuerça que por voluntad complíades mis desseos. Y en esto me fuestes algún tanto piadosa: por non me dar juntamente gloria que sofrir non podía. Pero con todo de aquí adelante ya seré usado de bevir alegre. Y querría por amor más que por fuerça recibáis servicios. Porque en tal caso por fuerça havidas merçedes dan pena a quien las faze: y ningún plazer a quien las recibe. Porque en los casos de amor non hay otro deleite: si non querer y ser querido. Y todo virtuoso deve procurar el deleite de su amiga más que de sí mismo. Y por esto yo non quiero de vos senyora merçedes: si la secreta voluntad non consiente en ellas. Que yo por amado procuro serviros. Que amar a vos sin vos ser en cargo: por mí me lo tenía. Y non quiero por fuerça aquello que sin amor non da gloria.

Respuesta de Braçayda a Torrellas

Muy complidas queréis Torrellas que se hagan todas vuestras cosas. Pues non creáis tan presto haver aquello sin trabajos: que otros affanando y moriendo haver non pueden. Ni queráis a vos hazer tan digno: que hayáis injuriándome lo que otros non han sirviendo. Non quiera vuestra soberbia forcejar amor. El qual más por servicios que por injurias se vençe. Y vuestro malvado propósito contra las mugeres non se contenta de haver nuestras honras en grande baxeza traído: sinon que presumáis por temor de vuestras malicias me vencéis.

Torrellas to Braçayda

My joy at my good fortune is so great that I should be happy to die now, for I fear the time will come when this pleasure I feel will desert me. Oh, how good it would be to die before changeable Fortune throws me down from this high throne! I will leave off extolling my victory to you, for you know its worth, but I want you to know this about me: if you had not said, when you wrote to me, that you were forced to love me, I should not have had the strength to live with such overwhelming joy, nor could I endure such high glory, for too much pleasure is no less fatal than unbearable pain is to melancholy hearts. Yet if I can keep myself alive and not die by the force of such great bliss, it is because you wrote that, unwilling, you feel forced to give in to my desires. Indeed, in this you were somewhat merciful to me, by not giving me all at once the glory that I could not endure. But for all this, from now on I will dare to live joyfully, and I want you to receive my service more from love than by force, because forced favors give pain to the giver and no pleasure to the receiver. In affairs of love there is no other delight than that of loving and being loved, and every virtuous man should seek to delight his beloved more than himself. For this reason, I want no favors from you, my lady, if your innermost will does not consent to them, and I, as a lover, will strive to serve you, to love you, without you owing me any debt. As for myself, I am indebted, and I do not desire to have by force that which gives no glory, if it is without love.

Braçayda's Response to Torrellas

You wish all your desires be carried out to the fullest, Torrellas. Now, do not believe that you, without travail, will receive so quickly all that others, by striving and dying, could not have. Nor should you consider yourself so worthy that you will earn, by insulting me, what others do not earn even by serving me. Do not let your pride force love, which is more easily won by service than by insults. Are you not content that your evil designs upon women have laid our honor to waste? Now you presume to conquer me because of my fear of your evil tricks?

Aquí podríades bien dezir como ya dixestes. Quando a los enemigos que havemos de dar pena damos gloria: a los amigos al respecto ¿qué les daremos? Pero set cierto que tal malicia en tal caso non haya lugar. Mas abréis segund vuestras obras la pena: y quitaos de amores y proveítvos de contricción verdadera y paciencia para la muerte. La qual de aquellas a quien offendistes cruelmente abréis de soffrir. Y aunque femeniles sean sus fuerças: ninguno las offendió: que sin offienza quedasse. Y porque la muerte vuestra ponga a los tales castigo: la havemos buscado tan cruel: aqueyo en pensar vuestros tormentos me spanto.

El Auctor

Estando Braçayda en tal razonamiento: vino la Reina con todas sus damas que en asechança estavan de Torrellas. Y aquell después de arrebatado atáronlo de pies y de manos: que ninguna defiença de valer se tovo. Y fue luego despojado de sus vestidos y atapáronle la boca porque quexar non se pudisse: y desnudo fue a un pilar bien atado. Y allí cada una traía nueva invención para le dar tormentos. Y tales hovo que con tenazas ardiendo: y otras con unyas y dientes raviosamente le despedeçaron. Estando assí medio muerto por creçer más pena en su pena non le quisieron de una vez matarle porque las crudas y fieras llagas se le refriassen: y otras de nuevo viniessen y depués que fueron ansí cansandas de tormentarle: de grande reposo la Reina y sus damas a çenar se fueron allí çerca d'éll porque las viesse: y allí praticando las maldades d'éll. Y trayendo a la memoria sus maliciosas obras: cada una dezía a la Reina que no les parecía que quantas muertes ad aquell mal hombre se pudiessen dar porque passasse largos anyos: non cumpliría aunque cada noche de aquellas penitencias oviesse. Y otras dezían mil maneras de tormentos cada qual como le agradava.

Y tales cosas passavan entre ellas que por cierto yo stimo que ellas davan al cuitado de Torrellas mayor pena que la muerte misma. Y ansí vino a soffrir tanta pena de las palabras: como de las obras. Y después que fueron alçadas todas las mesas fueron juntas a dar amarga cena a Torrellas. Y tanto fue de todas servido con potages y aves y maestresala:[50] que non sé cómo scrivir las diferencias de las injurias

Now you may well ask, as you did before, if we give glory to our enemies, whom we should punish, what then will we give our friends? But rest assured, your tricks will not work now. Rather, you will get the punishment that your deeds deserve; forget about love and arm yourself with true contrition and acceptance of death, which you will suffer at the hands of those women whom you so cruelly harmed. For even though our force be feminine, no one who offends women escapes injury. Now, so that your fate will be a lesson to all those who have harmed women, we have planned such a cruel death for you that the very thought of your torment strikes fear in me.

The Author

While Braçayda was thus speaking, the Queen and all of her ladies, who were lying in wait for Torrellas, came in. And seizing him, they tied his feet and his hands so he had no way of defending himself. Then they stripped him of his clothing and gagged him so he could not cry out. Naked, he was tied fast to a pillar and each lady invented a new form of torture for him: there were some who ferociously tore at him with hot iron pincers, while others furiously tore at him with their nails and teeth. When he was half-dead, in order to make his pain all the more painful, they decided not to kill him right away. And, rather than allow his harsh and brutal wounds to cool, more ladies came at him with new forms of torture. Now, when they grew tired of torturing Torrellas, the Queen and her ladies rested themselves and retired to dine near him so that he might watch. There, the ladies reviewed all of Torrellas's wickedness and recalled his sinful deeds, each lady saying to the Queen that however many deaths they might inflict upon the evil man, not even long years of such suffering penance would be sufficient, while still others discussed a thousand ways of torturing him, each one to her own taste.

The ladies spoke in such a way that I truly believe they inflicted a greater pain upon the miserable Torrellas than death itself; indeed, he was tortured as much by their words as by their deeds. When the tables had all been cleared away, the ladies went together to give Torrellas a bitter supper: he was so well served pottages, poultry, and "taster,"[50] by them all, that I know not how to describe the many varied insults and

y offienças que le hazían. Y esto duró hasta que el día esclareció. Y después que no dexaron ninguna carne en los huessos: fueron quemados. Y de su seniza guardando cada qual una buxeta por reliquias de su enemigo. Y algunas hovo que por cultre en el cuello la traían.[51] Porque trayendo más a memoria su vengança mayor plazer hoviessen.

Ansí que la grande malicia de Torrellas dio a las damas victoria: y a éll pago de su merecido.

Acaba el tractado compuesto por Johan de Flores. Donde se contiene el triste fin de los amores de Grisel y Mirabella. La qual fue a muerte condemnada: por justa sentencia disputada entre Torrellas y Braçayda: sobre quien da mayor ocasión de los amores: los hombres a las mujeres: o las mujeres a los hombres. Y fue determinado que las mujeres son mayor causa. Donde se siguió: que con su indignación y malicia por sus manos dieron cruel muerte al triste de Torrellas.

Deo Gratias.

injuries they heaped upon him, all through the night and until dawn. At last, when the ladies had left no flesh on his bones, the remains were burned and each lady kept some of the ashes, putting them in little boxes as relics of their enemy. Some of the ladies wore the relics in amulets about their necks in order to take greater pleasure in the memory of their revenge.[51]

Thus, Torrellas's great malice gave victory to the ladies, while he got what he deserved.

So ends the romance composed by Juan de Flores, which tells the sad story of the lovers Grisel and Mirabella: she was condemned to death by a just sentencing, in a case concerning who is more blameworthy in love—whether men make women love, or women men—argued by Torrellas and Braçayda. It was decided that women are the guilty party, and consequently out of their indignation and wickedness, women cruelly murdered Torrellas with their own hands.

Deo Gratias.

Notes

1. Although the lady to whom this epistle is addressed is unnamed, Flores's reference to working as a scribe for her may indicate that the dedicatee was none other than Isabel I, whom Flores served as official chronicler. In medieval Castilian, *tratado* referred to any piece of fiction writing. In the title here, I follow Keith Whinnom's translation of *tratado* as "romance" in his translation of *Cárcel de amor* (1492). However, it is worthy of note that the Spanish sentimental romances, as fictionalized intellectual inquiries, are related to the Latin genre of the *tractatus*, as both Edward Dudley and Armando Durán observe. Edward Dudley, "The Inquisition of Love: *Tratado* as a Fictional Genre," *Mediaevalia* 5 (1979), 233–43; Armando Durán, *Estructura y técnicas de la novela sentimental y caballeresca* (Madrid: Gredos, 1973).

2. This short dedicatory epistle was one of the most challenging parts of the romance to translate. All of the extant versions of the Spanish original contain multiple ambiguities. In the 1495 and successive printed editions, the first sentence of Flores's dedication is confusing to the point of illegibility: "Como en fin de mis pensanmientos concluir en que mejor serviros pueda mi voluntad busqué en que trabaje con desseo de más fazerme vuestro."

3. *Grisel y Mirabella* 1495: "por la comunicación de vuestra casa" [written on behalf of your family]. All successive editions read "por la comunicación de vuestra causa" [written for your cause]. In either case, if Isabel I was indeed the unnamed dedicatee, the phrase may be understood in the context of Flores's composition of the *Crónica incompleta de los Reyes Católicos*, which championed Isabel's claim to the throne of Castile.

4. Joseph J. Gwara offers an alternate reading of this ambiguous sentence, suggesting, in light of his detailed study of variants and errors in the textual transmission of the romance in both manuscript and print sources and Flores's style, that Flores means to say that "me he trabajado por haver una parte de las sobras de vuestra discreción para me aprovechar esta necesidad dellas," which might be translated into English in the following way: "I, in need of it, have endeavored to make use of the surplus of your intelligence." As Gwara points out, this interpretation is in keeping with the author's *captatio benevolentiae*. "Eleven Emendations to the Text of *Grisel y Mirabella*" in *Homenaje a E. Michael Gerli*, ed. José Manuel Hidalgo (Newark, DE: Juan de la Cuesta, 2011), 203.

5. The name *Mirabella* is clearly emblematic, combining the Spanish verb *mirar* [to look] or noun *mira* (sight), and adjective *bella* (beautiful).

6. The insertion of maxims is characteristic of Flores's style. Here Flores casts the saying ironically, since the King's preventative measures are no match for the power of love.

7. *Grisel y Mirabella* 1495 and successive printed editions identify both knights in these sections as "el otro caballero" [the other knight]. Here, for the sake of clarity, I follow the nam-

ing of the two knights in the manuscript versions. The similarity between the names Grisel and Grisamon reflects not only their intimacy and likeness, but also the fact that later in the romance Grisel will be made to stand for all men.

8. Here Grisel refers to the total servitude of a courtly lover.

9. In one of his more felicitous passages, the sixteenth-century English translator chose to render this passage: "Wherefore your love shall be discovered to be false, and your strengths (that were never strong) but of feebleness full." Although the translator was working from the Italian rather than the original Spanish version of the romance, he may have had access to a copy of the Spanish and have also sought to reproduce Flores's alliteration.

10. Grisel's reference to "passions" and "dying for love," dually expressions of religious feeling and erotic love, are commonplaces in fifteenth-century *cancionero* poetry and romances. Grisel is all too ready to be a martyr in the "religion of love." Flores's romance highlights and concretizes the metaphors of courtly love.

11. *Grisel y Mirabella* 1495: "la más plaziente que peligrosa batalla." Although the 1495 edition describes the battle of love as "more pleasing than perilous," most later editions say that it is a "no más plaziente que peligrosa batalla" [no less pleasing than perilous battle]. I find the later emendation more in keeping with the romance as a whole, since love is indeed dangerous for Flores's protagonists. The manuscript versions of *Grisel y Mirabella* do not contain either sentence.

12. *Maestresala*: see Volume Editor's Introduction, p. 35.

13. The extant manuscript versions report that Grisel and Mirabella are together in a chamber, a *camera*, rather than in a bed, a *cama*, as in the printed edition of 1495. Such a change could be inadvertent, or intended to heighten the drama and implicit sexuality of the scene.

14. The texts in the extant manuscripts make clear that both protagonists plan to claim responsibility: "cada un o por sí pensó de hazer la culpa suya, porque el muriese y salvase al otro," [each one thought to lay all blame on themselves, so that he or she might by dying save the other]. *Grisel y Mirabella*, ed. Ciccarello di Blasi, 225.

15. Ironically, Mirabella must take recourse to misogynist commonplaces about women in her attempt to save Grisel's life.

16. *Grisel y Mirabella* 1495: "pero aunque [el rey vuestro padre] del crimen quisiere enpeeçeros" [even if the king your father wanted to punish you for the crime], which does not make sense in the context of Grisel's speech. Some later editions emended the sentence to read "pero aunque del crimen quisiere empeçerme" [even if the king your father wanted to punish me for the crime]. The reading of the sentence in the manuscript version is given

above: "pero aunque del crimen *non* quisiere empeçceros" [even if the king your father *did not* want to punish you for the crime] (emphasis mine). *Grisel y Mirabella*, ed. Ciccarello di Blasi, 232 and 377.

17. Flores's term *desemboltura* is ambiguous. In the fifteenth and sixteenth centuries, *desemboltura* could refer to positive, courtly social graces, to ease and graceful behavior. However, it could also connote lewdness, or "loose" and "easy" sexual behavior.

18. Here Flores has Torrellas echo stanza II of the *Slander*.

19. Torrellas refers to the custom of knights who attended tournaments wearing a ribbon, sleeve, or other token from a lady as a sign of their love-service to the lady.

20. Here Flores seems to be alluding to sign language used by nuns who take vows of silence.

21. *Grisel y Mirabella* 1495: "non poder vos fallar" [not able to find yourselves].

22. *Grisel y Mirabella* 1495: "dar juicio al mal non amando" [decide evil without loving]

23. Flores' *Triunfo de Amor* envisions a world where women court men and Torrellas's hypothesis about women's ability and zeal in courting is proven to be true. See also Editor's Introduction, 40.

24. *Grisel y Mirabella* 1495: omits "estando enfrenadas" [held back by the bridle of shame].

25. *Grisel y Mirabella* 1495: "non lo avemos por tanto" [we do not give it much consideration].

26. *Grisel y Mirabella* 1495: "amando nos requestaís" [in love, you pursue us].

27. *Grisel y Mirabella* 1495: omits the word *partes*.

28. *Grisel y Mirabella* 1495: "desdenyadas" [disdained].

29. See Editor's Introduction, 39–40.

30. Here, once again, Flores draws the audience's attention to the metaphors of the language of courtly love.

31. *Grisel y Mirabella* 1495: "de medio" [middle].

32. *Grisel y Mirabella* 1495: "exem de pueblos." The omission occurs at a page turn and consequently is probably due to a typesetting error.

33. Flores has Torrellas refer directly to stanza VII in the *Slander*.

34. *Grisel y Mirabella* 1495: "differencia" [difference].

35. Here Flores has Torrellas play upon the saying "una golondrina no hace el verano" [One swallow does not a summer make].

36. *Grisel y Mirabella* 1495: "es possible" [it is possible].

37. This is another direct reference to the *Slander*, stanza III.

38. It is possible that Flores here plays upon the *double entendre* "secreto" [secret] in the same way that Torrellas does in stanza VI of his *Slander*.

39. This is another of Flores's many proverbial references. The Spanish proverb "el loco por la pena es cuerdo" can be translated as "punishment makes a madman wise."

40. *Grisel y Mirabella* 1495: "a mujeres" [to women].

41. Here Flores quotes Ecclesiasticus 16:22.

42. Two of the three manuscripts of *Grisel y Mirabella* specify that Mirabella was stripped of her rich gowns and left in nothing but a shift. *Grisel y Mirabella*, ed. Ciccarello di Blasi, 308.

43. Not only does Mirabella's assertion contain one of Flores's many plays on the opposition between *fuerza* and *flaqueza*; here Flores also plays upon the association of women with frailty and men with forcefulness.

44. *Grisel y Mirabella* 1495: omits the "no" in this sentence.

45. *Grisel y Mirabella* 1495: "mi ventura non salvo que den muerte a quien la mereçe" [my fate {decrees} nothing other than that they give death to one who deserves it].

46. *Grisel y Mirabella* 1495: omits the "no" in this sentence.

47. In his attempt to seduce Braçayda Torrellas speaks of his erotic "death" and "torture." Braçayda's ironic responses are the culmination of Flores's concretization of the language of courtly love.

48. *Grisel y Mirabella* 1495: "querrá" [will want].

49. *Grisel y Mirabella* 1495: "empero" [although].

50. To my knowledge, there is no dish dating from the period called *maestresala*. Flores may have listed *aves*, *potages*, and *maestresala* as an ironic reference to Torrellas's being treated to a multi-course banquet, complete with the ministrations of a master of ceremonies. In any case, the use of the term maestresala here may be Flores's joke, since the historical Torrellas served in a similar position as a "master of the knife" in the Aragonese court. The plot of the story itself provides an additional irony, as Grisel and Mirabella are exposed by the King's *maestresala*. A further implication in the final scene is that the Queen and her ladies eat the poet. See Volume editor's Introduction, 42.

51. In translating the Spanish *cultre* as *amulet*, I follow Joseph J. Gwara. "A Possible Hebraism in *Grisel y Mirabella* and its implications: Old Spanish *Cultre*," *Journal of the Early Book Society* 15 (2012): 1–40.

Bibliography

Spanish Manuscripts of Grisel and Mirabella

Nouela de Grisel y Mirabella. MS 940. Biblioteca Trivulziana, Milan, Italy. fols. 1r–76v.

Fragmento de Torrellas. MS 5-3-20. Biblioteca Colombina, Seville, Spain. fols. 69r–86r.

Grisel y Mirabella. [Frag.] MS lat. 6966. Biblioteca Apostolica Vaticana, Rome, Italy. fols. 68r–76v.

Early Printed Spanish Editions of Grisel and Mirabella

Grisel y Mirabella. [Lérida?]: Henrique Botel, [c. 1495].

La hystoria de Grisel y Mirabella, con la disputa de Torrellas y Braçaida. Seville: Juan Varela de Salamanca, 1514.

La historia de Grisel y Mirabella, con la disputa de Torrellas y Braçayda. Seville: Jacobo Cromberger, 1524.

La historia de Grisel y Mirabella, con la disputa de Torrellas & Braçayda. Toledo: Miguel de Esguía, 1526.

La historia de Grisel y Mirabella, con la disputa de Torrellas y Braçayda. Seville: Juan Cromberger, 1529.

La historia de Grisel & Mirabella, con la disputa de Torellas y Braçayda. Seville: Juan Cromberger, 1533.

La historia de Grisel y Mirabella, con la disputa de Torrellas y Braçayda. Cuenca: Juan de Canova, 1561.

La historia de Grisel y Mirabella con la disputa de Torrellas y Braçayda. Burgos: Philippe de Junta, 1562.

Fifteenth-, Sixteenth-, and Seventeenth-Century Translations and Adaptations of Grisel and Mirabella

ITALIAN

Historia de Isabella e Aurelio composta da Giouanni de Fiori alla sua signora in castigliano tradutta in lingua volgare Italica per Meser

Lelio Aletiphilo: e da lui dedicata al molto uertuoso L. Scipione Atellano. Milan: Giannotto da Castiglione, 1521.

FRENCH

Le iugement damour, auquel est racomptee Lhystoire de Ysabel, fille du roy Descosse, translatee de langaige Espaignol en langue Francoyse. Paris: Anthoine Bonnemere, [c.1520].

FRENCH AND ITALIAN

Historia de Avrelio e Isabella del Re di Scotia. Histoire d'Aurelio et Isabel, fille du Roy d'Escoce. Plus la Deiphire de M. Leon Baptiste Alberti, qui enseigne d'eviter l'amour mal commence. Paris: Gilles Corrozet, 1546.

FRENCH AND SPANISH

L'Histoire d'Aurelio et Isabelle, fille du Roy d'Escoce, mieux corrigée que parcy deuant, mise en Espagnole et François. Historia de Aurelio y Isabela hija del Rey de Escoia major corregida que antes, puesta en Español y Francés, para los que quisieren deprender una lengua de otra. Antwerp: Jehan Withaye, 1556.

FRENCH, ITALIAN, SPANISH, AND ENGLISH

Histoire de Aurelio et Isabelle, fille du Roy d'Escoce, nouvellement traduict en quatre langues, italien, español, françois & anglois. Antwerp, Juan Steelsio, 1556.

POLISH

Historja o Equanusie krolu skockim: nieznana powiesc Bartosza Paprockiego. Trans. Bartlomiej Paprocki. Cracow: Stanislawa Szarffenberg, 1578.

FRENCH, ITALIAN, AND ENGLISH

Histoire de Aurelio et Isabelle. The historie of Aurelio and of Isabell. London: Edward White, 1586.

GERMAN
Historia Von Aurelio vnd Isabella deß Königs in Schottland Tochter: Jn welcher ob der Mann dem Weib oder das Weib dem Mann grössere Vrsach zu sündigen geben geredt vnd außgeführet wird. Trans. Christian Pharemund. Nurenberg: Endter, 1630.

English Adaptations of Grisel and Mirabella

Green, Robert. *A paire of turtle doues, or, The tragicall history of Bellora and Fidelio. Seconded with the tragicall end of Agamio, wherein (besides other matters pleasing to the reader) by way of dispute betweene a knight and a lady, is described this neuer before debated question to wit: whether man to woman, or woman to man offer the greater temptations and allurements vnto vnbridled lust.* London: W. Jaggard for Francis Burton, 1606.

Swetnam, the woman-hater arraigned by women: a new comedie, acted at the Red Bull, by the late Queenes Servants. London: Richard Meighen, 1620.

Modern Editions and Facsimiles of Grisel and Mirabella

Grisel y Mirabella. Edizione critica, introduzione e note. Ed. Maria Grazia Ciccarello Di Blasi. Rome: Bagatto, 2003.

Tarp, Helen Cathleen. "*Aurelio et Isabelle*: An Edition and Study of the 1556 Antwerp Spanish and English Translations of Juan de Flores's *Grisel y Mirabella*. Ph.D. diss., University of New Mexico, 1999.

La Historia de Grisel y Mirabella. In vol. 2, Gwara, Joseph J., "A Study of the Works of Juan de Flores, with a critical edition of *La Historia de Grisel y Mirabella*," 503–708. Ph.D. diss., Westfield College, University of London. 1988.

La historia de Grisel y Mirabella. Edited by Pablo Alcázar López and José A. González Núñez. Facsimile. Originally published: Seville: J. Cromberger, 1529. Granada: Editorial Don Quijote, 1983.

Grisel y Mirabella: Sale nuevamente a la luz reproducido en facsímil por acuerdo de La Real Academia Española. Facsimile. Originally

published, [Lérida?]: 1495. Madrid: Real Academia Española, 1954.

Grisel y Mirabella. In Matulka, Barbara, *The Novels of Juan de Flores and their European Diffusion: A Study in Comparative Literature,* 331–71. New York: Institute of French Studies, 1931.

La historia de Grisel y Mirabella: Con la disputa de Torrellas y Bracayda. Facsimile. Originally published, Seville: J. Cromberger, 1529. Madrid: Sancho Rayón, 1874.

Principal Fifteenth-Century Cancioneros *Containing Pere Torrellas'* Slander against Women *and* Defense of Ladies against Slanderers

Cancionero de Herberay des Essarts. MS Add. 33382. British Library, London, UK.

Cancionero de Hixar. MS 2882. Biblioteca Nacional de España, Madrid, Spain.

Cancionero de Lope de Estúñiga. MS Vitrina 17–7. Biblioteca Nacional de España, Madrid, Spain.

Cancionero Coimbra Universitaria. MS 1011. Biblioteca Universitaria, Coimbra, Portugal.

Castillo, Hernán de, comp. *Cancionero General de muchos y diversos autores.* Valencia: Christofol Kofmann, 1511.

Modern Editions of Pere Torrellas' Works and Cancioneros *containing* The Slander against Women *and* The Defense of Ladies against Slanderers

Cancionero de Estúñiga. Edited by Nicasio Salvador Miguel. Madrid: Alhambra, 1987.

El cancionero del siglo XV, ca. 1360–1520. Edited by Brian Dutton and Jineen Krogstad. 7 vols. Salamanca: University of Salamanca, 1990–1991.

Castillo, Hernán de, comp. *Cancionero General.* Joaquín González Cuenca. 5 vols. Madrid: Castalia, 2004.

Castillo, Hernán de, comp. *Cancionero General.* Edited by Antonio R. Rodríguez Moñino. Madrid: Real Academia Española, 1958.

Le Chansonnier espagnol d'Herberay des Essarts. Edited by Charles Aubrun, Bordeaux: Féret, 1951.

Pere Torroella. Els Nostres Poetes. Edited by Martín de Ríquer. Barcelona: Llibrería Catalonia, 1935.

Torrellas, Pere. *The Works of Pere Torroella, a Catalan Writer of the Fifteenth Century*. Edited by Pedro Bach y Rita. New York: Instituto de las Españas en los Estados Unidos, 1930.

Torroella, Pere. *Obra completa*. Edited by Robert Archer. Soveria Mannelli, Italy: Rubbettino, 2004.

_____. *Obra completa*. Edited by Francisco Rodríguez Risquete. 2 vols. Barcelona: Barcino, 2011.

The Universities of Liverpool, Birmingham and Barcelona. "An Electronic Corpus of 15th Century Castilian *Cancionero* Manuscripts." http://cancionerovirtual.liv.ac.uk

Other Primary Works Cited

A Very Profitable Boke to Lerne the Maner of Redyng, Writyng, [and] Speakyng English [and] Spanish. Libro muy pronechoso para saber la manera de leer, y screuir, y hablar Angleis, y Español. London: John Kingston, 1554.

Antón de Montoro. *Cancionero*. Edited by Marcella Ciceri and Julio Rodríguez-Puértolas. Salamanca: Universidad de Salamanca, 1990.

Boccaccio, Giovanni. *The Decameron*. Translated by G. H. McWilliam. New York: Penguin, 1995.

_____. *The Elegy of Lady Fiammetta*. Edited and Translated by Mariangela Causa-Steindler and Thomas Mauch. Chicago: University of Chicago Press, 1990.

_____. *Famous Women*. Edited and Translated by Virginia Brown. Cambridge, MA: Harvard University Press, 2001.

Braçayda. *Poesía femenina en los cancioneros*. Edited by Miguel Ángel Pérez Priego. Madrid: Editorial Castalia, 1989.

Carvajal. *Respuesta en defensión de amor*. In vols. 2 and 4, *El cancionero del siglo XV, ca. 1360–1520*, edited by Brian Dutton and Jineen Krogstad, 2: 362 and 4: 56; 367–68.

Chaucer, Geoffrey. "The Wife of Bath's Prologue." In *The Riverside Chaucer*. Edited by Larry Dean Benson. 3rd ed. 105–122. New York: Oxford University Press, 2008.

F. A. d. C. *Triste deleytaçión: An Anonymous Fifteenth Century Castilian Romance*. Edited by E. Michael Gerli. Washington, D.C.: Georgetown University Press, 1982.

Flores, Juan de.

_____. *Grimalte y Gradissa*. Edited by Pamela Waley. London: Tamesis Books, 1971.

_____. *Triunfo de Amor*. Edited by Antonio Gargano. Pisa: Giardini, 1981.

_____. [Anon.] *La coronación de la señora Gracisla (BN MS. 22020)*. In *Dos opúsculos isabelinos: La coronación de la señora Gracisla (BN MS. 22020) y Nicolás Nuñez, Cárcel de Amor*. Edited by Keith Whinnom, 1–47. Exeter: University of Exeter, 1979.

_____. [Anon] *Crónica incompleta de los Reyes Católicos (1469–1476)*. Edited by Julio Puyol. Madrid: Tipografía de Archivos, 1934.

Gracián, Baltasar. *Arte de ingenio: tratado de la agudeza*. Edited by Emilio Blanco. Madrid: Cátedra, 1998.

Isidore of Seville. *The Etymologies of Isidore of Seville*. Edited and Translated by Stephen A. Barney, W. J. Lewis, J. A. Beach, and Oliver Berghof. Cambridge, UK: Cambridge University Press, 2006.

Lucena, Luis de. *Repetición de amores*. Edited by Jacob Ornstein. Chapel Hill, NC: University of North Carolina Press, 1954.

Luna, Álvaro de. *Libro de las claras y virtuosas mugeres*. Edited by Manuel Castillo. Valladolid: Maxtor, 2002.

Manrique, Gómez. *Respuesta al mal dicho de mossen Pedro Torrella catalano*. In vols. 1 and 2, *El cancionero del siglo XV, ca. 1360–1520*, edited by Brian Dutton and Jineen Krogstad, 1: 2–4 and 33–34; 2: 208–09 and 469–70. Salamanca: University of Salamanca, 1990–1991.

Martín de Córdoba. *Jardín de nobles donzellas*. Edited by Harriet Goldberg. Chapel Hill, NC: University of North Carolina Department of Romance Languages, 1974.

Martínez de Toledo, Alfonso. *Arcipreste de Talavera o Corbacho*. Edited by E. Michael Gerli. Madrid: Cátedra, 1992.

Mexía, Hernán. *Otras suyas en que descubre los defectos de las condiciones de las mugeres.* In vol. 5, *El cancionero del siglo XV: ca. 1360–1520*, edited by Brian Dutton and Jineen Krogstad. 196–200. Salamanca: Universidad de Salamanca, 1990.

Minsheu, John. *A dictionarie in Spanish and English, first published into the English tongue by Ric. Perciuale Gent. Now enlarged and amplified with many thousand words.* London: Edmund Bollifant, 1599.

Ovid. *Heroides.* Translated by Harold Isbell. London: Penguin Books, 1990.

———. *Metamorphoses: A New Verse Translation.* Translated by David Raeburn. London: New York: Penguin, 2004.

Pérez de Guzmán, Fernán. *Generaciones y semblanzas.* Edited by José Antonio Barrio Sánchez. Madrid: Cátedra, 1998.

Ribera, Suero de. *Respuesta de Suero de Ribera en defensión de las donas.* In vols. 2 and 4, *El cancionero del siglo XV, ca. 1360–1520*, edited by Brian Dutton and Jineen Krogstad, 2: 7–8 and 364–365; 4: 58 and 370. Salamanca: Universidad de Salamanca, 1990–91.

Rojas, Fernando de. *La Celestina,* Edited by Dorothy Sherman Severin. Madrid: Cátedra, 1987.

Ruperto de Nola. *Libro de guisados.* Edited by Dionisio Pérez. Madrid: Nueva Biblioteca de Autores Españoles, 1929.

San Pedro, Diego de. *Cárcel de Amor con la Continuación de Nicolás Núñez.* Edited by Carmen Parrilla García and Keith Whinnom. Introduction by A. D. Deyermond. Barcelona: Crítica, 1995.

Swetnam the Woman-Hater: The Controversy and the Play, ed. Coryl Crandall. West Lafayette, IN: Purdue University Press, 1969.

Tel-Troth, Thomas. [Joseph Swetnam]. *The Araignment of Lewde, Idle, Froward and Vnconstant Women.* London: Edward Allde for Thomas Archer, 1615.

Urriés, Hugo. *Señora discreta e mucho prudente.* In vol. 2, *El cancionero del siglo XV, ca. 1360–1520*, edited by Brian Dutton and Jineen Krogstad, 18–21. Salamanca: Universidad de Salamanca, 1990–91.

The Vidas of the Troubadours. Trans. Margarita Egan. New York: Garland, 1984.

Vives, Juan Luis. *The Education of A Christian Woman: A Sixteenth-Century Manual.* The Other Voice in Early Modern Europe. Translated by Charles Fantazzi. Chicago: University of Chicago Press, 2000.

Secondary Bibliography

Albuixech, Lourdes. "Utopía y distopía en tres ficciones de Juan de Flores." *Romania: Revue trimestrille consacrée à l'étude des langues et des littératures romanes* 120, no. 1–2 (2002): 176–191.

Antonelli, Roberto. "The Birth of Criseyde—An Exemplary Triangle: 'Classical' Troilus and the Question of Love at the Anglo-Norman Court." In *The European Tragedy of Troilus*, edited by Piero Boitani, 21–48. Oxford: Clarendon Press, 1989.

Aram, Bethany. *Juana the Mad: Sovereignty and Dynasty in Renaissance Europe.* Baltimore: Johns Hopkins University Press, 2008. Originally Published as *La reina Juana: Gobierno, piedad y dinastía.* Madrid: Marcial Pons, 2001.

Archer, Robert. *The Problem of Woman in Late-Medieval Hispanic Literature.* Rochester, NY: Tamesis, 2005.

_____. "'Tus falsas opiniones e mis verdaderas razones': Pere Torroella and the Woman-Haters." *Bulletin of Hispanic Studies* 78 (2001): 551–66.

_____. "Las coplas 'De las calidades de las donas' de Pere Torroella y la tradición lírica catalana." *Boletín de la Real Academia de buenas letras de Barcelona* 47 (1999–2000): 405–423.

Archer, Robert and Isabel de Ríquer. *Contra las mujeres: poemas medievales de rechazo y vituperio.* Barcelona: Quaderns Crema, 1998.

Benson, Pamela Joseph. *The Invention of the Renaissance Woman: The Challenge of Female Independence in the Literature and Thought of Italy and England.* University Park, PA: Pennsylvania State University Press, 1992.

Beysterveldt, Antony van. "Revision de los debates feministas del siglo VX y las novelas de Juan de Flores." *Hispania: A Journal Devoted to the Teaching of Spanish and Portuguese* 64, no. 1 (1981): 1–13.

Blamires, Alcuin. *The Case for Women in Medieval Culture.* New York: Oxford University Press, 1997.

_____. "Refiguring the 'Scandalous Excess' of Women: The Wife of Bath and Liberality." In *Gender in Debate from the Middle Ages to the Renaissance,* edited by Thelma S. Fenster and Clare A. Lees, 57–78. New York: Palgrave, 2002.

Blamires, Alcuin, Karen Pratt, and C. William Marx. *Woman Defamed and Woman Defended: An Anthology of Medieval Texts.* New York: Oxford University Press, 1992.

Boase, Roger. *The Troubadour Revival: A Study of Social Change and Traditionalism in Late Medieval Spain.* London: Routledge and Kegan Paul, 1978.

Breitenberg, Mark. *Anxious Masculinity in Early Modern England.* Cambridge, UK: Cambridge University Press, 1996.

Brownlee, Marina Scordilis. *The Severed Word: Ovid's Heroides and the Novela Sentimental.* Princeton, NJ: Princeton University Press, 1990.

Butler, Charles, ed. *Female Replies to Swetnam the Woman-Hater.* Bristol University: Thoemmes Press, 1995.

Cantavella, Rosanna. *Els cards i el llir: una lectura de l'Espill de Jaume Roig.* Barcelona: Quaderns Crema, 1992.

Casas Rigall, Juan. *Agudeza y retórica en la poesía amorosa de cancionero.* Santiago de Compostela: Universidade de Santiago de Compostela, 1995.

Checa, Jorge. "*Grisel y Mirabella* de Juan de Flores: rebeldía y violencia como síntomas de crisis." *Revista canadiense de Estudios Hispánicos* 12, no. 3 (1988): 369–382.

Crespo Martín, Patricia. "Violencia mitológica en *Grisel y Mirabella.*" *La corónica* 29, no. 1 (2000): 75–87.

Cruz Muriel Tapia, María. *Antifeminismo y subestimación de la mujer en la literatura medieval castellana.* Caceres, Spain: Editorial Guadiloba, 1991.

Cull, John T. "Irony, Romance Conventions, and Misogyny in *Grisel y Mirabella* by Juan de Flores." *Revista canadiense de Estudios Hispánicos* 22, no. 3 (1998): 415–30.

Dudley, Edward. "The Inquisition of Love: *Tratado* as a Fictional Genre." *Mediaevalia* 5 (1979): 233–43.

Durán, Armando. *Estructura y técnicas de la novela sentimental y ca-balleresca*. Madrid: Gredos, 1973.

Earenfight, Theresa. "Absent Kings: Queens as Political Partners in the Medieval Crown of Aragon." In *Queenship and Political Power in Medieval and Early Modern Spain*, edited by Theresa Earen-fight, 33–55. Burlington, VT: Ashgate, 2005.

Fenster, Thelma S. and Clare A. Lees, eds. *Gender in Debate from the Early Middle Ages to the Renaissance*. New York: Palgrave, 2002.

Forsyth, Cecil. "The Phagotus of Afranio" in *Orchestration*, 500–502. New York: Macmillan, 1944.

Francomano, Emily C. "Juan de Flores Delivers a Bull." In *"De ningu-na cosa es alegre posesión sin compañía": Estudios celestinescos y medievales en honor del profesor Joseph Thomas Snow*, edited by Devid Paolini, Vol. 2, 151–161. New York: Hispanic Seminary of Medieval Studies, 2010.

_____. "The Spanish Sentimental Romance." In *Women and Gender in Medieval Europe: An Encyclopedia*, edited by Margaret C. Schaus, 734–736. New York: Routledge, 2006.

Gerli, E. Michael."La 'religión del amor' y el antifeminismo en las let-ras castellanas del siglo XV." *Hispanic Review* 49, no. 1 (1981): 65–81.

_____. "Introducción." *Poesía cancioneril castellana*. Madrid: Akal, 1994.

_____."Toward a Poetics of the Spanish Sentimental Romance." *His-pania: A Journal Devoted to the Teaching of Spanish and Portu-guese* 72, no. 3 (1989): 474–482.

_____. "Introduction." In *Studies on the Spanish Sentimental Romance (1440–1550): Redefining a Genre*, edited by Joseph J. Gwara and E. Michael Gerli, xiii–xvii. Rochester, NY: Tamesis, 1997.

_____. Gender Trouble: Juan de Flores's *Triunfo De Amor*, Isabel La Católica , and the Economies of Power at Court." *Journal of Spanish Cultural Studies* 4, no. 2 (2003): 169–184.

Gerli, E. Michael and Julian Weiss, Eds. *Poetry at Court in Trastama-ran Spain: From the* Cancionero de Baena *to the* Cancionero general. Tempe, AZ: Medieval & Renaissance Texts & Studies, 1998.

Gómez, María A., Santiago Juan-Navarro, and Phyllis Zatlin, eds. *Juana of Castile: History and Myth of the Mad Queen*. Lewisburg, PA: Bucknell University Press, 2008.

Greer, Margaret R. and Elizabeth Rhodes. "Volume Editors' Introduction." In María de Zayas y Sotomayor, *Exemplary Tales of Love and Tales of Disillusion*, edited by Margaret R. Greer and Elizabeth Rhodes, 40–41. Chicago: University of Chicago Press, 2008.

Grieve, Patricia E. *Desire and Death in the Spanish Sentimental Romance, 1440–1550*. Newark, DE: Juan de la Cuesta, 1987.

_____. "Juan de Flores' Other Work: Technique and Genre of *Triumpho de Amor*." *Journal of Hispanic Philology* 5 (1980): 25–40.

Gwara, Joseph J. "A Possible Hebraism in *Grisel y Mirabella* and its implications: Old Spanish *Cultre*." *Journal of the Early Book Society* 15 (2012): 1–40.

_____. "Eleven Emendations to the Text of *Grisel y Mirabella*," in *Homenaje a E. Michael Gerli*, edited by José Manuel Hidalgo, 201–32. Newark, DE: Juan de la Cuesta, 2011.

_____. "Another Work by Juan de Flores: *La coronación de la señora Gracisla*." In *Studies on the Spanish Sentimental Romance (1440–1550): Redefining a Genre*, edited by Joseph J. Gwara and E. Michael Gerli, 75–110. Rochester, NY: Tamesis, 1997.

_____. "Preface." In *Studies on the Spanish Sentimental Romance (1440–1550): Redefining a Genre*, edited by Joseph J. Gwara and E. Michael Gerli, vii–xii. Rochester, NY: Tamesis, 1997.

_____. "A Study of the Works of Juan de Flores, with a Critical Edition of *La historia de Grisel y Mirabella*." Ph.D. diss., Westfield College, University of London, 1988.

_____. "The Identity of Juan de Flores: The Evidence of the *Crónica incompleta de los Reyes Católicos* (Concluded)." *Journal of Hispanic Philology* 11, no. 3 (1987): 205–22.

_____. "The Identity of Juan de Flores: The Evidence of the *Crónica incompleta de los Reyes Católicos*," *Journal of Hispanic Philology* 11, no. 2 (1987): 103–29.

Gwara, Joseph J. and Diane Wright. "A New Manuscript of Juan de Flores' Grisel y Mirabella: Biblioteca Apostolica Vaticana, Vat.

Lat. MS 6966, ff. 68r–76v." *Bulletin of Hispanic Studies* 77.4 (2000): 503–26.

Gwara, Joseph J. and E. Michael Gerli, eds. *Studies on the Spanish Sentimental Romance, 1440–1550: Redefining a Genre*. London; Rochester, NY, USA: Tamesis, 1997.

Jansen, Sharon L. *Debating Women: Politics and Power in Early Modern Europe*. New York: Palgrave Macmillan, 2008.

Krueger, Roberta L. *Women Readers and the Ideology of Gender in Old French Verse Romance*. New York: Cambridge University Press, 1993.

Mann, Jill. *Apologies to Women: Inaugural Lecture Delivered 20th November 1990*. Cambridge, UK: Cambridge University Press, 1991.

Martínez, Delmarie. "Mujer: dama o demonio en *Grisel y Mirabella*." *Mountain Interstate Foreign Language Conference Review* 6 (1996): 32–40.

Matulka, Barbara. *The Novels of Juan de Flores and their European Diffusion: A Study in Comparative Literature*. New York: Institute of French Studies, 1931.

McLeod, Glenda. *Virtue and Venom: Catalogs of Women from Antiquity to the Renaissance*. Ann Arbor: University of Michigan Press, 1991.

Nieto Jiménez, Lidio and Manuel Alvar Esquerra. *Nuevo tesoro lexicográfico del español (S. XIV–1726)*. 11 vols. Madrid: Arco, 2007.

Ornstein, Jacob, ed. *Repetición de amores*. Chapel Hill, NC: University of North Carolina Press, 1954.

_____."La misoginia y el profeminismo en la literatura castellana," *Revista de filología española* 3 (1941): 219–32.

Paster, Gail Kern. "The Unbearable Coldness of Female Being: Women's Imperfection and the Humoral Economy." *English Literary Renaissance* 28, no. 3 (1998): 416–40.

Pérez-Romero, Antonio. *The Subversive Tradition in Spanish Renaissance Writing*. Lewisburg, PA: Bucknell University Press, 2005.

Pettegree, Andrew. "Translation and the Migration of Texts." In *Borders and Travellers in Early Modern Europe*, edited by Thomas Betteridge, 113–128. Aldershot, UK: Ashgate, 2007.

Phillips, William D. *Enrique IV and the Crisis of Fifteenth-Century Castile 1425–1480*. Cambridge, MA: Medieval Academy of America, 1978.

Ríquer, Martín de. *Història de la literatura catalana*. Barcelona: Ariel, 1980.

Rodríguez Puértolas, Julio. "Introducción," in Antón de Montoro, *Cancionero*, ed. Marcella Ciceri, 14–15. Salamanca, Universidad de Salamanca, 1990.

Rodríguez Risquete, Francisco. "Del cercle literari del Príncep de Viana i unes poesies satiriques del *Cancioner de Saragossa*." *Revista de la Facultat de Lletres de la Universitat De Girona* (2002): 365–391.

———. "Pere Torroella i les corts dels Infants d'Aragó al s. XV (Conferència llegida al seminari de cultura catalana medieval i moderna de la Universitat de Barcelona 19 de descembre de 2000)." *Narpan: Espai de literatura i cultura medieval* http://www.narpan.net/bibliotecadigital/articles/cat_view/69-rodriguez-risquete-francisco-javier.html.

Roffé, Mercedes. *La cuestión del género en* Grisel y Mirabella *de Juan de Flores*. Newark, DE: Juan de la Cuesta, 1996.

Round, Nicholas G. *The Greatest Man Uncrowned: A Study of the Fall of Álvaro de Luna*. London: Tamesis, 1986.

Salvador Miguel, Nicasio. "La tradición animalística en las *Coplas de las calidades de las donas*, de Pere Torrellas." *El Crotalón* 2 (1985): 215–24.

Severin, Dorothy Sherman. "Cancionero: un género mal-nombrado." *Cultura Neolatina* 54 (1994): 95–105.

Smieja, Florian L. "A Sixteenth Century Polish Translation of Flores's Grisel y Mirabella." *Bulletin of Hispanic Studies* 35 (1958): 34–6.

Tarp, Helen Cathleen. "1495 to 1556: Flores Times Four." *Angles on the English-Speaking World* 6 (2006): 25–38.

———. "Legal Fictions: Literature and Law in Grisel y Mirabella." *eHumanista: Journal of Medieval and Early Modern Iberian Studies* 7 (2006): 95–114.

———. "*Aurelio et Isabelle*: An Edition and Study of the 1556 Antwerp Spanish and English Translations of Juan de Flores's Grisel y Mirabella." Ph.D. diss., University of New Mexico, 1999.

Turner, Alan. "Translation and Criticism: The Stylistic Mirror." *The Yearbook of English Studies* 36, no. 1 (2006): 168–76.

Walde Moheno, Lilian von der. *Amor e ilegalidad: Grisel y Mirabella, de Juan de Flores.* Publicaciones Medievalia. Mexico City: Universidad Nacional Autónoma de México, 1996.

Weiss, Julian. "Bibliography of Primary Texts in Spanish, ca. 1430–1520." In *Gender and Debate from the Early Middle Ages to the Renaissance*, edited by Thelma S. Fenster and Clare A. Lees, 275–81. New York: Palgrave, 2002.

———. "'¿Qué demandamos de las mugeres?': Forming the Debate about Women in Late Medieval and Early Modern Spain (with A Baroque Response)." In *Gender in Debate from the Early Middle Ages to the Renaissance*, edited by Thelma S. Fenster and Clare A. Lees, 237–74. New York: Palgrave, 2002.

———. *The Poet's Art: Literary Theory in Castile c. 1400–60.* Oxford: The Society for Mediaeval Languages and Literature, 1990.

Weissberger, Barbara F. "Isabel's 'Nuevas Leyes': Monarchic Law and Justice in *Triunfo De Amor*." In *Juan de Flores: Four Studies. Papers of the Medieval Hispanic Research Seminar 49*, edited by Joseph J. Gwara, 173–90. London: Dept. of Hispanic Studies, Queen Mary, University of London, 2005.

———. *Isabel Rules: Constructing Queenship, Wielding Power.* Minneapolis: University of Minnesota Press, 2004.

———. "'Deceitful Sects': The Debate about Women in the Age of Isabel the Catholic." In *Gender in Debate from the Early Middle Ages to the Renaissance*, edited by Thelma S. Fenster and Clare A. Lees, 207–36. New York: Palgrave, 2002.

———. "*A Tierra Puto!* Alfonso De Palencia's Discourse of Effeminacy." In *Queer Iberia: Sexualities, Cultures, and Crossings from the Middle Ages to the Renaissance*, edited by Josiah Blackmore and Gregory S. Hutcheson, 291–324. Durham, NC: Duke University Press, 1999.

———. "Resisting Readers and Writers in the Sentimental Romances and the Problem of Female Literacy," in *Studies on the Spanish Sentimental Romance (1440–1550): Redefining a Genre*, edited by Joseph J. Gwara and E. Michael Gerli, 173–90. London: Tamesis, 1997.

_____. "Role-Reversal and Festivity in the Romances of Juan de Flores." *Journal of Hispanic Philology* 13 (1988–89): 197–213.

Whinnom, Keith. *La poesía amatoria de la época de los Reyes Católicos.* Durham, UK: University of Durham, 1981.

_____. *The Spanish Sentimental Romance, 1440–1550: A Critical Bibliography.* London: Grant & Cutler, 1983.

Index